GREATER LAKELAND

BY THE SAME AUTHOR

POETRY
Five Rivers
Rock Face
The Pot Geranium
Selected Poems

VERSE PLAYS
The Old Man of the Mountains
A Match for the Devil
Birth by Drowning

TOPOGRAPHY
Cumberland and Westmorland
The Lakers
Provincial Pleasures
Portrait of the Lakes
Man and Literature
William Cowper
William Wordsworth—A Selection and an Introduction

Greater Lakeland

Norman Nicholson

Photographs by Tom Wright

ROBERT HALE · LONDON

First published in Great Britain 1969
Reprinted 1970
Reprinted 1975

SBN 7091 0951 2

Robert Hale & Company
63 Old Brompton Road
London, S.W.7

Printed and bound in Great Britain by
REDWOOD BURN LIMITED
Trowbridge & Esher

To
The Reverend and Mrs J. H. Eckersley
of Wreay Vicarage, Cumberland,

in gratitude for many years of
friendship, hospitality and
ready help in adversity,
up and down the diocese of Carlisle,

this book is affectionately dedicated

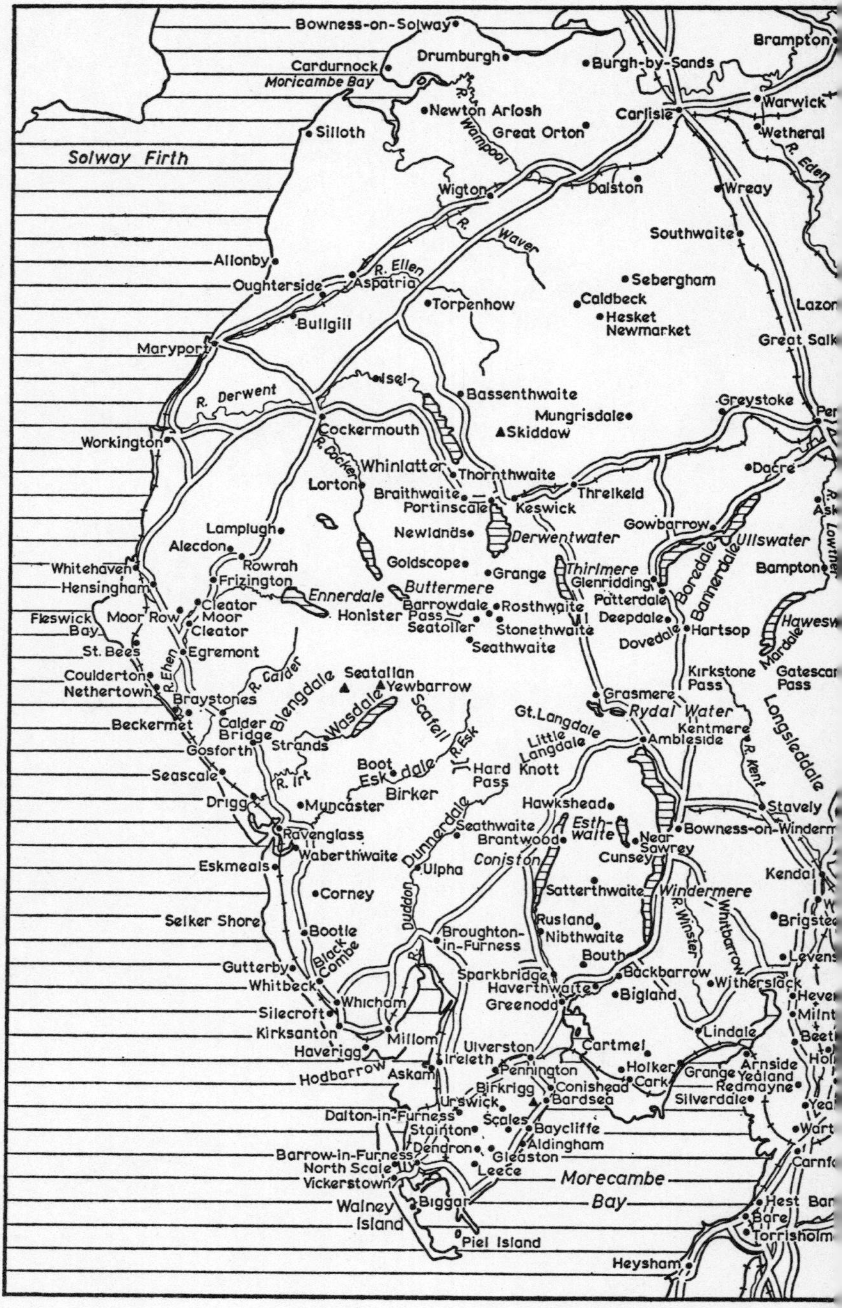
Bowness-on-Solway
Cardurnock
Moricambe Bay
Drumburgh
Burgh-by-Sands
Brampton
Newton Arlosh
R. Wampool
Carlisle
Warwick
Wetheral
Silloth
Great Orton
Solway Firth
R. Eden
Wigton
Dalston
Wreay
R. Waver
Southwaite
Allonby
R. Ellen
Aspatria
Oughterside
Sebergham
Caldbeck
Torpenhow
Hesket Newmarket
Bullgill
Maryport
Great Salk
Isel
Bassenthwaite
R. Derwent
Mungrisdale
Greystoke
Cockermouth
Skiddaw
Workington
R. Cocker
Whinlatter
Thornthwaite
Dacre
Lorton
Braithwaite
Portinscale
Keswick
Threlkeld
Lamplugh
Newlands
Derwentwater
Gowbarrow
Alecdon
Rowrah
Goldscope
Thirlmere
Ullswater
Whitehaven
Frizington
Grange
Glenridding
Bampton
Hensingham
Ennerdale
Buttermere
Patterdale
Boredale
Bannerdale
Cleator Moor
Barrowdale
Rosthwaite
Fleswick Bay
Moor Row
Honister Pass
Deepdale
Cleator
Seatoller
Stonethwaite
Hartsop
Dovedale
Mardale
St. Bees
Egremont
Seathwaite
R. Ehen
R. Calder
Couldertoń
Seatallan
Kirkstone Pass
Gatescar Pass
Nethertown
Yewbarrow
Blengdale
Scafell
Braystones
Grasmere
Rydal Water
Longsleddale
Wasdale
Gt. Langdale
Kentmere
Beckermet
Calder Bridge
Little Langdale
Ambleside
Strands
R. Esk
Gosforth
R. Kent
Boot
Hard Knott Pass
Eskdale
Seascale
R. Irt
Birker
Hawkshead
Drigg
Muncaster
Stavely
Dunnerdale
Esthwaite
Seathwaite
Ravenglass
Brantwood
Near Sawrey
Bowness-on-Windermere
Waberthwaite
Coniston
Cunsey
Eskmeals
Ulpha
Kendal
Satterthwaite
Windermere
Corney
R. Winster
Whitbarrow
Duddon
Selker Shore
Rusland
Brigsteer
Bootle
Broughton-in-Furness
Nibthwaite
Black Combe
Bouth
Levens
Gutterby
Sparkbridge
Backbarrow
Whitbeck
Haverthwaite
Witherslack
Whicham
Bigland
Greenodd
Silecroft
Lindale
Kirksanton
Millom
Cartmel
Haverigg
Ulverston
Holker
Arnside
Ireleth
Hodbarrow
Askam
Pennington
Grange
Yealand Redmayne
Birkrigg
Conishead
Cark
Urswick
Bardsea
Silverdale
Dalton-in-Furness
Scales
Stainton
Baycliffe
Dendron
Aldingham
Barrow-in-Furness
Gleaston
North Scale
Leece
Morecambe
Vickerstown
Walney Island
Biggar
Bay
Hest Bank
Bare
Torrisholme
Piel Island
Heysham

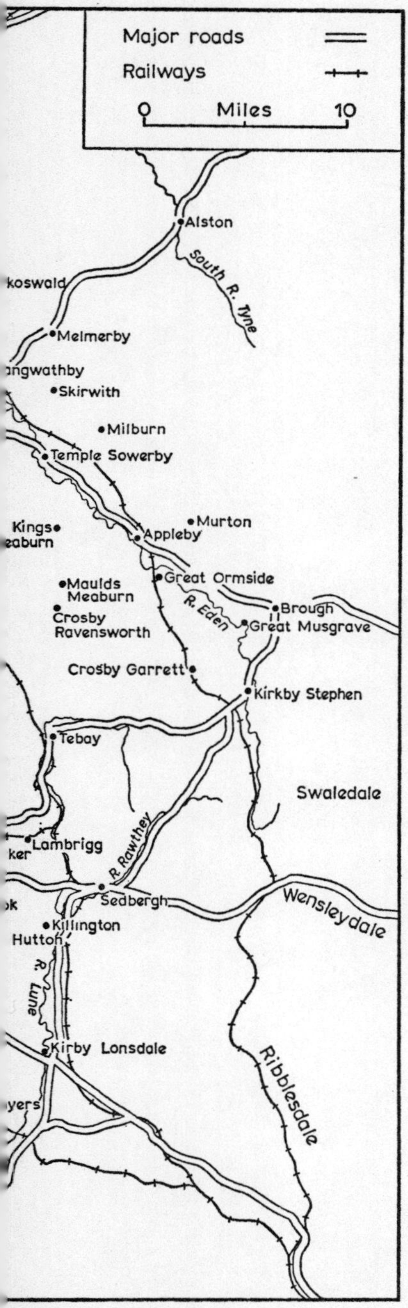
Major roads
Railways
0
Miles
10
Alston
South R. Tyne
koswald
Melmerby
ngwathby
Skirwith
Milburn
Temple Sowerby
Murton
Kings
eaburn
Appleby
Great Ormside
Maulds
Meaburn
Crosby
Ravensworth
R. Eden
Brough
Great Musgrave
Crosby Garrett
Kirkby Stephen
Tebay
Swaledale
R. Rawthey
Lambrigg
ker
Sedbergh
Wensleydale
Killington
Hutton
R. Lune
Kirby Lonsdale
Ribblesdale
yers

CONTENTS

ILLUSTRATIONS

INTRODUCTION AND ACKNOWLEDGEMENTS

THE English Lake District is one of the most famous tourist centres in the world, yet the part of it which is most often visited is quite small—only the inner circle of the higher fells and the upper reaches of the dales. Outside that inner circle there is a far larger area, less known but containing a wide variety of country-side, much of it of great beauty, together with a wealth of social, historical and human interest greater, even, than that of the Lake District itself.

It is to these outlying parts of Greater Lakeland, as well as to the better-known inner parts, that I want to introduce the visitor, remembering, of course, that those who live in one corner of the district become visitors when they go to the other corners. And because I have the visitor in mind, I have not overburdened my book with historical or archeological detail, which is often of interest only to the specialist or to the people who live in the parish concerned. Too many guide books seem to me to be stocked with such eminently forgettable things as notes on tenth-rate ruins and descriptions of the coat-of-arms of extinct families who bequeathed 17s 9d per annum to provide copies of *The Pilgrim's Progress* for the poor.

So, instead of offering the reader too much in the way of an-tiquities, family genealogies and local legends, I have tried to tell him what he may expect to see in the Greater Lakeland of today. For many people have lost the art of seeing what the countryside really looks like. They enjoy the fresh air, the sunshine, the space, the freedom and the view, but they no longer have the knack of seeing those differences of rock, soil and vegetation, of contour and texture, of methods of agriculture and styles of domestic architecture, even of the ways of building a wall, which help to make one dale so different from the next. Drop a Lakeland man, blindfold, anywhere south of Windermere, and, though he may not at once be able to tell exactly where he is, he will know, almost before he takes off the bandages, that he is not in Wasdale or Borrowdale.

In this book, therefore, I have chosen to lead the reader round Greater Lakeland, trying to make the landscape come alive before his eyes—sea-cliffs and salt-marshes, farms and woods, the lowland wastes and moors as well as the fells, and the industrial towns and ports as well as the villages of the dales. And I have taken for granted the fact that many visitors, perhaps most, come to the district by car. Of course, you cannot really see the Lakes from a car—that has been said before and will have to be said again. But a judicious use of a car can take you to places that would otherwise be beyond the reach of all but the most determined walkers—and how many of *them* discover the Caldbeck Fells or the Solway Marshes or the under-Pennine villages? The strength to be able to climb the rocks and walk the fells is much to be envied, but it is a luxury I have had to do without for forty years, and no one will persuade me that I have never seen the Lake District just because I have never climbed Nape's Needle.

To avoid having to make repeated acknowledgements in footnotes, I should like to say that all I have written about place-names in Cumberland and Westmorland is derived from those absolutely essential volumes issued by the English Place-name Society and published by the Cambridge University Press: *The Place-names of Cumberland*, by A. M. Armstrong, A. Mawer, F. M. Stenton and Bruce Dickins (3 vols. 1950-52); and *The Place-names of Westmorland*, by A. H. Smith (2 vols. 1967). This series does not yet include a survey of Lancashire, and, in the case of that county, I am indebted to *The Place-names of Lancashire*, by E. Ekwall (Manchester, 1922). For information on monasteries and churches I have turned largely to *The Victorian County History of Cumberland* and to the volume issued by the Royal Commission on Historical Monuments in Westmorland. Nikolaus Pevsner's volume on Cumberland and Westmorland in his Penguin 'Buildings of England' series did not appear until nearly all this book was written. Professor Pevsner seems to me to lack feeling for our native Lake District architecture, farms, barns, cottages and the like, and he finds less aesthetic pleasure than I do in some of our smaller towns, but he is, of course, a very useful guide to churches, castles, country mansions and the more notable of our town buildings. Finally, among publications of the last ten years, I should like to express my thanks for the pleasure and profit gained from William Rollinson's *A History of Man in the Lake District*, J. D. Marshall's *An Industrial History of Furness*, W. Heaton Cooper's *The Tarns of Lakeland* and *The Lakes*, and the several first-rate Lakeland books of A. H. Griffin.

I must also, as so often before, express my very great gratitude to the librarians and staff of the Carlisle City Library, the Whitehaven and Barrow-in-Furness Borough Libraries, the Westmorland and Kendal County Library and the Cumberland County Library, with its Millom Branch. Mr Kenneth Smith of Carlisle, Mr Donald James of Kendal and Mr Daniel Hay of Whitehaven have all gone to much trouble for my sake and used up much of the rate-payers' time. Mr Hay's letters, in particular, are always erudite little essays on out-of-the-way aspects of local studies, only a small part of which, unfortunately, could be packed into this book. My thanks are also due for information on special matters—mostly about churches—to the Reverend George de Burgh-Thomas, vicar of Bampton, the Reverend J. S. Whinerey, vicar of Wasdale, the Reverend Harry W. Mycroft, rector of Great Salkeld, and the Reverend J. H. Eckersley, vicar of Wreay; also to Miss N. Clutterbuck, hon. librarian of the Dove Cottage Library, Grasmere, to Miss Mary Burkett, Curator of Abbot Hall Art Gallery, Kendal, and to Dr J. Satchell, of the Kendal Civic Society, whose valiant efforts to save New Bank Yard seem not, alas, to have been successful; and, for help in various ways, to Mrs J. C. Cooper and Mrs J. Slack.

I want also to speak of my gratitude to all those friends whose hospitality has enabled me to widen my acquaintance with the district—especially Mr and Mrs Delmar Banner of Little Langdale, Dr Frances Taylor of Brough, Mr and Mrs Herbert Lawson of Arnside and the late Canon and Mrs Aiden Hervey, formerly of Great Salkeld. Lastly, to all friends and friends of friends who have shown me round houses, churches, castles, libraries, colleges, schools, steelworks, factories, farms and gardens, I tender my thanks; while to all non-acquaintances, on whose land and estates I have trespassed, I offer my cheerful and, if necessary, ready-to-be-repeated apologies.

Millom,
Cumberland

N.N.

CHAPTER ONE

MY GREATER LAKELAND

In 1867 my grandparents came from Cartmel in Lancashire to Millom in Cumberland. That is the beginning of my story, and Millom, for me, is the centre of what I have chosen to call 'Greater Lakeland'. Yet Millom is nowhere near the geographical hub of the Lakes, and it is nothing like what one expects a town of the Lakes to be. It is, in fact, a decaying Victorian settlement, standing beside abandoned iron-ore mines and what will soon be a derelict ironworks. A town more dead than alive, many would call it. Indeed, on the very day on which I write—Black Friday, 13th September 1968—the ironworks are to be closed down after just over a hundred years of iron making, and a quarter of the town's working population will be thrown on the dole. So that to call Millom the centre of Greater Lakeland will seem to most people to be absurd.

Yet it is easier to define the boundaries of the area than to decide where its centre is. Its extent is roughly that of the land between Carlisle and Carnforth, bounded on the west by the Irish Sea and on the east by the valleys of the Eden and the Lune. But its centre is different for everyone. Each man chooses his own centre, and for me it must be the place where I was born and from which, as I grew up, I became aware of the world around me.

In coming from Cartmel to Millom my grandparents brought memories of much that belonged to pre-industrial Cumbria. I use the term 'Cumbria' for convenience. Cartmel is in Lancashire, on the small peninsula that juts out into Morecambe Bay, yet nowhere in either Cumberland or Westmorland is there a place more thoroughly Cumbrian. Its lovely priory has been called the Cathedral of the Lakes, and the limestone valley in which it lies still rings with the Scandinavian vocabulary that the invading Vikings brought to the North-west over a thousand years ago. Fell, dale, beck, tarn are words familiar enough to any Englishman, yet they are not mere synonyms for hill, valley, brook and small lake. They have an unmistakably northern accent—you cannot think of a tarn in Kent or a beck in Tooting Bec. The Scandinavian trade-mark is printed the whole length of Greater Lakeland, from top to bottom. In the north, the Solway is entirely Norse, a *wath*, or ford, and a *sul*, or pillar; while, in the south, the Morecambe Bay valleys bristle with scales, slacks, becks and thorpes.

My grandfather, Richard Nicholson, and my great-grandfather, a farmer of Hard Crag, Cartmel, came from the men of Viking stock who, for centuries, spoke a dialect so packed with Norse words that it sounded like a foreign language to an Englishman of the south. As for my other grandfather, *his* name was Cornthwaite; and *thwaite*, or clearing, is the commonest of all the Scandinavian elements in our place-names.

My grandmother, Maria Brennan, derived, as her surname shows, from a very different breed. Her father was an Irishman who came to be gamekeeper at Dallam Tower on the other side of Morecambe Bay, where the little River Bela flows into the estuary of the Kent. Great-grandfather Brennan settled in Greater Lakeland in the nineteenth century, but the Celtic or British people had been there long before the Vikings or even the Romans. The early Celtic inhabitants of the Lakes belonged, however, not to the Irish but to the Welsh or Brythonic branch of the Celts, and after the collapse of the Roman Empire they joined forces with the other Welsh-speaking people of Galloway to set up the Kingdom of Strathclyde or Cumbria—the *cymry* being the name of one of the Welsh tribes, so that Cumberland is really the land of the Welsh.

But the Irish or Goidelic Celts also had their share in the history of Greater Lakeland, for it was from Ireland that the Norsemen came to Cumberland. And by the time they arrived there they were no longer Vikings in the popular sense of the word—i.e. men who ravaged the coasts of France and Spain and carried their raids as far south as the Mediterranean and as far west as America. They came to Cumberland not as pirates but as pioneers. For them the colonising of Iceland and the plundering of the Hebrides was already part of an heroic past. Their immediate ancestors for perhaps three or four generations had been living peacefully in Ireland or the Isle of Man, had married Irish girls, had picked up

Castlerigg Stone Circle and Saddleback

some of the gentler arts of civilisation and had probably accepted at least the outward forms of Christianity. If you want to see how fruitful was this fraternisation between Celt and Norseman, look at the mingling of Irish and Scandinavian ideas on some of our sculptured stone crosses, especially that at Gosforth in West Cumberland.

This meeting of the two races was re-enacted in the marriage of my grandfather and grandmother at Cartmel, and proved, in their case, to be almost equally fruitful, since they produced a family of fourteen sons. They were married in the priory where my grandfather signed his name in the register but my grandmother merely made her mark. And that, too, tells part of the history of Greater Lakeland, where only one generation divides a woman who could not read from a man who has at least enough schooling to write this book.

It tells, also, something about the history of my own family. For it would seem that my great-grandfather, of Hard Crag, disapproved of his son's marriage, maybe thinking he had married beneath him. Whatever may have been the case, my grandfather left Hard Crag and took his wife to live at Flookburgh, not far from Cartmel. From then onwards he seems to have had little to do with his father and brothers. All my own father's memories of childhood refer to the Brennan family, to Dallam Tower and Milnthorpe and Beetham Church, where my grandmother was baptised. At Flookburgh their first child, my eldest uncle, was born, and then my grandfather left the land and found himself a job in the booming new town of Barrow-in-Furness. Three months later he moved over the estuary to take charge of the haulage—then, of course, a matter of horses not just of horse-power—at the newly-opened Millom Ironworks. My grandmother joined him soon afterwards, crossing the Duddon at low tide in a carrier's cart. It is said that when she got near enough to the Cumberland shore to be able to see the miserable encampment of huts and sheds which was all that then existed of Millom Town, she told the driver to turn the horse's head round and go back to Lancashire. But, by that time, the tide had started to flow and had cut off their retreat, or this book might never have been written. Ten years after she arrived, my father was born, and, thirty-seven years after that, I came into Millom and the world.

Afforestation in Lickle Valley

And how much can I now recall of my first fresh impressions of what was to be the centre of my Greater Lakeland? Very little. My father kept a men's outfitter's shop, and we lived in the house behind it, and it is easy enough to remember the house because I still live there and am sitting two storeys above the shop as I write these words. But of the streets and the town, let alone the surrounding countryside, I remember, from that time, almost nothing.

In fact, my earliest recollection of anything outside the house belongs to the year 1918 when I was already 4. It must have been towards the end of the First World War, when my father was doing war work, three days a week, at the Millom Ironworks—or, as he used to say, wasting three days a week to save his country. I can recall that one afternoon he sprained his ankle and was brought home in the ironworks' motor-car—we still called them 'motor-cars' in those days. It was probably the car rather than the sprained ankle which impressed itself on my mind, since there cannot have been more than two or three cars in the town at that time. I remember, also, that he sat in front of the fire, bathing his foot in a tin bath. And from then onwards, the ironworks, which had not really existed before that, so far as I was concerned, became a real place—the place where my father had sprained his ankle. To a child, places take their meaning from people, hardly exist apart from people; which is something I must try to remember throughout this book.

(Some years ago I repeated this story over the radio, and a few days later a man stopped me in the street and told me that he had accompanied my father in the ironworks car, being at that time a boy of 14 who had just started work and joined the St John Ambulance Brigade. That is what life is like in a small town. You meet someone you think you have no acquaintance with and find that, years earlier, your courses had crossed or collided and that you are not strangers at all.)

'People' in my childhood meant, of course, my family. My mother died in the Russian 'flu epidemic of 1919, so that, after that date, I had little to do with her side of the family. But on my father's side my grandmother was still alive, together with nine of her fourteen sons—she did not have a single daughter, by the way. Six of the nine, including my father, still lived in Millom, and there was a time when I thought that our entire male population consisted of my uncles. Among them—though I was not really aware of this until I was older—they managed to touch almost every side of the working life of the town. The eldest, my Uncle Bill, was a blacksmith, working not at a smithy but at the ironworks foundry, making or repairing machinery. Tom was a cobbler at the Co-operative Society's boot-and-shoe shop. Arnold served apprenticeship as a painter and paper-hanger but worked as a labourer at the ironworks when I knew him. Bob was employed at a shop with the Biblical-sounding name of 'Elias My Tailor', where, round about the beginning of the century, he sewed fifteen-shilling suits at the side of a boy who was later to become mayor of Bournemouth. All four remained unmarried and lived under the stern maternal discipline of my crippled grandmother's wooden crutch. My Uncle Jim was the manager of the shoe shop where Tom worked as a cobbler. I would go in at the shop door, among the sky-scrapers of stacked boxes, and buy a pair of laces, and then my Uncle Jim would take me through to the back, where my Uncle Tom soled and heeled by the light of an open gas jet in an air thick as cow-hide soup. Another uncle, dead before I was born, had been the best-known of all: a cricketer and a footballer, who once had his collar-bone broken by the brother of George Steadman, Cumberland's most famous wrestler. He was killed in an accident at the Hodbarrow Mines, and for years his memory was cherished in our family like that of a war hero—the Nicholson who gave his life for his town. None of these brothers made much of a success of his life: only my father and my Uncle Jim achieved the four or five pounds a week that, in the 'twenties, was regarded as a comfortable income. But they and the thousands like them in Furness and West Cumberland made the world in which half the population of Greater Lakeland still lives.

It was when I started school that the landscape began to broaden out. The town of Millom is split in two by the railway line, a division characteristic of the two-sided life of all West Cumberland. South of the railway is Newtown, a flat peninsula linked to the mainland of Britain only by the railway bridge. (When the bridge was in danger of collapsing some years ago, it seemed that the whole industrial life of the town would come to a stop.) In

1850 this area, which was not yet even called 'Millom', was only a waste of dune, salt-marsh and swampy fields, but by the end of the century it had become a typical northern industrial town, with mines, blast furnaces, sheds, workshops, chapels, schools and a parallelogram of straight-ruled, tight-packed, slate-built terrace houses.

Holborn Hill, on the other side of the railway, is very different. Instead of being flat, it rises to over one hundred feet in a tough knob of Lakeland rock—the Coniston Flag of the Silurian strata. (Most of the houses of Newtown are built of slate quarried in Holborn Hill. In fact, Millom is the only industrial town of West Cumberland and Furness built mainly of the rock of the fells—the rest are of limestone, sandstone or just brick.) Holborn Hill's main street still follows the line of the eighteenth-century west coast route and contains all that is left standing of the two or three inns and the few cottages of pre-industrial Millom.

Now I lived in Newtown, but when I went to school I walked a quarter of a mile and crossed the railway into Holborn Hill. It was like moving from a town to a village. Most of the boys at the school had fathers who worked, if they worked at all, at the ironworks or Hodbarrow. But the farmers' sons attended the school, too. (I remember that in the infants' class I sat next to one of them—a genial lad who still farms in the district and asks me how the bloody hell I'm keeping whenever he sees me. And one day we were told to draw a turnip from memory. Most of us drew a kind of Mill's bomb with aspidistra leaves sprouting from the top. But I noticed that my companion was putting curly leaves on *his* bomb, and, judging that a farmer's son would know more about turnips than I did, I copied him and was commended for my observation.)

Out of school hours the boys went to play, not among the back streets and slagbanks as the Newtown boys did, but to the rough ground at the foot of the hills or the field called Billy Day Works, which means, of course, a field that Billy could mow or plough or reap in one day. When I went over the railway bridge I could look up to Duddon Estuary to the saw-edge sky-line of the fells, though my knowledge of their names was so hazy that once, when my father called me into the shop to meet a customer from Coniston, I asked him if he were Coniston Old Man. And when we took our PT we passed through a door in the school-yard wall into the cricket field, beyond which were meadows and then dunes and the sea. All around, in fact, was country as wild and open as any in England.

Yet this landscape had to wait another seven or eight years before it caught my full attention, for a new territory, far more exciting to a young boy, was opening up in front of me. When I was 8 my father married again, and my new mother, who is still living here in this same house, was the daughter of one of four Devonshire brothers who had come to Millom in the 1860s at the time of the decline of the West-Country tin-mines. This mid-nineteenth-century immigration was, indeed, the return of the Celts, for most of the miners were Cornish rather than Devonshire men, and the registers of the Millom schools are still well sprinkled with names like Pelleymounter, Penaluna and Trelore.

But whether they came from Cornwall or Devon, the West Countrymen were all Methodists and set up their societies, Wesleyan, Primitive or Bible Christian, with evangelical fervour and a rigid puritanism. By the time of the 1920s both the fervour and the puritanism were beginning to moderate, but Methodism and non-conformity in general was still a powerful force in the social life of the town. For people like my mother, friendships made sixty years ago at chapel or Sunday School are still the most lasting and most binding of all human contacts outside the family.

It was the weekday activities of the chapels that meant most to me. For, to the many people of that time to whom clubs and pubs were forbidden territory, the six or seven non-conformist bodies in Millom and the nearby village of Haverigg offered entertainment, amusement and the warmth of company and shared interests. Millom, in the 1920s, was certainly a place of unemployment and next-door to poverty, but it was also a place of concerts, choir practices, rallies, guilds, anniversaries, children's processions, bazaars, 'efforts' and the like. I was about 9 when I first began to take part. The Wesleyan Methodist Sunday School which I attended had arranged to give a children's concert and I was asked to be the chairman. I can remember to this day the satisfaction with which I announced: "The next item on the programme will be a recitation, entitled *Big Steamers*, to be given by myself."

The smugness, no doubt, was as irritating to the audience then as it will be to the reader now, but what really mattered was that, all at once, I found I could make myself heard. The fact that I eventually chose to become a poet is due, I think, at least partly, to that childhood success in the Wesleyan Sunday School in 1923 or 4.

Soon I became a regular performer—'elocutionist' I called myself—at concerts, chapel services and musical festivals. It was, no doubt, a dangerous encouragement to youthful conceit, but it meant that, by the age of 12 or 13, I felt that I had a place in the town, that I was known and accepted by my own people. I never had to go through the miserable experience of feeling that I was one of a generation which was misunderstood, neglected, resented or unfairly treated. It is this sense of belonging to a community which is my main debt to Millom. Without it, my Greater Lakeland would have had no real centre, would have been merely a huge, impersonal green belt.

Nor is this sense of belonging peculiar to Millom. Almost wherever I go in Cumberland and Westmorland I feel the same local loyalty. Of course, the area as a whole is not a community, even in the largest sense of the word. It does not, as do many of the Midland or south-country shires, centre on one market or cathedral town. The great unifying feature of the Lakes, the mountain dome, is a barrier that holds people apart instead of bringing them together. The inhabitants of the west coast may live all their lives without coming into contact with anyone from the Eden Valley. But all round the brim of the mountain dome there are communities, larger or smaller, which have much the same, ingrown, almost tribal self-centredness as that of Millom. Barrow and industrial Furness make up a region on their own. So do the West Cumberland mining towns, though there is a sharp split between the northern (Workington) half and the southern (Whitehaven) half. Carlisle and the Solway is yet another region, while, away in the east, Appleby, Kirkby Stephen and Kirkby Lonsdale are towns as isolated and clannish in their ways as Millom is in its way. To the people of all these places Greater Lakeland has a centre in one precise spot, in a shared background and a shared social experience.

This may sound appallingly self-satisfied and short-sighted, and I must admit that, until I reached my middle 'teens, I was scarcely aware of the world outside Millom. The town, of course, is remarkably inaccessible, as it is now finding out to its great discomfort. Throughout the nineteenth century it had been so isolated from Victorian England as to be to all intents an island. After my grandmother came to Millom, in 1867, she did not, so far as I know, ever leave it. I am sure that she never took a holiday, and I have been told that she never made a journey in a train.

Yet, even in its isolation, Millom is quite typical of Greater Lakeland as a whole. For the area has always been physically detached from the rest of Britain—divided from Lancashire and the Midlands by Morecambe Bay, from Yorkshire and the North-east by the Pennines, and from Scotland by the Solway. The Romans emphasised this isolation by planning their military roads, from Chester to Carlisle, to by-pass the main part of the area. The Celtic tribes emphasised it by forming the Kingdom of Cumbria. The Norsemen emphasised it still more by giving to the area what amounted to its own language. And, whatever the BBC and 'Secondary Education for All' may do to our accents, most of those of us who live in Greater Lakeland cannot help using our old Norse tongue every time we give our name and address.

I have said that an awareness of the world outside did not come to me until I was 13 or 14. Perhaps it began a bit earlier than that. I remember that, in one of my first geography lessons at Holborn Hill Boys' School, I was taught that the Pennine Chain is the backbone of England. Later on I was to learn that the Pennines are bone in a more matter-of-fact sense, for great tracts of them, especially where they lie within the boundaries of Cumberland or Westmorland, consist of limestone, formed of the skeletal remains of sea-creatures and sea-vegetation. The school itself had a bony look, being set like a mended fracture against a broken stump of a hill. It was cramped, dark, damp and built of slate quarried out of that same hill. Already in the 1920s it was half falling down and since then has been pulled down altogether. But, somehow, as I walked to school, I had got the idea that the hills I could see from the Railway Bridge were really the Pennines, which, of course, they were not. (I know now that if I had climbed a little way up the slopes of the fells just beyond the town, I should have been able to see at least the flat top of Ingleborough.)

To me, in fact, the Pennines seemed part of Millom, almost part of the school playground, and to be told that they were the backbone of England made me feel, even as a weak-kneed, weak-chested boy of 8, that I was somehow part of the backbone of the English nation.

That is what the Londoner will call typical, North-Country, provincial-minded prejudice, and, as a prejudiced, provincial-minded North Countryman, I will not bother to argue. But that the Pennines are the backbone of the North of England is not a matter for argument at all. They are also the cradle of the industrial world of today just as Greece is the cradle of our Western civilisation. Mining has been carried on for twenty centuries in the Pennines and in the hills of the Lakes, and the iron trade flourished in well-wooded districts such as the shores of Morecambe Bay, where charcoal was easily available for the smelting of the ore. And when, in the nineteenth century, coke took the place of charcoal in the furnaces, and coal replaced water-power in the mills, then the rocks of the North put England into the economic front-line of the world. All along the flanks and spurs of the Pennines lay great reserves of coal and iron-ore, often close together. In West Cumberland the two were found side by side, and, at Cleator Moor near Whitehaven, both were brought up from the same shaft. Add to this the fact that the limestone needed by the blast furnaces was also ready to hand; add again that the sea was nearby, for ports and the building of ships; and we can see our modern world taking shape among the northern hills. We may not like that world; we may think it strident and empty; but we cannot escape from it. And here, in the North, we can see where it all began—not in what are now the greater cities, nor among devastated areas of slagbanks, pit-heaps and back-to-back houses, but in small iron-ore mines among the crags and bracken of Eskdale, or the barn-like forges and saw-pits of the Morecambe Bay valleys, or the spoil-heaps of the lead-mining villages of Alston or Swaledale.

Of course, people do not usually come to Greater Lakeland looking for signs of the Industrial Revolution. Most of them are only too glad to forget it. Yet, in the whole of this area, industry and the countryside lie close together and have done so for centuries. When I was a boy I took a walk every Sunday morning with my father and my Uncle Jim. We always went the same way, through the old Hodbarrow Mines, which in the 'twenties were still employing 500 or 600 men, though this was only about a quarter of the number of the days of prosperity. We walked along cinder paths or kicked our way through the bracken, raising spurts of red ore-dust. All round us were the dingy bushes, willows, thorns and elders that are always avid to grab a root-hold wherever the surface of the soil has been broken by spade or steam-shovel. Down in the hollow there were swans and moorhens on the water pumped out of the flooded levels; behind the new sea-wall gulls and oyster-catchers nested; in the clump of mangolds planted by the mines manager partridges took cover. Rabbits scurried about everywhere; once or twice we saw a hare. And today, now that the mines are no longer working, there are foxes in the quarries among the screes of red rubble tipped out beside the old shafts.

Once past the mines, we came to the ruins of the old windmill which had served as the first company offices, and then moved out to Hodbarrow Point. There, if it were summer, I'd run to the patch of fragile, purple, chalice-like flowers, which, when I found them at that spot twenty years later, I immediately recognised as the bloody cranesbill (*Geranium sanguineum*). And beyond was the sea, with a small bay almost trapped between the limestone rocks of Hodbarrow Point and the limestone boulders of the new sea-wall.

This bay was a favourite spot with the children of Newtown in the 'twenties. It still is. In fact, it was not for many years that I came to realise that Hodborrow was not what most people would regard as typical seaside. For to me the grime and clutter seemed as much a part of the natural scene as the cranesbills and the sea itself.

It was the same when I climbed the old slag bank. All round was a Gobi Desert of slag, with smoking chimneys, roaring furnaces, the clang and bustle of machinery. But straight before me were the sands and tides of the Duddon Estuary and a view which is probably the most comprehensive of all the coastal views of the fells, from Scafell round to Coniston Old Man. The contrast was obvious to me, at least by the time I was old enough to climb the slag bank. But there was no incongruity. Scafell Pike and Millom Ironworks belonged to the same world, to my Greater Lakeland.

This sharp juxtaposition of industry and fell is, again, very typical and can be seen in many places along the western margin of the Lakes. From the shore at Askam you get much the same view up the Duddon as from Millom; from the bridge that joins Barrow to Walney Island you look to Black Combe; from the new secondary school at Hensingham you look across the decayed Cleator Moor minefield to the Ennerdale fells; from Workington Steelworks you look across the Solway to Dumfriesshire and Kirkcudbright. Even outside the area of heavy industry the contrast between urban and rural is just as startling. You can gaze out from upper windows of hotels in the centre of Carlisle and see the back of Skiddaw, while, in Kendal, the fells come so close that they almost hold up the traffic in the streets.

Everywhere in the urban and industrial areas the contrast is striking and insistent. Yet it is not the contrast that I am really concerned with. On the contrary, it is with the unity of the scene. To the vast majority of those who live in Cumberland, Westmorland or North Lancashire, one feature of the landscape is constant —a view of the Lakeland fells. For most of us, as for me, it is a distant view to begin with, which is one reason why I have chosen to start this book at what, for many people, will seem to be the extreme edge of the district. But now let me go to the geographical centre and work outwards.

CHAPTER TWO

THE LAKES: THE NORTHERN DALES

I BEGIN with the least Cumbrian town in Cumberland.

The site of Keswick is superb. It stands on a slope only a few hundred yards above the foot of Derwentwater. Southward, you look down the length of the lake into the wedge of Borrowdale, and beyond to the volcanic peaks of the Wasdale fells; northward, you are practically knocking your nose on the bottom steps of Skiddaw. It is a shop-window display, two of Cumberland's most characteristic types of landscape made accessible to the laziest passer-by.

It is this very accessibility which has ruined Keswick. As early as 1755, Dr John Dalton "enumerated the beauties of the Vale of Keswick" in a poem "addressed to two young ladies after their return from viewing the mines near Whitehaven". In 1767, Dr John Brown explained "that the full perfection of Keswick, consists of three circumstances, *beauty*, *horror*, and *immensity* united", to depict which "would require the united powers of Claude, Salvator, and Poussin"*.

Thomas Gray, who came to the Lakes two years later, was similarly intimidated by the 'impending crags', and hurried past without speaking in case his voice should dislodge the stones and bring down an avalanche. Soon the district became the resort of tourists less timid than Gray and less aesthetically-minded than Brown, and, by the end of the century, Derwentwater was claiming to be 'The Jewel of the Lakes', though some visitors, disappointed with the weather, called it 'The Devil's Chamber-pot'†. And before long Keswick began to acquire yet another kind of fame. In 1799 Wordsworth and his sister had settled at Grasmere, and soon first Coleridge and then Southey came to Keswick. Coleridge drifted away to Hampstead, but Southey stayed at Greta Hall for the rest of his life. The name of Robert Southey

* John Brown, *Description of the Lake and Vale of Keswick* (Newcastle, 1767)

† For more about the first tourists see N. Nicholson, *The Lakers* (Robert Hale)

means very little today. Even his one surely lasting contribution to English literature, the story of the Three Bears, is not usually associated with him at all. But in the early nineteenth century, in spite of Byron's ridicule, he was one of the lions, and helped to make Keswick into a place of literary pilgrimage, perhaps even before Wordsworth did the same for Grasmere. In fact, throughout the nineteenth century the Lake Poets acted as highly-effective unpaid publicity agents for the entire district. Today their names have lost their drawing-power: very few visitors, I imagine, now come to the Lakes primarily because of Wordsworth, let alone Southey. Yet, in the windows of the dining-room of 'The Royal Oak' at Keswick, the Lake Poets are enshrined in stained glass, like the patron saints of the region, each with his epistle or epigraph beside him—William and Dorothy Wordsworth, Samuel Taylor and Hartley Coleridge, Robert Southey and Thomas de Quincey, with a few part-residents and occasional visitors to fill up the empty panes. It seems a pity they could not have left one window blank in case another local poet turned up.

It was this growing fame which changed Keswick. From being a small market-town it turned into what is essentially an industrial town in an industrial society—a town given over to the manufacture of holidays. There is nothing in this to be ashamed of, and Keswick, like Blackpool, plays an important part in the economy of the North of England. In the dusk of the summer evenings, after business hours, the streets are crammed with sightseers, inspecting old prints, new photographs, local water-colours, local weaving, local pottery, local wood-craft, local jewelry, local toffee and all the hideous gimcrackery that people take home to ease their conscience with those they have left behind. For just as the new housing-estates of one industrial town are almost indistinguishable from those of another, so the shopping-streets of the country towns are becoming all very much the same, with their repetititive art-and-craftiness, their eager eye on the visiting tourist.

Obviously Keswick is not the only town in the district which has changed in this way. So, also, have Bowness-on-Windermere, Ambleside and Grasmere. What I have said about Keswick is, in fact, not so much a criticism of that town as a warning to all the others. At one time, when most people came to the Lakes by train, it could be said that the tourist towns—Keswick and Bowness, in particular—acted as collecting grounds for the visitors, where they were comfortably herded together like sheep in a fellside intake. The dales and dale-villages, then, were left to the walkers. The danger today is that the smaller villages, too, will lose their identity; that in trying to escape from the standardization of the cities men will impose merely another kind of standardization on the country. Already the two main roads into Keswick, through Braithwaite and Portinscale on the west and through Threlkeld on the east, have been turned into brutally-engineered bypasses, that disfigure the landscape like a hideous operation.

It would be wrong, however, to say that Keswick itself had lost its identity. For, long before it became a tourist town, it was a wool-market and a centre for the early mining trade. The copper mines hereabouts may have been worked even as long ago as the fourteenth century, and, by the end of the fifteenth, they were leased out to a colony of Dutch and German miners who ran them until the time of Queen Elizabeth. The mines where they worked were scattered across several of the nearby valleys—Borrowdale, Newlands, Threlkeld and Thornthwaite above Bassenthwaite—and produced not only copper, but lead, silver, zinc, and haematite iron, while Goldscope in the Vale of Newlands gave some gold as well as silver. Mining of copper died out, to all intents, during the Civil War of the seventeenth century, and most of the other mines lingered only half-heartedly or dwindled away, the one notable exception being the working of graphite or plumbago or black lead (locally known as 'wad') near Seathwaite in Borrowdale. This continued with great success well into the nineteenth century and was the foundation of Keswick's pencil-making industry of today*.

Historically, then, Keswick is as Cumbrian as the rest of the county, for, like the west coast, it springs out of the mines, out of the rock. Indeed, something of the town's industrial past can still be guessed at from the pencil-slim, late-Georgian town hall and the narrow, tightly-packed alleys where the pencil-makers lived. By the middle of the nineteenth century, however, Keswick was no longer a mining town and had become, instead, the main

* For more about the mines of Borrowdale and the Lake District see N. Nicholson, *Portrait of the Lakes* (Robert Hale)

junction for the Lakes, and, above all, the pay-box for Borrowdale.

Borrowdale is 'the dale of the fortress' (Old Norse *borg*), the name coming from a fort which is thought to have stood near Castle Crag. It is beyond argument the most theatrical of the dales. Derwentwater itself (the Derwent is the river of the oak), has none of the river-like character of, say, Windermere, but is more like a wide fore-stage to the back-cloth of the upper dale. Again, though the peaks round about are not on the whole as high as those of the western dales, they manage to look even higher. For everywhere the scene seems to have been touched up and exaggerated by a romantic artist—if any view at all in the Lakes resembles an eighteenth-century landscape print, it is surely that of Borrowdale.

The Lodore Falls, for instance, near the head of the lake, are neither particularly high nor particularly precipitous, but, after rain, the water comes gushing down as from a burst dam and can be seen from Portinscale, three miles away. As for hills, Castle Crag, above Grange, is less than 1,000 feet in height, but it juts up like a wigwam, making even Skiddaw look lumpy in comparison. And almost opposite Castle Crag, on the other side of the road and river, is the Bowder Stone, typical, one might think, of the many such boulders left by the retreating ice. But, while the rest are found mostly on remote fellsides or in the coastal farmland, far away from any road, here is the biggest of them all, only a few yards away from the bus-route, and perched on one corner like a performing elephant on one leg.

North of Rosthwaite, the valley branches into two: Borrowdale proper and Stonethwaite, from whence tracks lead over the passes to Wasdale, Far Easedale and Great Langdale. This is walker's country. But the road along the other tributary dale, that of Watendlath, the waters of which flow into Lodore, is often jammed with cars, while the view from Ashness Bridge is probably the most photographed of any in the district. For Borrowdale, like Keswick, has taken the full brunt of the crowds. Go there for solitude, for rural peace, for Wordsworthian tranquillity, and there's little hope of your finding them, or not, at least, in the holiday season. Instead, you will find every nook by the lake road along Borrow Bay stuffed tight with parked cars. You will find the river-side around Grange Bridge staked out by picnickers—tartan rugs spread on the rocks, transistors squeaking above the sound of water, children snaring tiddlers, and tubular chairs set up round the gas stoves. At Ullswater, I have seen a quartet in bathing costumes carry table and chairs into the lake and sit, knee-deep in water, eating their meal.

If you want to find quietness in Borrowdale, in summer, you must get up very early in the morning before the cars beam out from the town like starlings from the night's roost, or else walk beside the lake in the late evening after sunset. Then the fells are black cut-outs against the green of the sky, and the trees are huge haystacks of shadow at the foot of which the water gleams and flickers. And the young couples walk back to Youth Hostel or boarding house, the legs of the girls showing up clearly in the car headlights, though their black-clad companions remain almost invisible. On these narrow roads, short skirts must have saved many a life after dark, though they may not have saved anything else.

Skiddaw, immediately to the north of Borrowdale, is the foundation stone of the Lakes. For of the three main groups of rock which make up the Lakeland dome (Skiddaw Slate in the north, the Borrowdale Volcanics in the centre, and the Silurian slates and shales in the south) it is Skiddaw Slate which is the oldest. It was formed of the mud deposited at the mouth of a great river, and once, presumably, provided the base on which the volcanic rocks were laid. Today, owing to the bending and buckling of the strata, it appears only on the perimeter of the area, its main block being that of the Skiddaw-Saddleback range from whence it spreads westward to include all the country between Bassenthwaite and the lower end of Ennerdale Lake. The other major outcrop is in the south of the county, at Black Combe—a dark, inverted pudding-basin of a hill that makes Cumberland visible from well beyond Morecambe Bay.

Skiddaw Slate is essentially *the* Cumbrian rock, for, apart from one or two minor appearances in Westmorland (around the lower reaches of Ullswater) and one in Furness (Kirkby Moor), it does not occur outside the county. It is bare, solid, unvaried to the point of monotony. The fells of the volcanic rocks toss and break in stormy waves, but the Skiddaw fells heave up in a rounded, unbroken sea-swell. Compared to the solemn, poker-faced stillness of, say, Mellbreak above Loweswater, most of the volcanic fells, even Langdale Pikes, look quite fidgety.

The landscape of this northern block, therefore, is markedly different from that of the main dales. It is, in fact, almost dale-less —a huge dromedary of rock, with the hollow of Glenderaterra Beck between the humps of Skiddaw and Saddleback. The only rivers of any importance which cut back into it both flow out of its further side—the Caldew, which joins the Eden at Carlisle, and the Ellen, which reaches the sea at Maryport. How solid this mountain block is, how detached and free-standing, can be seen best of all from St John's-in-the-Vale. And, if you take the road through Mungrisdale and Hesket Newmarket, and back by Over Water Tarn and the Underskiddaw side of Bassenthwaite Lake, you will more or less have encircled Skiddleback, the name I'd like to give to this mountain area.

Back o' Skiddaw (pronounced Backer Skidder) is the barest country in the Lakes. Mungrisdale* and its small white-washed church look snug enough, with the phantom-haunted Souther Fell to the west, but once you get out of this valley you are travelling on a plateau open to all the winds from Scotland. On your left are the empty Skiddleback moors; on your right the mean-looking, inhospitable, middle-height upland that stretches to the edge of the Carlisle Plain. It is not bare as the moors are bare, for the land is partly cultivated, and there are birch woods and bushy wind-breaks along the side of the military-straight main road which runs diagonally across mid-Cumberland from Penrith to Wigton. Yet it looks as un-homely as the tundra. Such villages as there are, Caldbeck and Sebergham, seem sunk below ground level in little dug-outs of valleys. Caldbeck is famous as the home of John Peel, and there is a hideous gravestone in the churchyard with two carved hunting horns jutting out of the stone as if the hounds were going to haunt him through the after-life. The church itself is of great beauty, set back from the road among trees. As with the rest of the village it is

* The first syllable is probably derived from the name of St Mungo, or Kentigern, the patron saint of Glasgow and the apostle of Cumberland. The rest of the name is 'the valley of the pigs'

Derwentwater and Catbells

built of sandstone which is what makes both Caldbeck and Sebergham look different from the villages of the dales. The latter are one with the rock about them, man and nature working together. But Back o' Skiddaw, nature is less co-operative and man has to fight hard for comfort, building his defences of the warm stone of the plain. At Sebergham, two miles down river, where the hill-country finally peters out, there are some of the fine Georgian farm-houses which are typical of the Carlisle Plain; one, near the bridge, has two clipped evergreens in the front garden like an enormous pair of tympani. This village, though less known to the public than Caldbeck, has a better right to fame, for it was there, in the eighteenth century, that the curate, Josiah Relph, wrote his dialect poems while coughing his life away in the raw, fellside winters. Relph's *Pastorals,* after the classical model, were probably the first attempt in English to use the dialect for serious poetry, and his little book of poems 'embellished with the *Picturesque Engravings* of the ingenious Mr *T. Bewick,* of Newcastle' is a volume any Cumbrian should be delighted to own.

The road from Carlisle through Dalston and Uldale, which is now being opened up as an approach to the Lakes from the north, misses Caldbeck and Sebergham and also Ireby. Very few visitors to this part of Cumberland find Ireby at all, though it has the look of having once been the capital of Back o' Skiddaw and the place where the fell farmers met the men of the Solway hinterland. It still seems quite tucked away and off route, though a whole starfish of roads spikes out from it—one of them, to Torpenhow*, so narrow that if a motorist puts out his hand to signal he is likely to put it right through the hedge! Ireby has its little moot-hall and a butter-cross, and the whole village has the air of being comfortably unconcerned whether anyone finds it or not. It is well below the bilberry-line, yet still seems to belong essentially to the fells. Indeed, it continually surprises me to see how the fell character persists, westwards, as long as the land lifts itself even a score of feet above the level of the plain. Gilcrux†, for instance,

* Pronounced to rhyme with 'McKenna', with the 'Tor' like the 'Tre' in 'Trelore'. The name contains three elements—British *Torr* and *Pen* and Anglian *How*, all of which denote, roughly, 'peak' or 'ridge'

† Pronounced 'Gil-cruce'. The name is probably derived from Old Welsh '*cil cruc*', a retreat by a hill, the present-day spelling being due to accidental association with the Latin '*crux*', a cross

River Calder

which is only a mile away from the Maryport-Carlisle railway and the old colliery at Bullgill, is as stubbornly John-Peel-like as anywhere north of Skiddleback.

There are three passes which lead from the valley of the River Derwent to that of Buttermere or Lorton: Honister, from Seatoller to Gatesgarth; Newlands, from Portinscale to Buttermere Village; and Whinlatter, from Braithwaite to High Lorton. Of these, Honister is perhaps the finest of all the motorable passes in the Lakes. You climb rather blindly out of Borrowdale, seeing nothing much but a blank fell-side in front of you, until, at a sudden twist, you find you are already at the top, threading through a cleft you had not realised was there. The Youth Hostel is at your side, and the Buttermere green-slate quarries are high above you on the ridge leading to Fleetwith Pike. The road now slithers down below the shoulder of Honister Crag with its long running sores of purplish scree, so that, if you leave it and cross Gatesgarthdale Beck by any of its accidental stepping-stones, you will find yourself at the foot of a slow-motion waterfall of broken rock. Fragments of scree and an overflow of rubble from the quarries seem almost visibly to slide apart and together again in a kind of creeping avalanche. And everywhere, among the rocks, you can see the typical fell-side flowers: yellow tormentil, blue and white milkwort, eyebright, golden saxifrage and the alpine lady's mantle, deeply palmate and silvery with down.

Newlands, the middle of the three passes and the least frequented by motorists, runs along what used to be called Keskadale—a narrow desolate valley, which has much the look of those waterless troughs you sometimes find in the Pennine limestone. At the top of the pass the land flattens out for a short space, and you can park your car and look up at the feathery water-slides of Moss Force. Once over the watershed, you drop quickly, but Buttermere is hidden at first behind the flank of the fell, and you look back, instead, up the gill-like valley of Sail Beck below the precipices of Whiteless Pike and the Eel Crag group. It is Sail Beck, of course, which has made Buttermere, by washing down the acres of silt that have cut off the lake from Crummock Water. The division between the two lakes is only a mile long and frequently disappears under flood after heavy rain, yet the moment you descend to Buttermere Village, beside the almost too neat church, you feel that this lake, this upper-dale, is secluded and self-contained as no other. On the east, the Skiddaw Slates swell up in a row of rounded fells, solid as huge potatoes—Robinson, Whiteless, Grasmoor and Whiteside; while the western side is craggier—Red Pike, High Style, High Crag and Hay Stacks, making a jagged wall unbroken for four miles except for the dips between peak and peak.

The eighteenth-century tourists admired Buttermere above all the lakes. The 'butter' implies that the lake lies in green pastures, and, in fact, the tourists saw it as another Eden, complete with an unfallen Eve, Mary Robinson, daughter of the landlord of The Fish Inn.* But if Buttermere was Paradise Re-found, Whinlatter is Paradise Destroyed, for this, the third of our three passes, is the scene of the worst-planned afforestation in the Lakes. Whinlatter, which lies in the Thornthwaite Forest, was one of the earliest properties in the district to be acquired by the Forestry Commission. In the days when it was planted the commissioners had no thought for anything but the growth of commercial timber and little idea of the effect planting would have on the landscape. As a result, Whinlatter is a large-scale demonstration of how not to do it. The spruces have been set so thick and close that walking through them is like walking through a crypt. The trees seem to die as they grow, and their trunks are wrapped in disgusting old clothes of brown and withered boughs. The wood-floor is grassless, shrubless and weedless, piled high with poisonous needles, and this whole underbough world is as dark as a cupboard. When the road dips on the Bassenthwaite side, there are fine views of Skiddaw, but even here the commissioners have made their black marks. For all round the lake the conifers are stuck up in rigid blocks and rows, with long, naked ridges or fire-breaks that look as if a barber had run his clippers up the nape of the fell.

Just about the foot of the lake, Crummock† is augmented by the outflow from Loweswater, the smallest of the three lakes that drain into the Vale of Lorton. Loweswater is almost more closed-

* For the story of Mary Robinson, 'The Beauty of Buttermere', see N. Nicholson, *The Lakers* (Robert Hale)

† The name, British in origin, means 'crooked', and was given, in the first case, to the stretch of the River Cocker which links Crummock with Buttermere

in than Buttermere, and it has one very odd thing about it—it seems to be flowing the wrong way. For from almost any point along the shore road, you look down-lake to Carling Knott and Mellbreak (perhaps the most symmetrical outcrop of Skiddaw Slate in the Lakes), and up-lake to the gentle, low hills above Waterend. *This* is the end, your eye tells you, where the water must flow out. But, of course, it isn't.

As you pass down the Vale of Lorton the landscape suffers a sea-change. I call it a sea-change because the new landscape is a marine product, made up of the limestone which swings round the northern curve of the Lake dome until it joins the Pennines in East Westmorland. Cockermouth lies at the junction of the Skiddaw Slate and this limestone. It lies also at the junction of the River Cocker and the River Derwent, hence, of course, its name. The Derwent, coming from Bassenthwaite, reaches the town by way of the little village of Isel, with its entrancing largely-Norman church by the bridge. Cockermouth, too, has its Norman building—one of the castles founded by the conquerors to secure their hold on their Cumbrian estates. Yet the impression given by the town is less one of rural antiquity than of eighteenth-century, forward-looking urban elegance. Perhaps 'sobriety' would be a better word for most of the houses, though the one where Wordsworth was born does achieve a rather sedate kind of elegance, while one on the opposite side of the street, called the Grecian Villa, is positively perky. The present parish church, which has replaced that attended by the Wordsworths, is undistinguished except in its position, high above the waters-meet, which makes the spire the most scenically effective in the Lakes. But on the whole you can understand the complacent look about the statue of the town-planning Mayor Mayo, as he divides the traffic in one of the most spacious shopping streets in Cumberland.

Move off, however, into the side streets between the main road and the river, and you will find a different Cockermouth—old works and warehouses, alleys and courts, narrow as canyons, dark and stifling, many of them ready for demolition and maybe demolished by the time this book is printed. Anyone who knows West Cumberland will immediately be reminded of the older parts of Whitehaven, while the voices of the girls coming from the footwear factories have the unmistakable west-coast tang. For Cockermouth lies at yet a third junction—that between industrial Cumberland and the Lakes.

William Wordsworth, himself, was a product of this half-way-house society. His father was agent to Sir James Lowther, who owned or controlled half the coal and iron in Cumberland; and later on his son John married Isabella Curwen of Workington Hall, daughter of the man who owned most of the other half. His uncle, Richard, was Collector of Customs at the port of Whitehaven. It is quite wrong to think of Wordsworth as one born and bred among the fells, far 'from the taint of sordid industry', to use his own words. One of his earliest recorded memories, the lovely description of bathing in the Derwent*, is clearly that of a child to whom the fells still seem to belong to the distance, while the immediate foreground is made up of the smaller realities of house, terrace, mill-race and the yellow 'grunsel' (he means ragwort) growing by the river. At Cockermouth the Wordsworth children must have found themselves betwixt and between socially as well as geographically. They could not call themselves gentlefolk, yet, since their father was agent to one of the most unpopular men in Cumberland, they would hardly mix freely with the Cockermouth children. For a short while William attended the grammar school (now pulled down) which stood in the churchyard, but he seems to have made no friends there, though one of his contemporaries, six years older than himself, was Fletcher Christian, later to be famous as the leader of the mutiny on *The Bounty*. When their mother died, in 1778, the Wordsworth children left Cockermouth, and William and Dorothy went to Penrith, to the home of their uncle and aunt, William and Dorothy Cookson. From then onwards the poet's boyhood memories centred round Penrith or, much more, round Hawkshead, where he was sent to school in the following year. He began his life, however, at the perimeter of the district, awkwardly situated between the dales and the mines, between the old way of life and the new. When, eventually, he settled at Grasmere, it was an act of protest, a deliberate turning away from the kind of society the Industrial Revolution was producing.

Unfortunately that turning-away left industrial England

* *The Prelude*, Book I, lines 282-300

stranded. To most visitors, from Wordsworth's time onward, the coal-mines of Whitehaven just did not seem to belong to the same county as Derwentwater. Today, the two sectors are drawing closer again. Many people who live in Cockermouth work in the new industries of the coast, while Keswick and the tourist area rely to a considerable extent on the patronage of the day-visitors from the nearby industrial towns. The whole future of Cumberland, if it is not to stagnate into a gigantic holiday-camp, depends on a balance between town and country, industry and landscape. And Cockermouth stands, as it were, at the fulcrum, which makes it one of the most significant spots in the whole county.

CHAPTER THREE

THE LAKES: THE WESTERN DALES

To reach Ennerdale (the derivation of the name is obscure) from Cockermouth you take the Egremont road, turn off for Ennerdale Bridge, and then go by the track to the now demolished hotel at the water edge. From Buttermere it is better to go by Loweswater to Lamplugh and there take the narrow, under-fell road through Croasdale. Lamplugh itself is a paradoxical village, lying as snugly against the paunch of the fell as a fob-watch in a waistcoat pocket, yet looking as if it did not really belong there, since walls, barns, the old hall and the church are built, not of the slate they stand on, but of red sandstone carted in from the Cumberland plateau. The road to Croasdale runs almost along the bracken-line, and at Leaps Beck, beneath Murton Fell, you can see the red spoil-heaps of one of the earliest deposits of local haematite to be worked on a really commercial scale. The place is now silent and deserted, but it is one of the starting points of modern Cumberland.

The view from the foot of Ennerdale Water is a famous one, and since there is no motor road up the dale, it is the only view most people see. Instead of dwindling to river-width, as most lakes do, the bottom end of Ennerdale Water broadens out into an almost circular basin, about a mile in diameter. Above this basin, the lake narrows, pinched in between two out-jutting rocks—Bowness Knott on the left, and Angler's Crag on the right—each with a backing of still higher crags and fells. In sunless weather they make a black, forbidding front curtain, which, for theatrical effect, is not excelled even by Borrowdale. The upper half of the lake bends out of sight, behind Bowness Knott, but above it, six miles away, is Pillar, looking like an end-stop to the valley, though, in fact, the river and the track swing round it and beyond.

The upper dale is the country of the Ennerdale Granophyre, a beautiful, pinkish, igneous rock, very like its near neighbour, the

Eskdale Granite. It is a rock usually seen at a distance, as crag and peak. To see it close at hand, you should make your way from Croasdale to the beginning of the forestry road along the northern shore of the lake. If the gate is unlocked, you can drive a car carefully along the unmetalled track as far as Gillerthwaite. If it *is* locked, there is still a right of way for walkers to the top of the dale, and farther if you like, by Scarth Gap to Buttermere or by Black Sail to Wasdale. And all this way the granophyre will be round about you: in the walls, in the cobbles, and in the cuttings made by the becks as they bustle under the track on their way to the river.

Mention of forestry, however, brings us into the area of controversy. I did not know Ennerdale before the trees were planted. Those who did have complained that the valley is 'smothered by firs', or say that from the tops it now looks like a bath half full of dirty green water. What must once have been one of the barest and most Icelandic of the dales has now largely disappeared from view at river level. Yet what has come in its place seems strangely attractive. Indeed, by counteracting the erosion which was quickly turning all these western fellsides into barren scree and bracken, afforestation may help to restore the land to something like its former fertility. It would be better, of course, if the trees were oaks or chestnuts rather than conifers, but even the latter protect the soil from wind and frost and, above all, from the sheep. For sheep are the dust-bowl farmers of the fells. They extract the mineral content from the soil and store it in their wool, so that, instead of its being given back to the land as manure, it is carried away for ever in the year's clip. Sheep are essential to the economy of the dales, of course, and, acre for acre, they support more families than the forests. Yet it seems likely that the hill-farms will decrease in number and increase in size, so needing larger flocks and more capital but less labour. The forests, on the other hand, as they mature, should give work to such associated trades as saw-mills, rustic furniture and the like, bringing some of the all-the-year round employment that the Lake District so badly needs.

The question of the effect of planting on the Lake scene had better be left until we come to the areas where it has been carried out with some imagination. Ennerdale is not one of these. There is little variety in choice of tree, the upper line of the plantation is angular and mostly unrelated to natural contours, and the woods can seem monotonous if you insist on walking through them, mile after mile. Yet, if you are prepared to stand still or potter about, you will have no need to complain of monotony. The Ennerdale plantations have none of the black deadness of Whinlatter. For the most part, they are of Christmas tree evergreens, full of robins, blue tits and the blue jay, which, flashing among the boughs, always looks fawn and white, like a little flying deer. Chinks of birdsong glitter beneath the shadows. At every turn and dip in the track you can see Pillar or Steeple, spiring up above the dale, and, because this is not a public highway, you are not fenced about on either side, but enclosed by old stone walls or merely by grass verges. Where the little becks carve out their small gills, you can climb into the heart of the woods, along small waterfalls almost swamped under huge Niagaras of fern. Below you, often very close, is the river—called the Liza above the lake and the Ehen below it. And because Ennerdale is a heavily-glaciated dale with an almost flat valley-floor, the river at times moons about among loops and islands of shingle.

The same certainly cannot be said of the River Bleng, Ennerdale's next-door-but-one neighbour, and a tributary of Wasdale's River Irt, which can be approached from Wellington Brow, about a mile from Gosforth. Blengdale, too, is an afforested valley, smaller, narrower, more closed-in than Ennerdale and barred entirely to the motorist. The river here is rocky and raucous, and there is a good deal of the original timber still standing, ash and wild cherry, with the yellow water ragwort and big, ungainly, dandelion-like hawkweeds that seem to reflect back all the sunlight which has got through the mesh of the trees. The road winds with the beck, giving a succession of small vignettes, hirsute with pine trees. It is Scandinavia in miniature—chamber Sibelius.

Between Ennerdale and Wasdale lies the small valley of the River Calder which conceals one of the oddities of the Lakes—a snip of the general pattern printed on a different material. From Ennerdale Bridge you leave the River Ehen and cross Cold Fell to Calder Bridge. As you climb out of the valley there is one fine backward view of Ennerdale Lake, but afterwards you move across a rather formless landscape of a kind not often found so near the high fells. You pass, on the left, a partially reconstructed stone circle, marking a burial site, and find that you are running round the side of a huge smooth hump of hill-land, that seems to have been modelled in clay, for there is next to no sign of rock. On your right, every now and then, the land is scooped out into huge chutes, at the end of which you can see smoke drifting up from the iron and coal towns. Beyond is the Solway, and, when at last you begin the descent, the Isle of Man is straight before you. There has been a good deal of afforestation beside this road: geometrical clumps of dark evergreens, bordered by lighter larches, like patches that don't match. Some people dislike the plantations, but for me anything that breaks the monotony of this moorland is very welcome.

It is when you drop to the river at Calder Bridge that you first notice the change in colour. Here—as at Lamplugh, Beckermet and Gosforth—the walls and farms, the church and the older houses are all built of sandstone. But if you look over the wall by the church, you will see that at Calder Bridge this is not an imported stone, for the river runs through slabs and mouldings of red rock, smooth to the eye and rough to the touch. Sandstone is common enough in the northern parts of Cumberland and Westmorland and gives us some of our best river scenery. But the upper Calder Valley is the one place where this rock wedges itself right up among the mountains. You can sense the difference as soon as you leave the village by the road which runs past Calder Abbey. There are drystone walls, as in other parts of the Lakes, but they seem to be made of huge slabs of gingerbread, greened and mildewed with age. Even the farmers have joined in the wish to be different, for some of the field-hedges are planted with laburnum, which hardly seems the right tree to keep the sheep out, though it looks pretty as a birthday card in spring.

The abbey*, which is in private ownership though house and ruins are open to the public, was founded in 1134 by a colony of monks and lay-brothers from Furness—Benedictines who later adopted the rule of the Cistercian order. It was never one of the wealthier religious houses of the north-west, and the ruins

* For more about Calder Abbey see N. Nicholson, *Portrait of the Lakes* (Robert Hale)

are not nearly so extensive as those at Furness or Lanercost, but they are perhaps more romantically sited than either and are beautifully in scale and in tone with the valley to which they belong.

Above the abbey the road and river push their way through gone-to-seed plantations of almost black rhododendrons, until the road gives up the effort at Thornholme, and the river trowels out a steep-sided trough deep down below the plasterings of glacial clay. It is hard to remember that you are only a few miles away from the world's first atomic power-station at Calder Hall.

The next valley to the south is Wasdale, or Wastdale, not the 'westdale' but more probably 'the dale of the lake' from Old Norse *vatn*, water, and *dalr*. Wastwater, by the same derivation, is 'water water'! The most usual approach to the dale is through Gosforth on the Whitehaven-Millom main road. Like Calder Bridge, Gosforth is built mainly of dark red sandstone, and the square, phlegmatic houses along the main street have the look more of a mining-town terrace than of a typical dale village. In fact, it is far from typical. Historically, it belongs with the roots of Cumberland, for the church precincts contain some of our most important Norse antiquities: two hog-backs and three crosses, of which the standing cross in the churchyard is the finest of its kind in England. It is slim as a birch tree, round at the base, then cut into four faces and tapered to a small wheel-head cross at the top. The carvings represent both the Crucifixion and such conventional Christian symbols as that of a stag chased by hounds, and, at the same time, figures and scenes which seem to come from Norse mythology*.

Other signs of this vital cross-breeding between the two cultures, Irish-Christian and Norse-pagan, can be seen all along the West Cumberland coast. There are many place-names, for instance, in which an Irish personal name is joined to a Norse element. Aspatria is the most notable case. Here the Irish 'Patrick' is joined to the Old Norse *askr*, an ash tree, and the whole word is turned cart-before-the-horse after the Celtic fashion. Vikings who had not lived in Ireland would have put the man's name first, as

* For a fuller description see N. Nicholson, *Portrait of the Lakes*. The standard book on the subject is W. S. Calverley, *Early Sculptured Crosses of the Diocese of Carlisle*

in the present-day Ullswater, which is Ulf's lake. The practice was even continued by habit in names which have no Celtic associations at all. In the south of Cumberland, for instance, there is a whole batch of hamlets or farms with names of a similar form: Hallsenna, Hall Waberthwaite, Hallthwaites, each of which would probably have been called Senna Hall and so on in most other parts of England.

It should be remembered, however, that this Celtic-type inversion-compound is still an eccentric form, possibly adopted only by those Norsemen who had been overtouched by the blarney—those, in fact, who came rather late to Cumberland and so had an extra generation or two of Irish mothers-in-law behind them. As a general rule the Norsemen and the Danes continued to put the defined term second, as is still the case in English. Thus in Cumberland and Westmorland we say Scafell and not Fell Scar, Troutbeck and not Beck Trout. And if we want to differentiate between town and lake of the same name, let us speak of Windermere Town and Windermere Lake, and not twist our tongues into the ridiculous affectation of 'Lake Windermere'. As for such monstrous tautologies as 'Lake Ullswater' and 'Lake Derwentwater', I can only say that it would be as logical to speak of 'Mount Richmond Hill'.

The Irish influence on the Norsemen shows also in their devotion to the Irish saints. St Bega is commemorated at St Bees. St Bridget, the sister of St Patrick, can claim the dedication of the old church at Beckermet and is also remembered at Bridekirk near Cockermouth and at Kirkbride on the Solway, the latter being yet another example of a Celtic inversion. So also, at the opposite end of the county, is Kirksanton, the church of the Irish Saint Sancton.

But, in spite of all its early associations, Gosforth has recently been jerked into the twentieth century and is now the home of many of the scientists who work at Windscale and Calder Hall. The early effects of this impact of new upon old, of a technical-minded, urban-educated, off-comer group on a static, partly ingrown, rural community was the subject of a fascinating study made during the 1950's by Mr W. M. Williams*. His book

* *The Sociology of an English Village—Gosforth*, International Library of Sociology and Social Reconstruction (Routledge & Kegan Paul, 1956)

contained much detailed observation of the church-going, drinking and sexual habits of the villagers, their taste in furniture, their attitude to contraception and the like. Its most interesting pages, however, dealt with the social hierarchy which then prevailed and with the way the new suburban scale of social status, based largely on money, was clashing with the old rural scale, based partly on family, but partly also on a man's personal standing in the community, a thing to be gained neither easily nor quickly. 'They've got to summer you and winter you and summer you and winter you, afore you mak friends in Gosforth,' runs a local saying, and some say you must live in the parish for twenty years before you are accepted. Thus, a well-to-do off-comer was rated lower in the social scale than an impoverished member of one of the old county families who lived in a small cottage and did most of the housework himself. On the other hand, when a local farmer's widow bid up to a high price for a house, the revelation of her wealth caused surprise but did not raise her social status. Needless to say, when the study appeared in print it caused some annoyance among the local people who had not expected their back-kitchens to be thrown open to the public in this way. But for those who want to know what life in the Lake District is really like, this is a valuable and highly entertaining book.

The road from Gosforth crosses the River Bleng and reaches the western shore of Wastwater about a mile above the foot of the lake. There is a story in my family of an uncle from Durham who went to Wasdale by horse-drawn wagonette and said he was surprised that the sea came in so far. In fact, he was not very wrong, for Wastwater, more than any of the other lakes, looks like a Norwegian fjord. There is little of the usual margin of silt, willows and shingle between fellside and water-edge, while on the screeside the water cuts clean along the drop of the rock.

The view from this point is so familiar, even to those who haven't been there, that there is no need to describe it. An inventory will do as well. In the foreground, the lake; on the left, Seatallan, Yewbarrow and Kirk Fell; in the centre, the pyramid of Great Gable; on the right background, Lingmell, Scafell Pike and Scafell; on the right foreground, the Screes. It is one of the few views in the Lakes which looks as good in summer as in the other three seasons, for it is so much a matter of shape, proportion and balance that even the drab green of August does not smudge the effect.

But because the landscape is so very still, it is seen at its best when the air is moving, either in a storm, or in those times, between successive depressions, when moist clean air blows in from the Atlantic carrying foam-balls and tatters of cloud. Then, changing minute by minute, one peak will be blotted out and another in bright sunlight, or a huge waterfall of cloud will pour down the cleft between Kirk Fell and Gable, while the top of the latter floats like an island above the tide.

Wasdale is wonderfully typical of the landscape of the Borrowdale Volcanic rocks which make up the centre of the district and include all the highest peaks, except Skiddaw and Saddleback, and at least half of the lakes. These volcanics are still 'slate' in the common use of the term, but they were formed, not of mud, like the Skiddaw rocks, but of the lava and ashes thrown up by ancient volcanoes, probably under the sea. And this mixture of material that went to their making has produced rocks that vary greatly in degrees of hardness—the lavas, on the whole, forming rocks of greater durability, and the ashes, rocks which easily crumble. The result is often a terraced effect, of steep laval cliffs and gentler ash slopes. Where the volcanic ash has been subjected to pressure, however, it may turn as hard as iron; at other times it will split along the line of the cleavage and weather into mere scree.

This is what gives rise to the continual variation in the landscape of the inner ring of the Lakes—a restless swirling turmoil of peaks, crags, pinnacles, screes, gills, clefts, tarns and waterfalls. One side of a valley will be as hairy as Harris Tweed; the other will be glabrous as leather, with a dark green mould of moss in the creases. At one point in its course a beck will be oozing blackly through peat and bilberries and glacial clay; and, five minutes later, it will be head-over-heeling down a gill, through a fracas of dumped boulders and arthritic rowans. The most dramatic of all such scene changes is that of Wasdale. At one end of the lake there is the enormous west drop of Scafell, 3,000 feet of bomb-proof rock-walling; at the other end are the Screes, the biggest geological ash-heap in England, where a whole fellside is slithering away like the brick and plaster of a bull-dozed slum-clearance area.

Because it has been photographed so often, Wasdale seems to be more of a view than a real place. The familiar image of the lake, gathered from calendars and picture postcards before you ever go there, comes in between the eyes and the real thing. So that if you want Wasdale to become its true self, you should walk away from the picture-frame and see it from a less posed position. First of all go to the foot of the lake. This used to be the private estate of Wasdale Hall, but has now been bought by the National Trust, which has opened a public footpath along the shore of the lake and turned the hall, a pleasant nineteenth-century building of pink Eskdale granite, into a new Youth Hostel. From here you look square at the Screes, only a couple of hundred yards away across the water. In the morning it takes the sun a long time to slant over this skyline, and, while all the fells of Copeland Forest are swimming in sunshine, the lake remains black in shadow. And in the evening, when the western shore is settled into dusk, the Screes reflect the glow of the sky, volleying it down into the water, which glimmers dark purple and lilac and red long after the fells have lost all trace of colour.

To see the Screes still closer at hand, you either wade across the river, or go down to the bridge near Strands and take the lane to the pumping-house at the foot of the lake. From here there is a foot-path, not along the shore but running ten to fifty feet above it, the whole length of the lake as far as Wasdale Head Hall. The track is rough, needs firm feet and a head for heights, and the full three miles of it is more than I can manage to scramble. But even to venture only a quarter of a mile along it is to have a new view of Wastwater. Gable and the Scafells are out of sight, behind the running buttresses of the Screes, so that for once your attention is not held by that demanding centre-piece. The first thing you realise is that the Screes are not nearly so steep as they look from the other side. The second, is that they are by no means just bare rock. In among the slides of loose stones are scratchings or terraces of soil, covered with turf or bilberry or bracken. In autumn and winter, the Screes are like an enormous, old-fashioned school slate, chalked over in brown and red, and in spring they are chalked in yellow-green. This is a place where the alpine lady's-mantle grows, and, more surprising still, there are bushes and trees—gorse, juniper, holly and old hawthorns—which seem to wriggle out of chimneys and fissures like ferns growing in cracks of a wall.

Or go to Wasdale Head and take the track that leads along Mosedale Beck to Black Sail. You begin from behind the hotel, where there is a fine example of the kind of hump-backed, slate bridge usually called 'pack-horse'. And before you have gone very far up the rise, you see a splendid exhibition of one of the Lake District's native crafts, that of dry-stone walling. For the whole of this dead-flat upper dale is divided by stone walls into irregularly shaped fields, one of which, not otherwise different from the others, contains the church and the graves of fallen rock-climbers.

The earliest dry-stone walls were built not of quarried slate but of cobbles gathered up when a space was cleared for cultivation. The biggest boulders were then merely rolled to the edge of what was to be the new field and left there to become the base of the walls. When the long, wandering walls that mark out farm and grazing boundaries began to be built on the fells, the wallers opened small quarries in the fellside and brought down the slate in sledges. As each section of wall reached the level of the quarry, they opened another quarry, higher up, to avoid the labour of carrying the stone uphill.

A well-built dry-stone wall is really *two* walls, side by side, each made of stones carefully fitted one to the other, while the gap is filled with rubble and small fragments. It is this loose filling which allows the wall to settle and adjust itself to any movements in the ground beneath. To strengthen the wall, the builders laid a row of flat slabs that cross through from side to side, joining the two outer walls together. Often there are two such rows of through-stones in a wall, sometimes three, and they may project at the side, making a ridge running the whole length of the wall which people sometimes think is intended as a kind of stile.

Another type of stone-fencing to be seen in Wasdale (between Wasdale Hall and Strands) is that made by setting up slabs of slate side by side, like gravestones, sometimes strengthened by a row of thorn trees planted against it. There are a lot of these slab fences in the Hawkshead area.

It is Strands or Nether Wasdale which is the real village of the dale, though, as it lies between the two main lines of approach to the lake—from Gosforth and from Santon Bridge—it is missed

River Duddon, above Birks Bridge

by many visitors. It is built mainly of Eskdale Granite, is surprisingly spacious and has behind it a hill piled high with half-wild rhododendrons, which, around Whitsuntide, make the fell-side look like a florist's stall in a market. (The same can be said for Latterbarrow Crag beside the road to Santon Bridge.)

The church at Strands is less celebrated than that at Wasdale Head, lacking the romantic appeal of the climbers' graves, but it is a far more interesting building. Inside, it is quite surprisingly light for a dale church. There is a most agreeable wooden arcade to the north aisle, added in the 1830's, and a wagon roof with plaster bosses. The tables of the Creed, Lord's Prayer and Ten Commandments on either side of the little east window, date from the same time, and even the mid-Victorian wall-memorials, mostly of owners of Wasdale Hall and their families, show a surprisingly sober taste.

There is some older wall-writing, too, discovered in 1958, after having been under the plaster for many years; there is some medieval wood-work, rather injudiciously varnished, which came originally from York Minster; and there are also some amusing cherubs at the head of the pillars. And the Royal Arms of George III glares down from the west end on what in his day was still the high-and-dry Church that shut eyes and ears against Methodism, radicalism, the Industrial Revolution and the poetry of William Wordsworth.

I have spent some time on this church, partly because it is not sufficiently well known, but mostly because it is typical of the mid-dale churches in its simplicity, its unpretentiousness, its quiet self-composure, and, most typical of all perhaps, in the way in which it refuses to conform to type.

Below the village of Strands, Wasdale peters out and almost loses the character of a valley. There is perhaps a certain air of doom about these parts. Beside the road over Irton Pike, just above Santon Bridge, there is a stone commemorating the place where a Methodist local preacher collapsed and died on his way to a service. It bears the words 'Be ye also ready', while the little Methodist chapel on the other side of the village exhorts one to 'Flee from the wrath to come'. It is almost as if the nineteenth-century Evangelicals anticipated Calder Hall!

After Santon Bridge the river flows past Irton Hall (once a

The Pike, Duddon Valley

pele tower and now a school for spastic children) and begins to dilly-dally in the meadows by the isolated Irton Church and the equally isolated junior school. The *tun* of Irton, of course, shows that this was the site of one of the few English settlements along this coast, and the churchyard contains a splendid specimen of an Anglian cross, less historically important than the Norse cross at Gosforth, but even more satisfying as a work of art.

Then, a mile away, at Holmrook, the Irt runs beneath the main road and begins to ooze out into the salt marshes where it meets the Rivers Mite and Esk and leaks into the sea. It seems a tame ending to Wasdale's river.

Most people arrive in Eskdale at about mid-dale, and the middle stretch, from Eskdale Green to Boot, which cuts Eskdale into two parts, is comparatively populous and built on. This is mainly the result of the Eskdale Narrow Gauge Railway which, in the days before the motor-car, made Eskdale the most accessible of the western valleys. When I was a boy a ride on the Ratty was summer's special treat, and, once the train had arrived at the terminus, nearly everyone set off, past Dalegarth Hall, for Stanley Gill and the waterfall. The hall, at the foot of the gill, is one of those manor houses, not quite pele towers, that were nevertheless fortified against possible Scottish raids. Its chimneys are fine examples of the huge cylindrical structures which are the Lake District's own special contribution to English domestic architecture. Today waterfalls are out of fashion, and the path to the gill is much overgrown. The fifteen-inch gauge railway, on the other hand, is as popular as ever, and is kept going throughout the summer by bands of enthusiastic amateurs.

Above The Woolpack Inn, where for centuries the farmers have held their Shepherds' Meet and where I spent my honeymoon, the dale becomes barer and bonier. The river accompanies the road for about two miles and then swings left, by Brotherilkeld and Taw House, and eats its way like a woodworm into the core of the mountains. The track which runs beside it is surely the most private, overhung, utterly-locked-off right of way of any in England, though you can get an outsider's view of it from just beyond the walls of the Roman Fort half-way up Hardknott Pass.

This fort at Hardknott is less extensive than the one at Housesteads on the Wall, but it stands on a site of unparallelled impregnability. On three sides the land drops almost sheer; on the fourth, it slopes up less steeply to the Parade Ground with the fell beyond it. Hardknott is on the Roman route from Ambleside, via Little Langdale and Wrynose Pass, to the Roman port of Clanoventa, at Ravenglass, which, though the point has been disputed, is thought to have been the place from which the Romans planned to invade Ireland. The walls of the fort are now in the care of H.M. Ministry of Public Building and Works, and have been treated to the same kind of restoration which has roused so much controversy at Hadrian's Wall, and though I feel much sympathy with those archaeologists who argue that the ruins should be left as the Romans left them, yet I cannot forget that the Romans did not, in fact, leave them as ruins.

But Hardknott is not only a Roman road, it is on the line of the Lake District's most celebrated obstacle race—in fact, the twists and nearly one-in-three gradients of the pass make what is said to be the most severe classified road in Britain. At a busy weekend, one bad change of gear can force a long queue of cars to begin nervously reversing round precipitous bends, and on Bank Holidays the village children take their tea there to enjoy the fun.

The lower reaches of Eskdale, from the village to the estuary, were at one time little visited because of the lack of a road, but now the track from Forge House, where the Eskdale and Ennerdale foxhounds are kennelled, to Muncaster Bridge has been opened up and is well surfaced though narrow. At the bridge, on the Whitehaven-Millom main road, the river is still tidal, swelling and ebbing among Chinese rice-fields of man-high reeds, with yellow flags growing at the edge of the salt-flats. In many ways it looks a typical lower-end dale: the flat bottom, the stone walls, the birches and hollies on the slopes, and the clerestory of crags on the fellside. But the granite gives it a character of its own, and the view of the estuary, from the old Eskmeals Station, is one of the most Scottish-looking views in the Lakes—the heather-coloured, tumbling rock all round, the bristly conifers, the Scafells in the distance, and the sea-loch in the foreground.

In their upper reaches the Esk and the Duddon are separated

only by the almost conical Harter Fell, one of the craggiest, shaggiest, most scree-bitten peaks in the whole of the Lakes. Lower down, the division between them widens out into a roll of moorland culminating in the huge gumboil of Black Combe.

You can cross the ridge from Eskdale Green by Birker Moor, along an easy upland road, where you sometimes see the Highland cattle with which the farmers are experimenting as an alternative to sheep. To the west of the road, on the lower slopes of Hesk Fell, is the farm group of Woodend, where there was once a Quaker settlement that must have been one of the most isolated communities in Cumberland—above the snow-line much of the winter, below the cloud-line much of the summer, and walled off in a Quaker silence throughout the year.

Yet Birker holds a spot lonelier even than this, for Devoke Water is the least seen of all the lakes, though the bridle path to it is clearly sign-posted at the side of the road. From the signpost you have to walk about 500 yards before the lake comes into sight. One wonders whether to call it a lake or a tarn. In size it is as much a lake as, say, Grasmere or Rydal Water, but it has the bareness, the dreariness, the essentially up-land character of a tarn. The water looks as if it has been trapped there since the Ice Age, the last meltings of the last glacier. And apart from one half-ruined fishing lodge, built for the owners of Muncaster Castle, the place can have changed very little since then. If you go down the slope and squelch along the shore, the scene begins to look more cheerful, with the brown grouse revving up in the bilberries. The water, too, from here, has a glint on it and was once famous for its trout. But it is in the black of winter, when the night wind from the Irish Sea blows over my roof straight on to these fells that I think most often of Devoke. There are stories of tramps breaking into the fishing lodge, lighting a fire in the iron fireplace, and spending the night there, wrapped in their rags. The men of the Bronze Age, living in stone huts at Barnscar, not very far away, would scarcely have had cause for envy.

The other road joining Eskdale and Dunnerdale runs closer to Black Combe, from Corney to Loganbeck and Duddon Bridge. When I was a boy this was a green turf track, and I used to join it by the old 'workhouse road' (still a green track) from Bootle village, past the engagingly fussy waterfall of Gibson Spout. As you climb up from the Corney side there are views of the Isle of Man and Galloway, with the cooling towers of Calder Hall fuming romantically in the middle distance. And when you have crossed the ridge, if you watch out for a farm about a mile away on the right, you should be able to spot the Swinside Stone Circle, standing in its walled field.

Up to now the valley of the Duddon has not been seen, but soon you round a little swelling in the moor and suddenly you are looking right down into Dunnerdale. For me no view in the Lakes is more memorable. To the north is the hind-side of the Scafells, and across the valley the great mass of the Coniston group. All around is the sour moor, dabbed with the dark green of juniper bushes, which most people mistake for flower-less gorse. But you hardly notice any of this, for your eyes are drawn to the valley, the narrow aisle of cultivated land running up between the fells. There are cottages, farms, a church, fields, woods, and on either side is as rough a sea of crag and bracken as any in England. Even today it is not hard to sense the centuries of stubborn back-breaking work which have gone to making this valley habitable and homely. You are looking, however, at only about one fifth of the dale—the stretch between Ulpha and Seathwaite. Behind Wallabarrow Crag, which, from this viewpoint, seems to plug the dale like a cork, there are another five or six miles of meadowed riverside before the sheep take over completely at Cockley Beck. But if you want to understand the self-contained, ingrown, almost insular type of society which persisted in the dales until about the middle of the eighteenth century, then this view will help you more than any other.

I have written so much elsewhere about the Duddon that I will say little more about it now except to point out that of all the dales it is the most completely and consistently dale-like. Dunnerdale does not peter out. Stand on Duddon Bridge, looking upward, and you are in the 'jaws' of the valley, with steep, wooded hillsides jutting up on either side. Turn round, and only a couple of hundred yards away you can see the beginnings of the tidal marshes. The ruins of the eighteenth-century ironworks hidden among the trees of High Duddon mark the meeting-place of dale and sea, for the charcoal for the furnace came from the woods and the ore was brought up the estuary at high tide. The ruins themselves are as compelling to the imagination as those of any medieval abbey—vast and solitary, with the vent of the main furnace still intact. Already nature is fighting back, and the old walls are beginning to look more like screes than the work of man, yet the steel-works of Barrow and the iron-works of Millom lay latent in that old furnace like a tulip in a bulb.

To enter Dunnerdale from anywhere, top, bottom or side, you have to go over a hill—unless you walk the three miles through the Duddon Hall woods, where the water-side reeks of wild garlic in spring and itches with ants in summer. (Ants, in fact, are particularly troublesome along almost the whole of the Duddon.) And of all the side-approaches the most delightful is the road from Broughton Mills to Hall Dunnerdale Bridge, the final part of which lies between slate slab fencing and a huge twelve-foot-high wall made of rolled-away boulders the size of chests-of-drawers. Broughton Mills stands on the banks of the River Lickle, the Duddon's only tributary of any size, and is a pleasant village with two splendid specimens of tile-hung farm-houses—Hesketh Hall and Hobkin Ground. Above the village is one of the loveliest and least frequented of the smaller valleys, but the roads are claustrophobically narrow and hard to find, and I am not going to help anyone to find them. There is one place where a beck—not the Lickle—comes out of a plantation, flows under a bridge, in a typically off-hand manner, and on towards the ruins of an old farm. There it suddenly dives deep into the ground, making not so much a gill as a fifty-foot-deep trench, which worms through woods to meet the main river. In April there are daffodils as truly wild as they ever are in England, and later on you can find a flower more typical of the uplands—the yellow globe-flower, *trollius europaeus*, often balanced in mid-stream on clumps of soil no bigger than a bowler hat*.

The Lickle Valley is one of the places where the new forestry plantations have been planned with care and imagination. Here, and in upper Dunnerdale, the planting is asymmetrical and mixed—larches among the evergreens, with edgings of birch and oak. On the Hawk, a hill above the Lickle, the new line of the conifers follows the natural contour close to the former line of the bracken,

* This flower can be seen in profusion on the banks of the River Brathay just above Skelwith Bridge

while the larch changes colour with the seasons like the bracken itself. Walk in a larchwood before the worst of the winter storms, and you will see thousands of larch-needles caught on the spider-webs as if the spiders had turned vegetarian.

The 'sea' in the Borrowdale Seathwaite is probably derived from the Norse *sef* or sedge, but it has been suggested that the 'sea' of the Dunnerdale Seathwaite comes from 'sea' in its present sense, which, in this case, would be Seathwaite Tarn. This is the tarn which empties into the large beck that flows close by Seathwaite Church, where visitors often mistake it for the Duddon, as they sit in their folding chairs and watch the salmon leap up the waterfalls.

Many years ago, as a boy, I looked down on Seathwaite Tarn from the Coniston Old Man ridge, but since then such high places have been beyond my limit unless they are accessible by car. Seathwaite Tarn, however, is a reservoir for Barrow-in-Furness and can be approached from just above Holling House by a rough gravel road which is open to walkers but usually locked to cars. Late one summer evening, through circumstances which the Barrow Corporation will excuse my having forgotten, I found myself stranded in a car on the edge of the tarn while a companion walked back to Seathwaite to telephone for help. I walked across the wall of the small dam, beyond which there is nothing to show you that the place is in any way touched by man. The tarn veers to the right at the bottom of an enormous curving cleft, the walls of which, high above, are scraped and scabrous with scree. The sun had set, and a green reservoir of dusk seemed to be held in by the crags just as the black water beneath was held in by the dam. The damp rose up from the tarn, and I was driven back into the car to watch the clouds darken and discolour like rotting apples and the sheep sink into the mist. It was ten-o'clock-news-time and I had the smell of the twentieth century in my nose, but outside it was as bleak, lonely and frightening as it must have seemed to all who have lost their way in these hills any time during the last 2,000 years.

It may seem odd to count the Langdales among the Western Dales, since they run almost due east, yet in substance and character they belong with the Wasdale, Eskdale and Coniston fells, and have little in common with the Windermere country towards which they look.

I came to Little Langdale for the first time when I was a boy, having pushed a bicycle from Dunnerdale up what was then the gravel road of Wrynose Pass. I was not thinking of what I would see when I got to the top, for, since Cockley Beck, all my thoughts had been fixed on the source of the Duddon. For fifteen years I had lived beside that river, at the point where it ends and empties into the sea, and now I was going to find the point where it began. I did not find it, of course, for above Cockley Beck the river divides into half a dozen becks and tributaries, any one of which may reasonably be called the source of the Duddon. So that when I got to the top of the pass, I had a feeling of anti-climax. There was the Three Shires Stone, marking the place where Cumberland, Westmorland and Lancashire meet, but otherwise there was nothing much to look at—no view, only rough grass and bog-holes filled with a plant which I did not then know to be buckbean. I pushed my bicycle, rather grudgingly, for another hundred yards or so, and then, suddenly, Little Langdale opened before me like a crevasse—the deep grove of the upper-dale, the tree-less tarn, the little knoll of Birk Howe hiding the village, and, further off, Windermere and the fells beyond. I found I could not ride down after all, for the road was steeper than on the Cumberland side of the pass, and the surface little better than that of a stone wall pushed over. But that hardly seemed to matter. I reached the village and stopped for a glass of cider at the inn, then called The Tourist's Rest, but since imaginatively re-named The Three Shires by a relative of mine.

'You'll fall off your machine', said the inn-keeper, and gave me a non-alcoholic imitation.

Since then the track over Wrynose has been well-surfaced, though anyone who crossed it a few days after the storm of 13th-14th August 1966 could see it much in its old rough state. At that time in a matter of hours a huge reservoir of rain poured down a small area centred around the heads of Dunnerdale, Borrowdale and the two Langdales. Damage in Borrowdale was estimated at £100,000 and farmers reckon that some of their fields have been lost to cultivation for ever.

In Dunnerdale damage was less extensive, though the beautiful

Birks Bridge, which normally stands about thirty feet above the river, was snapped in half, the walls on the Lancashire side being swept away with only the arch left standing. Above Cockley Beck cart-loads of boulders were tipped four feet deep on the water pastures, beck-side walls were tossed away, and huge scallops bitten out of the river-banks. All the little fell springs seemed to have erupted, pouring out lava-like gushes of clay. Other spots looked as if a rake, twenty or thirty yards wide, had been scraped down the fellside, leaving long sores of raw, blue scree. At one farm in Little Langdale the water poured in one door and out of another, dropping the débris of the Ice Age on the fitted carpets. And those of us who live only a dozen miles away thought of it only as a rather wet night!

In ordinary summer weather, however, the only blockage on the Wrynose-Little Langdale route is likely to be from the eruption of cars, in spite of which I hope the planners will not be tempted to 'improve' this road. For Little Langdale, as it still remains, is one of the most perfect of the dales, where a way of life that took centuries to evolve can be sensed from the relation of house to house and house to rock—the village with inn, post-office, the old school (with a church-room upstairs), the beautiful, largely seventeenth-century farm-houses of Birk Howe, Bield and Fell Foot, merging into the fellside as if they had grown out of it, the quarrymen's cottages and the quarrymen's bridge, called Slaters Bridge, which is a combination of the typical hump-back of the Lakes with the clapperstone of the Pennines. Driving a full-size motor road up this dale would be as senseless as laying a tarmac footpath through Westminster Abbey.

Great Langdale, too, has been threatened with a wider road, and, though I hope it will not happen, I admit that it would be less disastrous than in Little Langdale. For Greater Langdale lacks the privacy of its smaller neighbour. It is more of a corridor than a valley, so that as you ascend all you notice is the magnificent twin-tower elevation of the Pikes like the west end of a cathedral. The trouble is that once the cars have reached Dungeon Gill or thereabouts, there is really nowhere else for them to go, and if the road is enlarged there is a danger that Mickleden will be turned into a giant carpark. (Already the valley has become an Easter meeting ground for campers, some of whom have flashed knives in the inns, pulled down signposts and damaged gates.) Alternatively, the cars will grate and groan their way up the twisting road towards Blea Tarn and down through Little Langdale. In *The Excursion*, Wordsworth placed the house of 'The Solitary' beside Blea Tarn. It will not remain very solitary if this new excursion becomes popular.

The two Langdales demonstrate very clearly the effects of the ice on the scenery of the inner Lakes. The district had, in fact, taken its present ground-plan long before the Ice Age, for when rain falls on a dome-shaped object it is bound to flow downwards and outwards, so that the rivers will carve out valleys radiating roughly from the centre, as Wordsworth put it, like the spokes of a wheel. There may have been no lakes in pre-glacial times, but you could probably have found your way rather blunderingly from dale to dale with the aid of a modern Ordnance Survey map.

Yet the Ice Age brought an immense change. Up to then, the landscape had been shaped mainly by the erosive power of running water; now it was to be chiselled by ice. Greater Lakeland underwent glaciation both from the outside, from the great Scottish glaciers which slid down the coast, and from the inside, from the home-bred glaciers, which formed on the tops of the fells and descended along the lines of the valleys till they met the 'Scotch' ice of the coast.

It was these dale glaciers which were the real sculptors of Cumberland and Westmorland. Towards the foot of the valleys they flowed over the lower ridges, leaving them smooth, rounded and upholstered by thick cushions of boulder clay. In the upper valleys, where the ridges were higher, they dug deeply into the groove of the dale, flattening the bottom and chopping off the sides, turning it from the more normal V-shape to the characteristic U-shape. Great Langdale is a splendid example of this, with beckside meadows, flat as a tennis court, running the whole length of the upper dale, from Chapel Stile to Mickleden. Often, too, the ice would scoop down into the floor of a dale and then plane up again, leaving a hollow, which, when the ice melted, became a lake or a tarn. That is what happened in Little Langdale, and the result is Little Langdale Tarn. At other times it would pluck at the rocks of the floor-bed until they snapped away in one solid piece. And that is what happened at Skelwith Force, below the meeting-place of the two Langdales, where the River Brathay drops clean away, the whole width of it in one break, giving the Lakes one of their most spectacular waterfalls, as well as one of the most accessible. The other kind of Lake District waterfall, of which Dungeon Gill in Great Langdale is one of the finest examples, is yet again a product of ice engineering, but in a different way. For when the glaciers carved off the sides of a dale, the little tributaries were left hanging in the air, and the becks, which before then had trundled evenly down to the main stream, either dropped sheer, in one long streak, as at Dungeon Gill, or cut back into the rock in a series of minor falls and chasms as at Tilberthwaite. What the ice did, in fact, was to exaggerate all the native characteristics of the Lake rocks, making the steep hills steeper, the round hills rounder, the crags craggier and the dales more cleft-like and secluded. And nowhere was its over-emphasis carried out with more exuberance and effect than in the greater and lesser valleys of Langdale.

CHAPTER FOUR

THE LAKES: THE CENTRAL DALES

I CALL them the Central Dales for convenience, but the long hollows which hold the lakes of Thirlmere, Grasmere, Rydal and Windermere are not true river-carved dales at all. Instead, they lie along the line of the Lake District's main geological fault, though, like the river-dales, they were enlarged and deepened by the action of the ice.

The northern section of the fault is, admittedly, very like a normal dale, and must have been still more so when Thirlmere was narrow enough to be bridged in the middle. By now, of course, the lake has been dammed, the water-level raised, and a slag-heap of detritus tipped along shores shame-facedly screened off by conifers. Manchester has a conscience about Thirlmere. There have been well-intentioned schemes to give more access to the public and to save what can be saved of the lake's still considerable beauty. But it remains—as does Haweswater—a dammed and damning example of what must not be allowed to happen to any of the others.

Yet once you get above the dark green tide-mark of trees you begin to see what the early tourists saw in Thirlmere, once called Wythburn Water or Leathes Water after a local landowner. It was dale-like, undoubtedly, with a rather dainty and river-like lake in the bottom, but from the little Wythburn Church to Legburthwaite it ran straight as a street. None of the dales proper is nearly so stiff. Indeed, the Thirlmere—i.e. the 'fault'—side of Helvellyn is perhaps the most solid, least fractured wall of volcanic rock in the whole district.

This rock spreads over the Raise, too, so that the small, reedy lakes of Grasmere (the grass lake) and Rydal (the valley of the Rye) are cupped like a thistle-head in a calyx of green and spiky fells. But just below Ambleside the volcanics fall away and give place to the gentler Silurian rocks, and the effect is as if the fault had widened out to include the whole of the central southern area, Coniston and Esthwaite as well as Windermere.

The importance of this geological fault in the history of the Lakes is enormous. From the very beginning it offered what was obviously the best line of communication. By the end of the Middle Ages it had become the main route for the wool trade; in the eighteenth century it was the way by which the tourists discovered the district; and today it carries the heaviest road traffic in the Lakes. And when the eighteenth-century tourists followed the route they found not just lakes and mountains but a string of towns and villages—Kendal, Bowness, Ambleside, Hawkshead, Grasmere—whose existence, from the beginning, depended on sheep.

Tourists apart, sheep have been the mainstay of Lake economy for at least 1,000 years, and the characteristic local breed, the Herdwick, might almost be regarded as part of the indigenous fauna. It is as much at home on the fells as the fox. It is sure-footed as a goat, and can leap over most walls when driven to it, though, for convenience in herding, the field-walls are often pierced at the bottom by gaps or hatches known in my part of the district as 'hog-holes'—a 'hog' being a sheep before its first shearing. Each farm has its own 'heaf' or right of pasture on the fells, and each flock goes with the farm, so that when a farmer gives up his tenancy he has to leave a specified number of sheep behind him. It is said that the sheep have a territorial instinct and will stick to their own 'heaf'. But because strays are inevitable the farmers have evolved a system of identification known as smits* (i.e. body marks made with tar or red ruddle) and lug-marks (i.e. various ways of cutting the ear), which has gone into the folk culture of the Lakes.

Today metal tabs are gradually taking the place of lug-marks, while the Herdwick is no longer the only sheep to be seen in the dales, the Swaledale and various cross-breeds having almost superseded it in some parts. Yet the dalesman still owes much of his social life to the sheep, whether the Herdwick or any other breed. Straying sheep have often been at the bottom of arguments

* For more about smits and lug-marks see N. Nicholson, *Portrait of the Lakes*. The use of a vein of red ore for marking sheep led to the discovery at Hodbarrow, Millom, of the richest deposit of iron ore ever worked in Great Britain

and quarrels, but they are also the reason or the excuse for some of the happiest events of the dale year—the Shepherds' Meets, at which the strays used to be gathered together to be sorted out and claimed by the owners, with proper exchange and recompense. Nowadays, a farmer who finds a stray will probably look at the lug-mark and telephone the owner right away, leaving him to collect it in his van, but the Shepherds' Meets still go on, a ripe Cumbrian mixture of business, gossip, song, drink and tatie-pot supper which has so far managed to survive even the attentions of the B.B.C. Outside Broadcasts department.

The main thing provided by the sheep, however, was work. In the later Middle Ages the wool trade was well established in Kendal, where Flemish weavers had settled, probably by the end of the fourteenth century. It expanded under the protection of the Parr family of Kendal Castle, and by the early sixteenth century had spread south to Milnthorpe, and north and west to Staveley, Ambleside, Grasmere and Langdale.

It was, basically, a cottage industry. The wool was sorted and washed in yards or gardens, and then spun by the housewife and woven by the husband. As late as the eighteenth century, Wonderful Walker, vicar of Seathwaite in Dunnderdale, used to keep a spinning-wheel at his side as he taught in the village school, which was held, of course, in the village church. For the most part, however, the spinners worked in their own homes, and many of the farms had a spinning-gallery attached to the outside of the barn, though it was probably used for drying the wool rather than for spinning. One fine example can still be seen at High Yewdale, beside the Ambleside-Coniston road, and another at The Farmer's Arms, Sparkbridge, an inn with an interior which might have come out of an eighteenth-century print.

Once the cloth was woven the weavers took it in to Hawkshead, Ambleside or one of the other towns, where it went through the later stages of manufacture: fulling, bleaching and dyeing. In Tudor times, the boom years in the Lakes, there were little walk-mills or fulling-mills all along the banks of the Rothay. But in the seventeenth century the trade suffered a slump. The coarse Westmorland cloth went out of fashion, and many of the cottage weavers died of the plague. Kendal kept going, by turning to exports, but elsewhere the trade began to dwindle and eventually disappeared altogether, except for the modern revival of expensive handloom tweeds which are about as genuinely local as ice-cream.

Nevertheless, it is to the old wool trade that the tourist towns owe their physiognomy. Hawkshead,* in particular, began as a huddle of weaving-rooms, one-shop warehouses, little mills, markets and inns. It is as quaint as a Christmas card, yet to walk through it, especially in winter when the streets are empty, is to walk not through the sham picturesque of a colour-supplement, but through a world of imaginative geometry: squares, rectangles and prisms of slate in pavements, gables, porches, chimneys, archways, outdoor staircases and the like. Even the roads round about—up-dale to Outgate or down-dale to the lake—are fenced, not with the usual walls but with up-ended slate-slabs. The whole village could be fitted into the boundaries of a large agricultural show; yet it contains enough corners, angles, alleys and entries to keep the eye happy for hours. The celebrated German artist, Kurt Schwitters†, who settled in Ambleside during the Second World War, spent the last years of his life turning the inside walls of a barn or potting-shed at Elterwater into a work of abstract sculpture (he called it a Merzbau) which has since been transported, at enormous cost, to Newcastle University. Hawkshead is just such another work of abstract art. Let us hope that no-one wants to shift this, too, into an art gallery.

They can't shift the parish church however, for it is perched, like a glacial erratic boulder, on its own hill high above the roofs of the village. In Hawkshead the dead don't wait for Judgement Day but go half-way to heaven as soon as they are buried. The building, dating from the fifteenth and sixteenth centuries, is as typical a piece of local stone-work as any wall or stile, though it is coated with plaster and at one time was white-washed. It is also a kind of art gallery in itself, for it retains the old wall texts and geometrical decorations, mostly painted in the seventeeth and early eighteenth centuries, which used to be very common in this part of the Lakes. One of the texts, painted in 1711 by William

* i.e. Hauk's shieling: a personal name plus a corruption of Old Norse *saetre*

† Born at Hanover in 1887. He escaped from the Nazis, first to Norway and then to Ambleside, where he died in 1948

Mackreth of Hawkshead, is sometimes pointed out as an example of the Westmorland dialect in church:

> In the beginning was
> the Word, and the Word
> was with God, and t'Word
> was God. John. j.j.

Personally, I think the painter merely ran short of space.

Of the other wool towns, Bowness* has practically disappeared under a tidal wave of tourism. Yet it has its old church (with medieval glass in the windows taken from Cartmel Priory after the Dissolution), while something of the home-spun dignity which the eighteenth-century visitors admired still hangs about the curve of the road up the hill to Windermere station, and, here and there, in the side-streets, where Victorian boarding-houses rise up steep as spoil-heaps at a slate quarry.

Ambleside†, on the other hand, though taking as much of the holiday surge as Bowness, has managed not to be swamped. For one thing, the landing-stage and the promenade under the tulip trees are at Waterhead, three-quarters of a mile from the centre of the town. For another, in spite of all the thousands of visitors in summer, Ambleside remains stubbornly local. Go there in winter and you'll find it getting on with its job of catering for the all-round-the-year population of the district. There is nothing picturesque about it—except for the old mill, now a studio, and the little house on a bridge which is surely the National Trust's dottiest property. Yet the four-storey slate terraces—superbly built or they would have fallen down under the vibration of modern heavy traffic—seem to me as essentially Cumbrian, or Westmerian, as any of the lichened fell-farms of Eskdale or Little Langdale.

Grasmere is another case altogether. It is at the very hub of the dales, and the lake lies in such a dolly-tub of hills that you are puzzled as to how the water can leak out. The dream-like double valley of Near and Far Easedale—as perfect and unspotted as if it had been preserved under glass—is only an after-supper

* Accent on the first syllable—the name means 'Bull's headland'. In contrast, Bowness on Solway is probably the 'rounded Headland', being derived from Old Norse *bogi*, a bow, and *nes*, a cape

† Sheiling on a sandbank by a river. Old Norse *á*, river, and *melr*, sandbank, plus another corruption of *saetre*

Logan Beck, South Cumberland

stroll from the hotels, with a waterfall so convenient for viewing that it might have been rigged up by the Water Board. Stone for stone, Grasmere has changed little since the last century. The church, more than any of the larger churches of the district, has the look of belonging to the fells, even of accepting the fells as part of the congregation. For when the building was enlarged, the north wall of the nave was modified into an arcade, to carry the roof

> . . . upheld
> By naked rafters intricately crossed,

as Wordsworth accurately said. So that you sit in the pews with a fell wall at your side, not quite knowing whether you are indoors or out.

Yet, though the stones may be the same, Grasmere has changed so enormously that you can hardly call it a village any more. In winter it is an abandoned encampment of empty hotels; in summer, a fairground. For the part of it called Town End has become that most embarrassing of all tourist attractions, a literary shrine. Of course, Hawkshead has its connections with Wordsworth as well as Grasmere. He attended the grammar school there and lodged with Anne Tyson at her cottage at Colthouse, about a quarter of a mile from the village*. The years at Hawkshead, in fact, when he boated and skated and robbed birds' nests and walked round Esthwaite Lake nearly every morning before breakfast, are of far greater importance for the understanding of the poetry and the man than the time he spent at Grasmere. But at Hawkshead the memory of the poet has been ousted from popular favour by that of Beatrix Potter, so that it is Grasmere which has to take the full brunt of the part-bored, part-curious, part-sniggering pilgrims. To me, Wordsworth is one of the supremely original minds of all English poetry, and for many years I conscientiously refused to join the queue at Dove Cottage. But one day, when I was visiting the nearby Wordsworth library to examine its superb collection of manuscripts, one of the trustees took me into the cottage at lunchtime when it was closed and empty. The rooms are small and dark, opening so abruptly, one

* And NOT, as used to be thought, at the cottage she later occupied in the village itself. See Mary Moorman, *William Wordsworth: The Early Years* (Oxford, 1957)

Bowfell from Crinkle Crags

into the other, that there can have been little privacy, especially when the place was full of children. The garden at the back rears up, steep as a fellside, with one great rock from which you can gaze down on the upstairs windows. You can imagine a female relative in every room industriously copying out poems. It is not primarily of the poet that you think, though much of his best verse was put on paper at Dove Cottage, for his great days of experience and vision had come and gone before he ever went to Grasmere. It is the rest of the household who come to mind—Dorothy, his sister; Mary, his wife; Sara Hutchinson, his sister-in-law; the children; the visitors; Coleridge; De Quincey and later Hartley Coleridge who became tenants of the cottage after the Wordsworths had left. Dove Cottage was not the only house the family lived in. There was Allan Bank, where the chimneys smoked, and Grasmere Old Rectory, and Rydal Mount, where the children grew up and Dorothy declined into senility and the poet into his old age. But it is Dove Cottage which seems so closely packed with powerful personalities that you wonder it did not explode.

Coniston (King's *tun* or farm) is the one considerable village of the central dales which comes not from wool but directly from the rock. In the sixteenth century copper was mined in the combe in the side of the Old Man, smelted by charcoal in bloomeries in the woods, then shipped down the lake to Nibthwaite and thence carted to Greenodd and Ulverston. As late as the last century hundreds of men still worked at the mines, and even today, now the ore has run out, there is work from the rock at the Broughton Moor Slate Quarries, which produce some of the finest quality building stone, much of it being shipped abroad to face modern buildings in many parts of the world.

The lakes of Coniston, Windermere and Esthwaite all lie within the area of the third main group of the Lake District rocks, that of the Silurian Slates and Shales. These southern rocks are rather more recent in origin and, like the Skiddaw Slates, were formed of estuarine mud. The boundary between the Borrowdale Volcanics and the Silurian Slates is almost a straight line. Start at Broughton-in-Furness, on the Duddon Estuary, take the main road to Coniston and on to Ambleside, and most of the way you will have the volcanic rocks on your left and the country of the Silurian Slates on your right. Lump by lump, there is not much to choose between the two rocks. Both are slaty and slivery; both modulate through undertones of grey, green, blue, purple and even, at times, red—as in the large quarry at Wreak's End on the Foxfield-Grizebeck road. (Some of the purple samples are keeping the rain off my head as I write this page.) Yet the difference between the scenery of each is obvious, as you can see from almost any point on the Broughton-Coniston road. On your left, the buttressed castle wall of Dow Crag and Coniston Old Man; on your right, the brackenny pasture sloping down to Coniston Lake, and, beyond the lake, the low ridge of moors, wooded up to the waist, which divides Coniston from Rusland.

This landscape of the Silurian rocks is the least rhetorical in the Lakes—the kind which the early tourists used to call 'sylvan'. It contains none of the higher peaks and no great crags, screes or waterfalls—in fact, the land rarely rises above 1,000 feet. Compared to the magnified prehistoric barrow of Skiddaw or the cathedral steeples of the Langdale Pikes, the Silurian Slates may seem tame and unexciting. But this is only if we think in terms of views. In terms of human life and history the southern valleys are in every way typical of the Lakes, and nowhere has the Scandinavian influence been stronger.

Coniston village, however, seems to belong far more to the volcanic rock than to the gentler country round the lake, and the visitor, coming here for the first time, will find himself impelled almost irresistibly towards Old Man and Wetherlam. He can climb the former either from the Walna Scar road or from the track which runs from The Sun Inn, past the old copper-mine buildings (now a Youth Hostel) and the two tarns that lie in the kangaroo-pouch of the fell. But for me a stealthier, more intimate way of worming into the secrets of these rocks is offered by Tilberthwaite Gill. Take the Ambleside road along Yewdale, turn left at the signpost to High Tilberthwaite, then left again at the track to the gill. For the first hundred yards or so the rise is steep, wriggling among old rubble-heaps until you come out on the shoulder of the hill overlooking the beck that flows from the gill. From thence the track is easy, until you reach the first of the bridges at the foot of the gill itself.

But first you should explore the quarries that lie just to the left of the track. There are larger quarries in the district (that above Little Langdale, for instance, which is known as The Cathedral), but I know of no spot which shows more clearly the way in which the human landscape was shaped from the rock. For it was not just mass-produced, amorphous stone which was dug out of these quarries; it was cottage walls, roofs, lintels, the coping-stones of doorways and the arch-stones of bridges. Some signs of working can still be seen—a broken fragment of a tram-way, or an up-turned bogie rusted to the red of sheep's sorrel. And, toppled over on the floor are one or two split-pillars of rock, left unshaped and unsold, like fallen menhirs at a prehistoric burial site. For the most part, however, the quarries have reverted to wild rock gardens. Rowans and birches jut out of the fissures—hosepipes playing a spray of green. The purples and yellows of bell-heather, harebell, tormentil and assorted hawk-weeds occupy the ledges, with lousewort, bog asphodel and the pale cross-leaved heather in the sumps. Everywhere the angular, almost cubist, man-made façade of the rock is being smudged back into the unobtrusive smoothness of nature.

The path continues, keeping fifty or a hundred feet above the level of a beckside splintery with larches, though the fell above the gill is treeless and surprisingly uncraggy. This is a spot which is at its best in mid-October, when the bracken is red and the birches are spurting out like fireworks all along the screes.

The path now drops to the beck and crosses it at the point where it turns sharply round the corner into the upper staircase of the gill. What happens round the corner I can tell only from the memory of over forty years ago, for my legs will no longer carry me beyond the bridge. I remember, then, a chasm narrow as a Hawkshead alley, with the path edging round rocks and the roots of trees; cascades, shoots, dubs, scoops and swirls of water; planks thrown from side to side, with rickety hand-rails here and there. I remember, as a small boy, that my foot went right through the rotten tread of one of the little bridges, and I was left, clinging to my father's hand, only an inch or two above the water. Some months later, reading in bed with the mumps, I decided that Tilberthwaite must be the place of Ruskin's *King of the Golden River*, only when I had been there I hadn't been king.

The three lakes of the central dales are all predominantly parklike and pastoral, and to these may be added the little artificial lake generally known as Tarn Hows*, which is so popular with summer visitors that the woods round about have become concealed car parks. The tarn itself, which, before the dam was built at the head of Tom Gill, was just a cluster of ponds, is too stagily pretty for Cumbrian taste. It looks, in fact, like a wide-screen setting for *Rose Marie*. But from its elevated position it gives magnificent steeple-jack views of the Yewdale, Tilberthwaite and lower Langdale country, while, if you climb the hillside to the south, you can look along the whole length of Coniston Lake to Morecambe Bay.

Coniston Lake (once called, more attractively, Thurston Water, after the Norse name Thor) looks rather dull when seen from the village side, with a backing of shapeless moors now cardiganed in conifers that do little either to improve or to harm the view. But once you cross over to the Monk Coniston side, the lake takes on another aspect altogether, with Old Man and Wetherlam giving it a backing as dramatic, almost, as Wastwater's, while Coniston Old Hall, with its enormous cylindrical chimneys, diversifies the middle distance, as the eighteenth-century travellers might have said. Moreover, the eastern shore turns out, when you get there, to be a chain of changes and surprises—rocks, knotts, nabs, coves, little bays and bulges of woodland. This eastern or Brantwood side has become a popular motor-run in summer but at other seasons is almost deserted. I remember especially one brilliant February day, when I drove between shining banks of snow among sugar-stick trees and dead bracken frosted to white paper doilies. The lake was frozen, the ice covered with a thin layer of snow, and foot-print, skate-print, dog-pad, bird-track and even tyre-tread showed how it had become a new kind of thoroughfare, though a greener shade in the centre marked the edge of danger. It seemed warmer than on many a day of August, yet the sun had already set for cottages at the foot of the Old Man, and the refrigerator door was beginning to swing close for the night.

Esthwaite Water†, between Coniston and Windermere, is the

* In fact, the tarn has no name. 'Tarn Hows' is the name of a nearby hill. Had it been intended to be the name of the tarn it would, of course, have been Hows Tarn

† Old Norse *ees-thveit*, the clearing by the water

most park-like of all the lakes. With its little peninsulas, two on either side, it looks on a large-scale map like a gap in an otherwise-finished jigsaw puzzle. It was created, in the first place, by a side-loop of the Langdale-Rydal-Troutbeck ice, and the entire lake has the character of a gravelly, waterlogged glacial moraine. At both the top and bottom end there is a dub or large pool, cut off from the main body of the water by a hundred or so yards of silt. In fact, with its shallow, reedy shores and the cows grazing in the waterside fields, it resembles one of Capability Brown's lakes, an embellishment in a country seat.

This is not intended as disparagement. Esthwaite preserves an eighteenth-century, pastoral beauty and is one of the most lived-around of all the lakes. If only it were less accessible—if, perhaps, it were in another part of the district—it would surely be counted a spot of special charm. As it is, Beatrix Potter's rabbits have left droppings of sentiment all round its shores, though it is not the little books themselves which are sentimental but the readers. Esthwaite, in fact, like Hawkshead and Near Sawrey, would be none the worse for an outbreak of literary myxomatosis.

Windermere was once the queen of the Lakes, but she abdicated long ago. Of course, to people from cities, so used to cars and crowds that they scarcely notice them, Windermere may still seem both pretty and peaceful; but to one brought up as I was, in the country of Black Combe and the Duddon, it seems not so much a part of the Lake District as an ambitious municipal park, with drives, walks, seats, kiosks, sailing-boats, rowing-boats, regattas, long-distance swims and tame ducks.

Yet it is still a pleasure to cross the lake by the ferry, sliding close to the oval, Georgian house on Belle Island, which was named after Isabella Curwen of Workington, whose husband, John Christian Curwen, bought it for her as a wedding-present. A pleasure again to turn off just before you reach the ferry on the Cunsey side, and drive through the National Trust property beside the lake. Here, with the two umbrageous little islands called 'Lilies of the Valley' between you and Belle Isle, you are in a placid backwater with a floating suburb of houseboats. Any South-countryman should feel thoroughly at home.

A North-countryman, however, had better push beyond the metalled road into the woods, where the view is fragmented into tiny bays and scoops, with becks and sykes dripping into the water every few yards. The banks are chock-full of the wild and half-wild flowers of planted woodland: creeping Jenny, tutsan, enchanter's nightshade, and pink purslane (*Claytonia alsinoides*), a native of North America, and the small yellow balsam (*Impatiens perviflora*)—the huge Himalayan balsam, so common beside the canals of industrial Lancashire, is also beginning to invade the dales, notably at Colwith.

But perhaps the best way to see the lake for the first time is to take a trip on one of the pleasure boats, from which you see it at the right speed, neither too fast to miss much, nor too slow to be bored. And if the boats seem rather archaic, that is all the better, for Windermere is now a period piece. That, indeed, is how I most enjoy it, on a bright afternoon between Christmas and the New Year, motoring along the Newby Bridge-Bowness road, where every now and then you come out into wide open bays and then sheer back into woods full of large, self-satisfied, slate-built nineteenth-century villas, closed-up boarding-houses, hibernating among rhododendrons, and expensive modern weekend bungalows, slid in wherever planning permission can be wangled. It is a scene as Victorian as Carlisle Railway Station.

But mention of winter brings me to the weather. The Lake District is one of the wettest parts of England, and presumably most of those who come there are prepared to put up with a few wet days. But too many still believe that they need clear, bright weather before they can really enjoy themselves.

I blame photography for this. The photographer must have a clear amosphere for most of his effects; he looks out for bold shapes, for sharp detail, and contrasts of light and shade. And those who first learn about the Lake District from photographs come expecting the real thing to be like that.

The travellers of the eighteenth and nineteenth centuries, on the other hand, learned about the Lakes from paintings, engravings and prints. They looked, not for precise detail and hard shapes, but for hints and ambiguities, for dimness and shimmerings and the golden glow of Claude Lorraine. There was a lot of stock romanticism in this attitude, of course, but it did equip them to enjoy the Cumberland weather. Thomas Gray, for instance, came in October, one of the best of all months in the Lakes, when there is a cloudy, Michaelmas daisy sky, and all the reds and browns and purples are toned down as if under a smudge of wood smoke. And there are quiet, dark, drizzling days in the dead of winter, when the evergreens seem to ooze beads of water, and the bracken sulks a deeper and deeper red the wetter it gets, and the besoms of the broom glow with a dark, intense green. A view, then, would be a distraction.

Rusland, lying to the east of Coniston Lake, is really a double valley made by two parallel streams, Colton Beck and Rusland Pool, both of which flow into the estuary of the River Leven between Haverthwaite and Greenodd. Colton Beck is only a few miles in length (its lovely upper stretches can be reached by the rough road from Nibthwaite Grange), but Rusland Pool is considerably longer, and above Rusland Church it is split into two tributary streams, Force Beck or Grizedale Beck and Dale Park Beck.

The roads in Rusland take the form of a capital 'H'. The left down-stroke, coming from Hawkshead, follows Grizedale Beck to Satterthwaite, passes Whitestock Hall (a tile-hung, Georgian mansion, grey-yellow beside beeches) and meets the main Barrow road at Greenodd. The right-hand stroke comes from Esthwaite Water, down Dale Park to the Haverthwaite cross-roads. And, about the middle of the valley, there are a whole scribbling of little transverse roads which make up the horizontal stroke of the letter.

I have given all these precise and perhaps rather prim-sounding directions because Rusland is a valley which has to be searched for. You can't just drive your car straight at it, as you can at Wasdale, knowing that, if you don't fall in the lake, you are bound to reach the dale-head in the end. It is not, of course, in the least inaccessible, but it has the luck to lack most of the features which would have turned it into an obvious tourist target. It has no lake, and its streams are mostly enclosed in farm-land or forest. It *has* a waterfall—a beautiful asymmetric arrangement of delayed drops and dawdlings at Force Mills—but this so discreetly screened that many people drive past without noticing it. Rusland has none of the higher hills, no crags, not a great deal of open fell at all and, in fact, not many views in the picture post-

Coniston Old Man from Appletreeworth
(overleaf) *Westmorland Cottages, at Colwith and* (facing) *at Crosby Ravensworth*

ELTERWATER

card sense. Yet it is a dale which has retained much of the look and tone of what southern Lakeland must have been before the tourists discovered it.

This does not mean that it has not changed. Nor does it mean that it is uninhabited or untouched by man. In fact it has very much the look of being lived in, which is the look these valleys have had for centuries. Today, no doubt, the dale people are not all country people, for Rusland is handy enough to Ulverston and even to Barrow to house men from the Glaxo works or Vickers. But the townsman has not yet taken over the place. The half-a-dozen little villages are still almost entirely unselfconscious, with only a few infestations of lilac doors, Venetian blinds and ornamental ironwork among the whitewash and brown-wash, the slate roofs and milk-churn stands, the weed and mould and lichen colours of barn, farm, cottage and church.

Most of the villages are more scattered than one expects, but Bouth, in the lower dale, is compact, with a pub, a post-office, cross-roads and even what might be called one or two streets. All round about there is a monkey-puzzle of narrow roads, some of them single-track and interrupted by gates—an excellent arrangement which discourages crowds but is no obstacle to people like me who have the patience to open and close. Here, and round Oxen Park, Bandrake Head and Colton Church, you have the feeling, rare in the Lakes, of sneaking into the villages by the back way, running between stone walls and shippons and through damson orchards with the washing hung out. Here and there, as you climb above the 200-foot contour—the land is never much higher—you come into rough pasture with the bracken fighting it out with the grass, and with bluebells in spring, harebells* in summer, and patches of gorse in bloom practically all the year round.

Because it is so well-wooded, Rusland is at its dullest in high summer, yet, at all times of the year, it seems to me to be a particularly pleasant spot for a wet day. You walk or drive around corner after corner, finding at every turn a new vista, too small for the rain to blanket out, yet full of surprise and interest. On the Haverthwaite-Rusland side, where you will sometimes see a

* The harebells are, of course, the bluebells of Scotland, and that is what I was taught to call them as a child. Bluebells we called wild hyacinths

Patterdale

whole pride of peacocks walking along the road, you pass beside beech woods, with old trees standing shin-deep in red leaves for much of the year. On the other side of the valley, near Bandrake Head, the woods are scruffier, though large tracts are now being felled and tidied for forestry planting. They stink and steam and sting with ants in summer, but in the winter you can squelch through the mud or crackle over the frost, gathering holly berries and the first hazel and alder catkins long before Christmas. And there is about one week, towards the end of April or the beginning of May, when these woods are tasselled with bird cherry—the northern cherry with small, buddleia-like blossoms, which Dorothy Wordsworth called 'heckberry'.

Above Force Forge most of Rusland is given over to the Forestry Commission. The delightful little road through Dale Park sails along a two-or-three-hundred-yard-wide canal of pasture between steep banks of trees. The other road, through Satterthwaite, runs in the heart of the forest.

The planting, here, has not been as imaginative as that beside the Duddon or the Lickle, yet I do not think it need rouse controversy. The Monk Coniston Moors were pretty dreary beforehand, and the humps and heavings of dark green conifers and lighter green larches are certainly no less appealing to the eye, and give a rounded, repetitive, upholstered sky-line most uncommon in the Lakes. And, by careful agricultural planning, the farms produce about as much on their reduced acreage as they did before the coming of the trees.

Grizedale Hall, the mansion of the former owners of the estate, was pulled down soon after the commissioners took over, and, so far as I can remember it, this is no great architectural loss. It served as a prisoner-of-war camp during the last war, and the famous German escaping officer, 'The One that Got Away', got away from here. Today there is an extremely well-run camping site not far from where the old hall stood, with planned nature trails and fire-watching towers which provide a wonderful chance to watch the three species of deer.

For all this, the forest is not a garden, and the trees, however slow in growth, are really just a crop. One day they will have to come down. The thinnings may be sent to the new pulp mill just outside Workington, and some of the mature timber will go to the new saw-mill near Penrith. The forests may look raw and even alien to some people, but, like the traditional industries of mining, quarrying, sheep-farming and the rest, they are part of the practical economy of the district and are doing much to keep it alive.

The name of Force Forge in Rusland reminds us that man's mark on the area is not entirely agricultural, for these southern dales were one of the earliest centres of the iron trade. At first this was on a very small scale. The ore was smelted by charcoal—Ashburner is still a common name in the district—and, since it seems to have been easier to take iron to the woods than charcoal to the mines, the first bloomeries sprang up along the shores of Coniston and in the valleys of the Duddon and the Crake. By the seventeenth century large furnaces were being built, together with small forges, and could be found at Coniston, at Cunsey Beck, close to Windermere, at Ulpha in Dunnerdale, at Hackett, near Colwith on the Brathay, at Burblethwaite on the Winster and at Low Wood and Backbarrow on the Leven. Yet, in spite of all this enterprise, methods of manufacture remained rather primitive and lagged behind those used in some other parts of England.

In 1711, however, a group of Cheshire ironmasters decided to take advantage of the Lake District's potentially large supply of charcoal by setting up a more modern furnace at Cunsey on the west shore of Windermere. Local industrialists responded with enormous spirit to this challenge from the off-comers, and four of them immediately founded the Backbarrow Company, where they were to introduce the most advanced smelting techniques of the time*. Two and possibly three of the four were Quakers, and their society gave them valuable links with other iron centres at Bristol, Warrington, Lancaster and Whitehaven, so that the Backbarrow Furnace soon became one of the most successful and forward-looking in the North of England.

Similar furnaces were established at Nibthwaite and Penny Bridge on the Crake, at Leighton near Arnside, Newland near Ulverston, and Duddon Bridge in South Cumberland. At Lindale a small foundry was set up by Isaac Wilkinson and his son, the great John Wilkinson, who also had a share in the Low

* See J. D. Marshall, *Furness and the Industrial Revolution* (Barrow in Furness, 1958)

Wood ironworks at Haverthwaite, which was later to be the site of a factory producing gunpowder for the local mines and quarries. Eventually, as the Industrial Revolution rolled on, coke replaced charcoal, and the eighteenth-century plants closed down—all, that is, except Backbarrow, which until very recently, remained the oldest working ironworks in Europe.

They still stand, close to the 'Blue' works—an almost irresistible temptation to the colour photographer—and below the brutal by-pass which has slashed the old village in two. They look as endearingly toy-like as Stephenson's 'Rocket', though they are a hundred years older, and the part they played in the industrial history of the area makes them one of the most fascinating—and even, when you think of it, one of the most frightening—relics of the past to be found anywhere in the Lakes. For, though the pacifist Quaker iron-masters could never have foreseen it, the road from Backbarrow leads straight to the shipyards of Barrow-in-Furness and the atomic-armed *Polaris* submarine.

CHAPTER FIVE

THE LAKES: THE EASTERN DALES

PATTERDALE (Patrick's dale) is the only dale—apart perhaps from Little Langdale—which should be approached from the head rather than the foot, for by far the finest scenery lies between the lake and Kirkstone Pass. If you come from Pooley Bridge you have a long drive through rather ordinary waterside parkland, and it is not until you get nearly to the turning for the Cumberland Troutbeck that the curtain begins to go up on the highly effective last act of the lake. If you come from Kirkstone, the tributary dales begin to open out, one after the other, as soon as you reach Brotherswater—first, Dovedale on the left; then Hartsop with its village on the right; then Deepdale on the left. The fells begin, surprisingly, to close in as you get nearer to the lake, which keeps tantalisingly out of sight most of the way. Patterdale village and Glenridding are both truly home-grown, with scarcely a stone anywhere that has not come out of local quarries, yet they are now so given over to the holiday trade that they have a forlorn look in the off-season.

Patterdale, in fact, after having once been one of the out-of-the-way valleys, has now become one of the main tourist centres. Visitors come by car from Windermere, by coach from Keswick, Carlisle and even Newcastle, and every now and then the steamer calls at Glenridding Pier, and a batch of usually elderly people moves slowly over the lakeside gravel to cups of tea and post-cards. The still-narrow road swarms like an open-air market—children rushing for ice-creams, fathers trying to find a car park or a lavatory. Where the road comes close to the lake girls wade out into the water, and transistors drop their little bags of aural dye into the once-clean silence. On patches of grass between the birches mothers spread rugs and ground-sheets, and set up folding chairs and tables, and soon, I fancy, they will bring portable gnomes and bird-baths to make the lakeside look still more like the back-garden lawn.

Yet, somehow, all this is the kind of cheerful family clutter that can be put away at bedtime. Go along the same road in the late evening, and you will find a heavy impasto of stillness on the lake—the surface like a breathed-on mirror, moist and steely, with the eastern, roadless shore rising out of the water, black and fjord-like. Or go, at almost any time of the day, into any of the by-valleys or gills on either side of the lake—Martindale, for instance, on the Howtown side, beyond which you can push on to Boredale and Bannerdale, two hidden-away, north-looking valleys, where in winter the sun scarcely even knocks at the door.

My own chief memories, however, lie a little way outside the romantic, *Swan Lake* setting of Ullswater. If you follow the road which runs beside Aira Force (perhaps the finest water ballet in the Lakes) and then branch left to Cockley Moor, you leave behind the crags and glooms and come out on a slouching moorland, like the Back o' Skiddaw except that this is Front o' Skiddaw. Here, in a house which looked from the outside like a sanatorium, there lived from 1940 to 1965 one of Cumberland's most remarkable personalities of recent times. You climbed the hill on to the sour, peaty moor—perhaps at dusk or in a thick drizzle—if you were invited to one of Helen Sutherland's musical evenings, then entered the house to find that the primitive world of water and rock were shut out and you were surrounded with twentieth-century art at its most elegant: Barbara Hepworth, David Jones, Ben Nicholson and the Cumberland-born Winifred Nicholson, a descendant of the Earls of Carlisle. From this house, beside Aira Beck, I have gathered the equally elegant mountain pansy (*Viola lutea*), though always the blue variety and never, unfortunately, the yellow.

My last memory of Cockley Moor is of a summer evening, when friends had collected there from all over Cumberland and Westmorland to listen to a Pergolesi one-act opera. Miss Sutherland sat on the stairs and said goodbye to us like an eighteenth-century duchess, knowing, as we did not, that she would see few of us again. We drove out, through the cloudy backwash of the sunset, into the same world of water and rock, leaving behind us a wilderness that, for twenty-five years, had been one of the richest places in Cumberland.

Ullswater is a spot which supplied everything that could be asked for by the eighteenth-century travellers in search of the picturesque. They sailed along the lake as if they were circumnavigating unexplored Africa, fired brass cannons to set the echoes pealing and amused themselves listening to stories of the Mounsey family, the so-called 'Kings of Patterdale'. On the western banks of the lake the Duke of Norfolk built a hunting lodge, called Lyulph's Tower, in the form of a fortified china cabinet, and Wordsworth obliged with a poem beginning 'List, ye who pass by Lyulph's Tower', the style of which adequately matches that of the architecture, though it has done his reputation much less harm than the hackneyed O-level piece on the daffodils of nearby Gowbarrow. Wordsworth's verses, a mock medieval ballad about a sleepwalking girl, really had their setting not at Lyulph's Tower but at Aira Force, a gill which still holds much of the mystery and shadow which appealed to the Gothic fancy. Wordsworth merely made a mess of the story—it was not the kind of thing he could take very seriously. But de Quincey, telling another tale of Aira Force*, catches so much of the ambiguity, the *frisson* of the genuine Gothic that he makes Aira Force seem as much an eighteenth-century invention as Lyulph's Tower itself:

> There is, on the western side of Ulleswater, a fine cataract (or, in the language of the country, a *force*), known by the name of Airey Force; and it is of importance enough, especially in rainy seasons, to attract numerous visitors from among 'the Lakers'. Thither, with some purpose of sketching, not the whole scene, but some picturesque features of it, Miss Elizabeth Smith had gone, quite unaccompanied. The road to it lies through Gobarrow Park; and it was usual, at that time, to take a guide from the family of the Duke of Norfolk's keeper, who lived in Lyulph's Tower—a solitary hunting lodge, built by his Grace for the purposes of an annual visit which he used to pay to his estates in that part of England. She, however, thinking herself sufficiently familiar with the localities, had declined to encumber her motions with such an attendant; consequently she was alone. For half an hour or more, she continued to ascend: and, being a good 'cragswoman' . . . she had reached an altitude much beyond what would generally be thought corresponding to the time. The path had vanished altogether; but she continued to pick out one for herself amongst the

* In *Recollections of the Lake Poets*

stones, sometimes receding from the *force*, sometimes approaching it, according to the openings allowed by the scattered masses of rock. Pressing forward in this hurried way, and never looking back, all at once she found herself in a little stony chamber, from which there was no egress possible in advance. She stopped and looked up. There was a frightful silence in the air. She felt a sudden palpitation at her heart, and a panic from she knew not what. Turning, however, hastily, she soon wound herself out of this aerial dungeon; but by steps so rapid and agitated, that, at length, on looking round, she found herself standing at the brink of a chasm, frightful to look down. That way, it was clear enough, all retreat was impossible; but, on turning round, retreat seemed in every direction alike even more impossible. Down the chasm, at least, she might have leaped, though with little or no chance of escaping with life; but on all other quarters it seemed to her eye that at no price could she effect an exit, since the rocks stood round her in a semi-circus, all lofty, all perpendicular, all glazed with trickling water, or smooth as polished porphyry. Yet how, then, had she reached the point? . . . Finding herself grow more and more confused, and every instant nearer to sinking into some fainting fit or convulsion, she resolved to sit down and turn her thoughts quietly into some less exciting channel. This she did; gradually recovered some self-possession . . . Once again she rose; and, supporting herself upon a little sketching-stool that folded up into a stick, she looked upwards, in the hope that some shepherd might, by chance, be wandering in those aerial regions; but nothing could she see except the tall birches, growing at the brink of the highest summits, and the clouds slowly circling overhead. Suddenly, however, as she swept the whole circuit of her station with her alarmed eye, she saw clearly, about two hundred yards beyond her own position, a lady, in a white muslin morning robe, such as were then universally worn by young ladies until dinner-time. The lady beckoned with a gesture and in a manner that, in a moment, gave her confidence to advance—*how* she could not guess; but, in some way that baffled all power to retrace it, she found instantaneously the outlet which previously had escaped her. She continued to advance towards the lady, whom now, in the same moment, she found to be standing upon the other side of the *force*, and also to be her own sister. . . . The guiding sister began to descend, and, by a few simple gestures, just serving to indicate when Miss Elizabeth was to approach and when to leave the brink of the torrent, she gradually led her down to a platform of rock,

> from which the further descent was safe and conspicuous. There Miss Smith paused, in order to take breath from her panic, as well as to exchange greetings and questions with her sister. But sister there was none. All trace of her had vanished; and, when, in two hours after, she reached home, Miss Smith found her sister in the same situation and employment in which she had left her; and the whole family assured her that she had never stirred from the house.

Such writing shows, better, perhaps, than any picture, how very different the Lake landscape looked 150 years ago in the eyes of the people of the time, even though, in a place like Aira Force, the actual sticks and stones may be almost the same as they are today.

Soon after you leave Ullswater, at the Pooley Bridge end, you come upon the eastern end of that sickle of limestone which curves round the northern rim of the Lakes from the coast to the Eden Valley. The castled villages of Dacre and Greystoke (pronounced Greystock) lie in this limestone, the second of the two with a most beautiful collegiate church built largely by the Hudleston family, who were benefactors also to the Old Church at Millom.

Much of the limestone seems to fit easily into the Lake scene—a variation rather than a contradiction. But as you take the little road over Barton Fell to Askham on the way to Mardale and Haweswater you come upon a new kind of country altogether. Askham itself (from Old Scandinavian, 'ash trees') looks familiar enough at a first glance, since it is shaped out of the red Permian sandstone that gives us so many of the villages immediately to the north of the Lakes. But it is set round a green, or common, which is rare in a Lake village, and it has that well-behaved, consciously-tidy look that you often find in the neighbourhood of a great estate. The estate, of course, is that of Lowther Castle (though the present Lord Lonsdale lives at Askham Hall), and the estate village of Old Lowther has still more of the tidied-up, deliberately picturesque look as if it had been designed with more thought to outdoor appearance than indoor sanitation. The Church of St Michael, just inside the park gates, has been tidied up in a different way, for here a building of the twelfth and thirteenth centuries was entirely encased in a late-seventeeth-century overcoat, so that the Lowther of the time could feel pious and medieval within and an enlightened man of the Renaissance outside.

The castle itself, the work of Robert Smirke, has been a roofless shell since 1936, like an enormous box-barracks for toy soldiers left out on the carpet after the children have gone to bed. It is set in miles of parkland, with huge, open swards and carefully sited trees, and commands the middle Eden over to Cross Fell. Even today it still calls all eyes to it by the sheer scale and impudence of its rhetoric.

But a Cumbrian brought up as I was during the Depression of the 'twenties, cannot but look somewhat ironically on that hollow façade with its back to the mines that made the money to build it. The Lowthers, of course, were well-established on the Cumberland-Westmorland border before the Norman Conquest, and for centuries played an important part in the politics of the North-west without, however, attaining the front rank in either power or wealth. In 1696 Sir John Lowther was made a Viscount, but it was not until the middle of the eighteenth century that the family's fortunes began their spectacular up-thrust. That was the time when Sir James Lowther of Whitehaven began to realise, more clearly than his predecessors, the vast potentialities of Cumberland coal and iron. It was he who planned Whitehaven New Town, built his house at The Flatt (rebuilt by the next baronet as Whitehaven Castle, now an old people's home) and then died, in 1755, one of the richest men in the country. His wealth went to another Sir James Lowther, the fifth Baronet and later first Earl of Lonsdale. This 'little contemptible Tyrant of the north', as his Whig opponents called him, had his 'henchmen' all over the county and nine Members of Parliament in his pocket ('Lord Lonsdale's Nine-pins'), any one of whom might be ordered to apply for the Chiltern Hundreds if he did not vote as he was told. He had no pretensions to aristocratic grandeur, but he bought estate after estate until he made iron-ore mining in Cumberland practically a Lowther monopoly. Eventually he became the bugbear of local legend, was reputed to have the evil eye, drove through his villages at headlong speed and kept the embalmed body of his mistress in a glass-covered coffin.

When he died in 1802 the earldom died with him but was re-created in 1808, and it was the new earl who built the present

Lowther Castle—a romantic folly which took itself far too seriously—and made handsome amends to Wordsworth for the first earl's miserly treatment of the poet's father. In spite of its blown-up magnificence, Lowther Castle was never really a home. The nineteenth-century Lowthers lived most of the year in London or the Midlands, fanatically devoted to hunting. 'William the Good', the first earl of the second creation, was, in fact, one of the pioneers of modern fox-hunting, and if Cumberland's reputation is to be associated with that miserable sport, we ought more properly to sing 'D'ye ken Lord Lonsdale' than 'D'ye ken John Peel'. Then, in the early twentieth century there emerged a new kind of Lord Lonsdale: Hugh Lowther, 'The Yellow Earl', who survived several Victorian scandals, knocked out John L. Sullivan (at least, by his own account) and became 'Britain's Ambassador of Sport' and perhaps the best-known English peer in the world. In 'Lordy's' time entertaining at Lowther was about the chief source of employment between Penrith and Shap. He had his regiment of yellow-liveried servants, who observed among themselves precedence and protocol as strict as that of any eighteenth-century German court. He had his fleet of yellow motor-cars and his pack of yellow dogs. He flattened twenty farms to make his park the largest in England, and when the Kaiser stayed at Lowther in 1895 hundreds of rabbits were let loose in a nearby fir-wood so that the imperial guest could have an easy shot. Finally, in his old age, with cigar in mouth and gardenia in buttonhole, he became a kind of Coniston Old Man of Lakeland sports, patron of hunting, hound-trailing, wrestling and fell-running, whose annual visits to Grasmere were welcomed like those of royalty. And outside Cumberland scarcely one in a hundred of those who were familiar with his name and appearance connected him with the collieries of Whitehaven or the iron-ore mines of Millom.

The present Lord Lonsdale, it should be said, is a patron of the arts, a keen supporter of conservation of wild life and the countryside and one of the most forward-looking agricultural landlords in the county.

To move from Askham along the banks of the River Lowther to Bampton and the foot of Mardale is like travelling along the eastern coast of the Lake District. The slate fells at the back of High Street end as abruptly as the spurs of Black Combe above the Irish Sea, while eastward there are rolling tides of sea-formed limestone. That is what makes Mardale (mere dale) so isolated. Unless you approach it on foot from Kentmere or Longsleddale, you have to go right out of the Lakes to get there. Indeed, Bampton and Bampton Grange, the two halves of the village built where Haweswater Beck joins the Lowther, have the look of only just having been discovered by the outside world, or of having been discovered long ago and then forgotten. They were once, in fact, a place of some consequence, out of the way of the main Scottish raids, and under the care and protection of Shap Abbey. Boys from the village were probably taught in the parish church by monks from the abbey, though later it had a grammar school, founded in 1623.

The present church—to my mind one of the most attractive small churches in the diocese—is not, of course, the one where the monks taught, having been built not until 1726, with the east end and chancel arch rebuilt in 1884-5. Outside, it is modest, rather puritan—though close to the village inn!—and looks, perhaps, a little earlier than its actual date. Inside, it is most surprisingly urban. There is nothing here of the barn-like character of, say, Grasmere. The heavy stone columns which one expects when entering almost any country church are replaced by slender oak pillars, carrying round wooden arches, and the whole arcade, though hardly to be called imposing, is neat, precise and almost smugly comfortable.

The contrast between this interior and the washed-up, forgotten landscape outside is hard to understand until you remember that Bampton was once the centre and meeting-point of a dale community that no longer exists. I did not know Mardale before it was flooded, and was not one of those who flocked to the valley in the 'thirties for a last drink in The Dun Bull or a last pull on the old church bell. So I will not be sentimental about it.

It is a dead valley, nevertheless. The only inhabited building is the Haweswater Hotel—and why *that* should have been allowed there, I cannot think. There is not even that passing bustle of cars and lorries which gives a kind of mechanical life to Thirlmere. Haweswater is a dead lake. The shores are littered with a kerb of detritus which makes it look from a distance like a half-empty swimming pool, and all along the side of the one road there is a police force of conifers forbidding you to go near the water.

In fact, it is no longer a lake but merely a reservoir. The dale it stands in is almost dead straight, like Great Langdale, though narrower, less craggy and more monotonous. And, like Langdale, it leads up to a magnificent dale-head, second only, perhaps, to that of Wasdale. On the western shore the fells stretch out one huge paw between Riggindale Beck and the water-head, and behind this the crags of Harter Fell and Ill Bell erupt upwards in tensely-controlled violence, among which the paths pick their way, on either side, to the passes of Gate Scarth and Nan Bield. Old photographs show a shore-line curved and indented far more than would now seem to be possible, with alders and ashes amicably disposed around a little boathouse, and the turf creeping up to the very edge of the water. Haweswater, as I said, may be merely a reservoir, but, when it was still a lake, it must surely have been one of the finest of them all.

CHAPTER SIX

KENDAL AND SOUTH WESTMORLAND

KENDAL is, of course, Kent-dale, by which I mean the country drained by the River Kent and its tributaries, including those which flow into the Kent Estuary. The chief town of this region was one of Westmorland's three Kirkbies or 'Church towns', called, more precisely, Kirkby Kendal to distinguish it from Kirkby Lonsdale (in the Lune Valley) and Kirkby Stephen (named, originally, from its owner, though later associated with St Stephen to whom the church is dedicated). Time, unfortunately, has chosen to drop the 'Kirkby' from Kirkby Kendal, so blunting a pleasing, nomenclative right-angled triangle, and at the same time making it impossible to use the name 'Kendal' for the valley of the Kent without causing confusion.

North of the town almost the whole of Kent-dale lies in the Silurian slates and shales, which stretch from the Duddon Estuary to the Howgill Fells above Sedbergh and, east of Troutbeck, swell up into bare, solid, bulbous hills quite unlike those round Windermere and Hawkshead. The upper Kent and its two main tributaries, the Sprint and the Mint, flow among these hills in three almost parallel valleys—Kentmere, Longsleddale and Bannisdale—which make up the three south-western spokes of the great broken cartwheel of the Lakeland dales.

None of the three is much visited by tourists, though two of them are well populated and easy to reach. Luckily, in either case, the road comes to a stop at the head of the dale, for if it did not, the trip by Kentmere over Nan Bield to Mardale and back by Gatescarth and Longsleddale would be as popular as the run round the two Langdales, via Blea Tarn. Kentmere has another effective tourist deterrent in the form of an industry—the mining and processing of diatomaceous earth of the kind used in the manufacture of both face powder and heat-insulated bricks. The tourist who is not deterred, however, will pass up a very agreeable valley, once the site of a lake—hence the name—to a splendid dale-head of volcanic rock, which, in fact, is the hind-side of the view at the head of Haweswater. The church stands on a little knoll, raised like a conductor's rostrum in front of the huge orchestra of the Mardale fells, while near by is Kentmere Hall, birthplace of Bernard Gilpin, 'The Apostle of the North', whose preaching in the sixteenth century led men back to religion. It was another member of the same family, William Gilpin (born at Scaleby Castle, near Carlisle), whose writings in the eighteenth century led the tourists to the Lakes, though most of them have not discovered Kentmere even yet.

Longsleddale is a farming valley. You can look into it from one point on the Shap road, above Garnet Bridge, where it has the appearance of a long narrow trench dug right into the foundations of the hills. This, indeed, is what it was in danger of becoming when the Manchester Corporation wanted to lay a pipe-line from Haweswater to run down the whole length of the valley. The pipes would have gone underground, but it was estimated that 70,000 tons of soil would have had to be shifted, and that 200 lorries a week would have used the dale road while work was in progress. It is hard to see how contracts on that scale could be managed without leaving the road hacked and widened and the face of the landscape scarred in a way that would take years to mend. A government decision of 1965 has saved the valley for the present, but one cannot feel altogether confident about the future.

The threat to Bannisdale* was even greater, for here Manchester wanted to build a dam and turn the valley into a new reservoir. This scheme, too, has been dropped, though every now and then there are warning signs that the water-mongers are still in business. It is true, of course, that if Bannisdale were to go under not many people would miss it. There is no metalled road along the valley, but only one that enters it about mid-dale, near Dryhope Farm, and then succumbs to mud and gravel at the little bridge over the deck. From above that point, Bannisdale is a back-water in time—a shallow hollow lying between fleshy, muscled hills with here and there a sparse, fluffy beard of oaks, blond in autumn and black-stubbly in winter. There is no village, no church, no pub, no tales of the 'Kings of Bannisdale'; nothing,

* Name from an Old Norse nick-name: 'the man who curses'

in fact, to rouse romantic nostalgia. Yet this is not one of the deserts of England. It is a valley that has been lived in and worked in for centuries. Every meadow and in-take, every wall and barn is the result of many generations of toil, struggle and grim persistence. As I said when the controversy about the proposed dam was at its height: if you drown Bannisdale, you drown history.

Kendal lies at the junction of the Silurian Slate with the Mountain Limestone. South of the town the limestone occupies the whole of the east bank of the Kent, from Levens Bridge nearly to Morecambe. West of the river the outcrops are more broken, giving the landscape a variegated, continually surprising look.

The first of these outcrops starts almost in the centre of the town. Climb Beast Banks and take the road towards Crosthwaite, and very soon you will be out on typical, open, Persil-washed limestone upland. You pass an old quarry with a radio mast close by and find yourself on the brow of the long escarpment of Underbarrow Scar. Here the road begins to twist downwards among woods, to the valley of the River Gilpin*, beyond which is the second of these limestone outcrops, that of Whitbarrow. In between are the drained, silted mosses of the lower Gilpin, so that you look from limestone to limestone across a valley bottom made up of mud washed down from the slate of the higher hills.

To me, coming from the coast, this Underbarrow outcrop has a particular fascination, for it is the first spot in Westmorland where I meet typical limestone flowers. All along the roadside, near the radio mast, you can find the hoary plantain (*Plantago media*), the one decorative member of an unpopular family, sticking up little pale green rabbit-tails dusted with lilac and pink. There, too, grows the large field scabious, and when you drop into the Gilpin valley the hedge-banks are awash with the opulent corollae of meadow cranesbill (*Geranium pratense*), that vary from blue to pink almost acre by acre.

The upper part of the Underbarrow and Lyth district shows the southern slates at their most cheerful—rather like Rusland, but more prettified, more dimpled and dented, an old-fashioned parlour beside Rusland's old-fashioned kitchen. 'Lyth', however,

* Named from the family to which Bernard and William Gilpin both belonged

Lowther Castle

(overleaf) *Ullswater, looking down lake and* (facing) *looking up lake*

is a misleading name. Most people who visit the Morecambe Bay area in spring will have seen advertisements for bus tours to 'THE DAMSON BLOSSOM IN THE LYTH VALLEY'. But where and what is Lyth? It is not a village; it is not a river; and it is certainly not a valley. The 'Lyth Valley' tour, in fact, covers two different valleys. It begins in that of the River Gilpin at Gilpin Bridge (often called Sampool Bridge on maps) about a mile west of Levens and runs below Whitbarrow until it joins the Kendal-Gummer's How road, where it crosses into the valley of the River Winster and on to Bowness. Traffic to the Lakes is now being diverted on to this road to avoid Kendal, and as a result much of the Gilpin-side stretch has been widened and straightened and given verges broad as a tennis-court. The coach driver, who looks well over the top of all this, is better off than the car driver, but, unless his tour brings him back from Bowness south to Lindale, he will have missed the best of the Winster. For this middle stretch of the river lies in a liquorice allsort of a valley, having for the black layer the slate of Cartmel Fell, and for the white, the limestone of Whitbarrow Scar. Nowhere else are the two rocks laid one against the other in such an orderly, such a neatly-cut manner. The difference is obvious on the two-and-a-half-inch map of the district from the very shape of the escarpments. You can see it best, however, not from the valley, but from the slopes of the fells to the west, where you look across the dip and the low hog-back of hill beside Witherslack and see the full, clear length of Whitbarrow.

This is not walkers' country. Most of the land is enclosed, and much of the road is cluttered in woods, but for the cyclist or the motorist it offers the quite unusual choice of four roads up the valley, or, if he takes them all, the chance of writing a large capital 'M' on the landscape.

The left-hand upstroke begins at High Newton and keeps well up the fellside until it dips into the valley near Cartmel Fell church. From this road you can see why the middle Winster has attracted the attention of the Manchester water engineers, for, in almost every respect except ugliness, it is a reservoir already. All that is needed is the dam. When the project to flood the valley was still being debated, the Winster Protection Society set up notices at various spots telling the visitor that, if Manchester got

Abbot Hall Art Gallery, Kendal
Sizergh Castle

its way, he would then be standing in twenty feet or so of water. And after a fortnight of wet weather he is quite likely to be standing in two feet even now.

From this road, too, if you turn your back on the valley, you can thread your way past the farms of Foxfield and Sow How and eventually come out just below Gummer's How—an intricate, unpublicised, agreeably aimless journey, open to walkers and cyclists, and even to motorists if they can balance on two strips of tarmac and do not mind opening and shutting many gates, though the farmers will not thank me for saying so. St Anthony's, on Cartmel Fell, is one of the most visited of the small dale churches, containing two beautifully-carved box pews, a three-decker pulpit, and some fifteenth-century stained-glass which is said to have come from Cartmel Priory, though the pieces depicting St Anthony and his pig seem likely to have been intended for his own church. St Anthony himself is the patron saint of herdsmen, basket-makers and charcoal-burners, so that it is not surprising that a corruption of his name, 'Tyson', is about the commonest surname in the dales.

The left down-stroke of the 'M' is the main road of the valley, much used by the more discriminating damson seekers. Running down it, they have the steep, wooded or brackeny hillside on their right, and on their left the almost absurdly flat riverside fields. In fact, the river, which only a couple of miles back was a rumbustious dale beck, is now as lackadaisical as a cut in the saltings at low tide. At Helton Tarn, a 200-yard-wide reedy sump, it almost gives up altogether, in which case Manchester would not have needed to build a dam.

About a quarter of a mile below Helton Tarn you should turn left at the guide post, cross the river by Bleacrag Bridge and begin the second up-stroke. You are very close to the limestone, now, though the escarpment is so thickly wooded that you hardly notice it. This is a road for the grocery van and the deliverer of paraffin, not for anyone in a hurry. You progress from farm-yard to farm-yard, through damson trees, black as ebony in winter and newly white-washed every spring, until eventually you reach Cowmire Hall, a farm-house built round a very late (sixteenth-century) pele tower. Its seventeenth-century front—three storeys, seventeen windows, and huge cylindrical chimneys

—is rectangular, entirely undecorated and splendidly unapologetic, a like-it-or-lump-it building that the neighbours have been lumping for 300 years.

You turn round at Cowmire Hall for the final down-stroke, and retrace the line for about half a mile, after which you strike left, past Witherslack Hall, now a school, into a little side valley. Witherslack Church—an externally plain, seventeenth-century building with a quite delightful interior—looks east from below precipitous woods across the open meadows of the lower Winster, and its churchyard stands on rock so solid that every now and then they have to use dynamite to blast a space for new graves.

You are now approaching the last southern bluff of Whitbarrow, where it rears with almost blatant exhibitionism high above the Foulshaw and Sampool Mosses. I have left this cornerstone of the Winster and Gilpin valleys to the last, though most visitors come across it first. In fact, to those who drive up from Lancashire, aiming for Newby Bridge or Ulverston, it is the first Lake rock they have time to notice. (Those who travel by train, however, will get a good view of Warton Crag, just outside Carnforth Station.) At Levens Bridge, ten miles north of Carnforth the road swings due east, across the Gilpin levels. This is a stretch I do not like: it is too fast, too flat, too busy and too straight. But for about two miles it is trained like a telescope plumb on to the gable-end of Raven's Crag and White Scar.

This is an exciting moment, especially for those who are coming to the Lakes for the first time. The rock leans forward like the hull of a ship, a dirty, weather-worn off-white for the most part, with ochre-yellow dribblings of scree and lower buttresses powdered grey with dust from the quarry and crushing-plant. The road veers left and runs along the base of the escarpment. Here the land is beautifully wooded between the road and the rock, and a whole tidal wave of larches breaks half-way up the face of the cliff, green as sphagnum moss in spring, but most of the year as yellow as the limestone itself. It is, to anyone who loves rock, a thrilling welcome, an exhilarating promise. And, of course, it is a promise which is not kept, for if the visitor wants to see anything else quite like White Scar and Whitbarrow he must go, not to the Lakes, but to Wharfedale. White Scar, in fact, is Westmorland's Kinsey Crag.

The limestone which covers practically the whole of southern Westmorland is nowhere else as spectacular as at Whitbarrow, but on Farleton Fell and Hutton Roof Crag it rises to nearly 1,000 feet. There are crustings of limestone pavement, and ten-or-twenty-foot-high escarpments that run horizontally along the hillside, and look, at a distance, like a row of ivory-backed prayerbooks on a bookseller's shelves. And there are abandoned quarries above Holme and Burton where you can sit in the sun, sheltered from the wind even in a breezy April, and stare across the estuary to Grange. And nowhere is spring greener than among the limestone, with the vivid turf and hawthorn spurting out of crumbles of rock. In these, and in the hills just south of the Lancashire border, you can find—I will not say precisely where—herb paris, gentians and genuinely wild lilies-of-the-valley.

For the most part, however, South Kent-dale is not hill-country. It is not quite lowland, either, though it has something of the easy-going look of the lowlands. Its main stream is the River Bela, which for much of the way potters between mud-banks and seems of just the right kind of amiable, trusting temperament to accommodate (as it does) an open-prison camp. But the principal water-course is really the old Lancaster Canal, begun in 1792 with the aim of linking Kendal to Wigan, though, in fact, it got no further than Preston. It did, however, link both Kendal and Lancaster to the sea, by an extension to Glasson Dock, and for a time, beginning in 1833, it ran an express passenger service, from Preston to Kendal and back. The boat held about seventy people; the fares were from four shillings to six shillings; and the time taken for the fifty-seven miles was about seven hours, the boat being drawn by two horses, changed every four miles. It must have been a good deal more comfortable and not noticeably slower than a journey along the A6. Today the canal is one of the most peaceful places in Westmorland—a long, curving, engineered lake crossed by innumerable, hump-backed, limestone bridges. Perhaps the deserted motorway will look something like that when we all take to the air.

If you come to this country from the upper dales you feel that the tension has slackened. Agriculture is no longer such a hand-to-mouth affair. There are more hedges than walls; the sheep are of lowland breeds; and the pasture often stays green and almost lush all the year round, for this district enjoys one of the mildest winter climates in England. The farms are bigger and the manor-houses are not just glorified farms as they usually are in the dales.

I am not very fond of paying money to traipse round other people's homes, especially when I remember that at one famous house visitors are led through the late-Victorian wing while the family sit comfortably in the Tudor rooms. But lower Kent-dale possesses two of the Lake District's most visitable homes, Sizergh* and Levens, both of them originally pele towers of the fourteenth century. At Sizergh, the Stricklands added Elizabethan wings to the old fortress-dwelling, making it into a house of enormous presence. At Levens, Sir James Bellingham embellished the building, in the late sixteenth and early seventeenth centuries, with plaster-work ceilings, staircases, wainscots, carved fire-places and overmantles of almost indigestible richness. Later, after the Glorious Revolution of 1688, Mons. Beaumont, who had been gardener to the deposed James II, came and laid out the gardens with bowling-greens, lawns, box-edgings and clipped yews in a great variety of formal or fanciful shapes. The present owner of Levens is an amateur of the harpsichord, and the visual delights of house and garden are now frequently augmented by the formal or fanciful shapes of baroque music.

Much of lower Kent-dale falls within the elipse made by the two roads from Carnforth to Kendal. The more westerly of these, through Milnthorpe and Levens, is now the most hideously over-crowded thoroughfare in the two counties, taking all the traffic from the M6 bound for the Lakes, Furness, West Cumberland and Scotland. Milnthorpe has been sawn in half by this traffic. It was once the capital of its little region—small, but very town-like, with climbing terraces of yellow-grey limestone, the chimneys of which throw an almost Edinburghian reek over the hill on a misty winter day. Most passers-through see nothing but cafés, lavatories and lorries, yet, in its more modest way, Milnthorpe is a Kent-dale equivalent of Lonsdale's Kirby. Perhaps, when the M6 is continued to the east of Shap, the village may lose some of its traffic and regain some of its serenity.

Beetham and Heversham, formerly on the road, have both been by-passed, though nobbut just. Each is exceptionally pretty,

* Sigrith's *erg* or shieling

and each has an interesting church—that at Beetham being one of the loveliest of our small Norman buildings. But both are within sight and ear-shot of the rush and roar of the traffic, and seem more like archaic lay-bys than genuinely independent villages.

Burton, at the more easterly of the two roads, has preserved more of its independence. For one thing, this route takes much less traffic, though the amount increases each year. For another, it was, from the start, a road-based village and is therefore the better able to stand up to intrusion. The little stage-set of a village square is, in fact, laid out, plumb and obvious, to catch the eye of the road-user. When the old houses were built, in the eighteenth and early nineteenth centuries, they cannot, of course, have expected to see so much traffic, so heavy and so fast, but they are not going to let themselves look surprised about it.

The more rural villages lie away from the main roads: Brigsteer and Levens in the north, overlooking the Gilpin levels; Yealand Redmayne, Yealand Conyers and Warton in the south, among the hills;* Holme right in the middle. I find it hard to think of one apart from the others. They are all built predominantly of limestone, though often rough-cast and lime-washed. They are full of nooks and angles, of big round chimneys and heavy porches. There are gardens sheltered by fat walls, often piled high with water-worn sculptures, miniature Henry Moores and Barbara Hepworths prised away from the limestone clints on the fellside. (Hundreds of tons of such weathered stone have been carted off to make rock-gardens in the Lancashire holiday towns.) The walls are matted over with white and purple rock, with ivy and the ivy-leaved toadflax, and often there are clipped yews (copied from Levens Hall) in front of the houses and sprawling orchards at the back. Limestone is one of the more workable materials, so that the local builders have been able to tackle structures that would have been risky in slate. Levens, for instance, has one of those little white church spires that gleam like a pillar of salt in the evening light. (There is another at Field Broughton, near Cartmel, and one at Bardsea, near Ulverston.)

Warton in Lancashire is the most southerly village in Greater Lakeland and is now being much built-about and suburbanised.

* The name Yealand, in fact, is derived from Old English 'high land'

It is the ancestral home of the Wahsington family, and their coat-of-arms, three mullets and two bars, which became the pattern of the Stars and Stripes, can still be seen, in the wall of the tower of the surprisingly large parish church. Formerly the arms were in the outward wall, but they suffered so much from the off-bay weather, that, a few years ago, they were literally pushed through the wall to the inside, where they are now rather faintly visible in the choir vestry.

Holme is perhaps the most typical village of them all, precisely because it has nothing special about it. It stands at the centre of the elipse, between the main London-to-Glasgow railway line and the old canal—fast trains at one end of the village and slow boats (or, now, *no* boats) at the other. Few of the houses are very old or very handsome, but in September the yellowing greens of plum and pear merge with the yellowing grey of stone until it is hard to tell which is garden and which is house. And, for all its rural look, it has a carpet factory tucked out of sight—indeed many of the Kent-dale villages are, or once were, partly industrialised, and even Milnthorpe (the *thorpe* or hamlet with a mill) did not get its name for nothing.

I remember Holme, however, more particularly because of an incident that shows how close is the link between the Lake countryside and the industrial coast. One summer evening I was walking through the village when a man called to me over a garden wall and asked if I remembered Jim Buckett. Ten years later Lord Birkett was to ask me the same question. For in the 1890's, when Lord Birkett and the old man in the garden had been young, Jim Buckett was the star player in a Millom Northern Union rugby team, which provided eleven of Cumberland County's thirteen men. I did, in fact, remember Buckett as a very old man, twisted with rheumatism, while my father had often told me of a cup-tie in which Millom had been drawn at home against one of the powerful Yorkshire clubs. One minute from the end the visitors were leading by three points to nil when the ball was passed to Buckett, who, with his very long reach, gathered it well in front of him and went over the line. But the referee thought he had knocked-on and disallowed the try.

And now this old man began to tell me about the same match. I listened abstractedly as the smoke of his pipe floated over the antirrhinums and early Michaelmas Daisies. It was an old story; it had not lost much in the telling; and, anyway, I suspected that my acquaintance, like my father, was talking only from hearsay, and had not seen the match at all.

'It should have been at least a draw', he went on. 'The referee knew he had made a mistake the moment he had blown his whistle, but there was nowt he could do about it then'.

'Did you see it?' I asked, somewhat sceptically. 'Were you a spectator?'

'I was not. I was the referee.'

Yet the place which, for me, most represents the character of Lower Kent-dale is a house of which I have no personal memories and which I have seen only from the outside. This is Dallam Tower, the eighteenth-century mansion in its splendid park, lying along the banks of the River Bela just above the viaduct of the old Arnside-Kendal railway. In the early nineteenth century my great-grandfather came to Dallam from Ireland to be gamekeeper to the wealthy Wilson family, and since the man who rears the pheasants seems to me to have as much right to call the land his own as the man who kills them, I do not hesitate (without asking anybody's permission) to look on Dallam Tower as my ancestral home.

My great-grandfather must have found plenty to do. Dallam Park had—still has—its herd of deer, and the Kent Mosses were famous for rabbiting, ferreting, fishing, wild-fowling, fox and otter hunting and cock-fighting. The Kent Estuary, in my great-grandfather's time, was much more of an arm of the sea, and small trading ships came up as far as the mouth of the Bela, bringing grain and coal to Milnthorpe. The building in 1857 of the Arnside Embankment and Viaduct for the Furness Railway put a stop to this sea traffic and led to the gradual silting up of the channel, so that today this part of the Kent looks less like the sea than a salt, inland lake, full or nearly empty according to the state of the tide.

Nevertheless, the shooting and gutting and netting and worrying still goes on. Peter Scott used to shoot geese at Sandside before he decided that it was more profitable (both for him and for the rest of us) to paint them. Anglers still lean over the promenade wall at weekends or sit in their cars, one hand holding a Sunday newspaper, and the other, a fishing-rod. No doubt the

Sea-washed turf, Silverdale

poaching still goes on, too, and, in spite of loyalty to my great-grandfather's memory, my sympathies are largely with the poachers.

('It was very good of the Chairman of the Bench to pay your fine for you,' said a friend of mine to a man who had been brought up in court for poaching salmon.

'So he bloody well should,' the man replied. 'It was him that got the salmon.')

Another thing which still goes on is cock-fighting. Mr R. D. Humber, in *Game-Cock and Countryman,* tells some of the old, almost legendary tales of cockfighting policemen and magistrates, of daring escapes from the law at Foulshaw Moss and Blea Tarn and among the ruins of Millom Castle, and of dead cocks hidden in straw and live ones shut into milk churns and driven innocently past the raiding police. There was a time when nearly every farm in the dales had its game-cocks, and mains were fought regularly, though in secret. Today it is probably the very illegality of the sport which is its chief attraction. It is hard not to feel a kind of grudging admiration for men who, to follow their hobby, will cross half a county and gather at dawn or by the light of car-headlamps on some cold, misty moors or marshes—just as it is hard not to feel admiration for the pluck of the birds themselves. (If a game-cock refuses to fight, the owner immediately wrings its neck to teach it to know better next time.) The admiration sometimes comes from unexpected quarters. A few years ago Foulshaw Moss, immediately opposite Sandside on the Gilpin shore of the estuary, was the scene of one of the most notorious of post-war cock-fighting meetings, where the police took the names of hundreds of spectators.

'I hear you were at Foulshaw the other day,' said a constable, interviewing an acquaintance of mine.

'No, no. You're wrong. I never left the house.'

'But your car was seen.'

'I tell you, I never left the house.'

'Stick to that story,' said the constable, 'and you'll hear no more about it'.

What interests me most about Kirkby Kendal is not its early history but the way the town has adapted itself to the present day.

Cartmel Priory, from the south and from the north-east

Of course, the history is interesting enough. There are traces of a British settlement at Castle How, near the County Hospital, while the Roman Camp beside the river at Watercrook was both an important station on the system of supply roads between Chester and Hadrian's Wall and a link with the coast via Ambleside and Hardknott. In the late twelfth century, the barony of Kendal was created by Richard Coeur de Lion, who later divided this in three, giving the portion with the castle to Sir William Parr.

It was during the time of the Parr family that Kendal rose to be the main commercial centre of the Westmorland wool trade, which I mentioned in the last chapter. Much of the cloth, woven on cottage looms, was brought into the town by pack-horse, and the streets and yards were bustling with stables and inns. 'Kendal Cottons', a coarse, hard-wearing *woollen* cloth, was worn throughout England by the poorer classes of Elizabethan times, and the town was equally famous for its dyes. Early travellers tell of tenter-fields all round the town where the dyed or bleached cloth was stretched out to dry. And 'Kendal Green', the colour worn by Falstaff's 'three misbegotten knaves', was, in all probability, the colour of the English bowmen at Flodden—the dye being obtained from the blue of woad and the yellow of dyer's greenweed (*Genista tinctoria*), a small, broom-like plant of the pea family which still grows abundantly in the area, especially near the sea.

It was in the seventeenth century, when the Westmorland homespun went out of fashion and the trade declined in the villages, that Kendal began that course of adjustment which so rouses my admiration. First, it shipped its goods to the plantations of America, where the owners were not unduly fastidious about the kind of cloth worn by the negro slaves. Then it began a reciprocal import business, more particularly in tobacco and snuff, and still remains one of the main centres of snuff manufacturing. (You can see one of the snuff warehouses in Lowther Street, with a painted negro snuff-taker jutting out from the wall like a ship's figure-head.) Today the wool and clothing trade continues, though on a reduced scale, and there are light engineering industries and the important K-shoe factory. The town also houses the head offices of the Provincial Assurance Company and has been the administrative centre of the county of Westmorland. It looks like a market-town and, in fact, has a lively, Saturday market. It looks, also, like a tourist town, and many travellers stop there overnight on their way to Scotland or the Lakes. Yet for all this it is essentially an industrial town and one of the most remarkable in England. It is relatively small, with just under 20,000 inhabitants, and, unlike similarly situated country towns such as Harrogate or Clitheroe or Hexham, it has no large area of population lying fairly close at hand. (Hexham, in particular, has become a kind of outer shopping centre for many of the people living on the eastern edge of Newcastle.) So Kendal has to rely on itself and on its immediate environment, and it is just this that has made it so self-sufficient, so self-contained and so proud of itself. When Cornelius Nicholson published his admirable *Annals of Kendal*, in 1861, he added a long supplement of 'Biographical Sketches of Many Eminent Personages Connected with the Town': Katharine Parr, and her brother William; Richard Brathwaite, author of *Drunken Barnaby's Journal;* William Hudson, a distinguished eighteenth-century botanist; John Gough, 'The Blind Philosopher'; and, of course, George Romney, who was born at Dalton-in-Furness but served his apprenticeship at Kendal and returned in his old age to die in a house near the parish church.

Kendal is, in fact, the best example in the Lakes of a town which has held on to its true character and refused to decline into a mere holiday centre. At the same time it has brought work and independence to South Westmorland and saved this part of the Lakes from having to sell out to the tourists. Of course, there is always the danger that the town's comparative prosperity will turn the nearby villages into suburbs, but so far this does not seem to have happened, and if there were two or three more Kendals scattered about the Lake District I should be much more optimistic about the future of the whole area.

Because the journey from my home to Kendal is a difficult one I knew the town for many years only as an occasional, tip-and-run visitor, and it seemed then to be all one street. The road bends and bumps from the southern end, called Kirkland, to the middle section, Highgate ('gate' meaning 'street'); then climbs gently up to the town hall, and sweeps downhill along Stricklandgate (the name, in this case, coming from that of the family of

Sizergh Castle). This long, three-jointed road, is met only by one side-road of importance—the narrow Finkle Street, curving and sloping into Stramongate and on towards the river. ('Finkle Street' is, of course, a name which occurs all over the North of England—it has been thought that it may be copied from the Finkle Street in York—and there are examples in Carlisle, Workington and St Bees, and one, now lost, at Appleby. Among the various suggested derivations are those from *fenkel*, a bend; from fennel, the garden herb which may have been sold in the shops; from a word meaning a rubbish-dump; and, more endearingly, from an unrecorded Middle English word meaning 'cuddle' or the like so that the name would be the equivalent of 'Love Lane'.)

Just north of Finkle Street is the market place, joined to the Finkle both by the narrow passage called the New Shambles, and by the corkscrew-twisting Branthwaite Brow. This for the quick visitor is the most obviously attractive part of Kendal. The market place is constricted and rectangular: it has a beautiful chemist's shop at the corner, but on the whole is rather austerely Georgian, though now most pleasantly coloured and cared for. The New Shambles is just what you might expect—overhung, cobbly and shadowy, with boutiques, coffee bars and all the latest old fashions. Branthwaite Brow, foot by foot, is one of the most delightful streets in the Lakes, with two or three handsome inns, a pair of charming houses at the Finkle end (looking as if they'll soon need careful preservation, however) and a Unitarian Chapel in a little courtyard approached through fine iron gates. From this courtyard, looking over walls and roof tops, you can see one of the two views that hang over the back doors of the town—the eastward view to the castle and the bare hills that divide Kent-dale from Lonsdale.

As was almost inevitable, Highgate-Stricklandgate has had to endure the treatment usually handed out to the shopping streets of any busy town. Once-elegant, eighteenth-century houses have have had shopfronts shoved into them like ill-fitting false teeth, and one or two of the larger stores flaunt façades that hit you in the eye like a slap with a wet fish. Nor has Kendal been much more fortunate with its newer non-commercial buildings. The town hall amounts almost to an architectural caricature, while the tunes played on its bells make me thankful that I am rather deaf. As for the public library, it has so many lintels, sills, coping-stones and medallions of red sandstone let into its basically limestone walls, that it looks like a man who has just pushed his face through a car wind-screen*.

In spite of all this, the main road has a dignity about it—partly from the limestone in which most of it is built, and partly from the good upper storeys which often remain. Moreover, there are still plenty of whole buildings well worth looking at. It is not my intention to provide a house to house inventory of the notable architecture of Kendal, for this has already been done by Professor Pevsner in his *Buildings of Cumberland and Westmorland*. But a walk of not much more than a hundred yards along the west side of Highgate will give you a good idea of what the town still holds.

Start at The Fleece Inn—once The Golden Fleece, a name that remembers the town's early prosperity and the motto: *Pannus mihi panis* (wool is my bread). This is the one remaining specimen of a type of building which once ran all along this part of Highgate, with a projecting upper storey of lath and plaster supported on wooden posts. Through the archway to the north of the inn you look up the Old Shambles, built in the late eighteenth century and leading to a still handsome, though now rather dilapidated, building which was once an inn. Beyond this you look at the other Kendal view—the westward view to the steep, wooded hill of Fellside, against which the Victorian houses, all of limestone, seem no more intrusive than outcrops of rock. This towering leafiness, only a few hundred yards from the main nerve of the town, makes the Lake country seem very near.

A few yards to the south of 'The Fleece' is the treble-bow window of the shop where Cornelius Nicholson worked at his *Annals*—the premises are now the offices of the Westmorland printer, Titus Wilson. Almost opposite is the eighteenth-century Angel Inn, and lower down on the 'Fleece' side is the Sandes Hospital. Here a prim, seventeenth-century frontage, seeming even older than its 300 years, gives entrance through an archway (notice the iron collecting box with the inscription, 'Remember the poore') to a long, flowery courtyard where live eight widows,

* But, in a building as in a person, a rough exterior can hide a heart of gold, for in no library have I received readier help and kindlier courtesy than at Kendal

in Victorian almshouses which look as if they had been stolen from a Cotswold village. I don't know if they find their homes very comfortable or convenient, but the little gardens, with the old Blue Coat School beyond, have a quietness which seems quite incredible when you remember that the second-busiest road in Westmorland is only about ten yards away.

You can walk on, finding interest in every third or fourth building. Beyond Sandes Hospital, for instance, is the New Inn, with its yard, once the site of a malt kiln, that now contains the Zion Chapel, looking as big as a cathedral in its very restricted confines. And beyond the New Inn, further down Highgate, is the fine brewery built by the Wilsons of Dallam Tower. And beyond the brewery—well, somewhere beyond this is the spot where you will decide to cross the road, and when you do, you will have to adjust yourself to a new view of Kendal.

For the idea that the town is one long street is quite wrong. If you climb above Fellside to the Serpentine Road you can see something of the plan on which the old town was built. Behind Highgate, on this western side, are row after row of narrow streets and alleys, known as the Kendal Yards. The Old Shambles, beside the Fleece, is the most spacious of them. Others are barely as wide as a lobby and reached from the main street by archways or entries. From above, you can see them, jammed closely together, back to back, the roofs irregular and higgledy-piggledy, looking like a picture-map of a medieval city, though, in fact, they are not nearly so old, and there is no truth in the legend that they were built as a defence against the Scottish raids.

There has been much rebuilding, of course—jobbing up and knocking down. Not many people live in the Yards nowadays, though on this western side you will sometimes find quite commodious eighteenth-century houses squeezed into a space where now you could not get permission to build a hen-hut. Mostly, however, you will find only workshops and warehouses and the back premises of the Highgate buildings, though here and there your nose will warn you of demolition and decay.

On the other side of Highgate the conditions are much worse. Walk through almost any of a score of entries, and you will come across acres of rubble—yard after yard bull-dozed down, with plaster and dust fuming in the sun, old fireplaces and chimney flues gaping from broken gables and weeds growing among fallen walls. That, at least, is how it was when last I explored this area. How soon and how well the town council will rebuild, I cannot tell.

Some of the Yards still remain as if perched precariously on the side of a volcano. I walked down one of them, New Bank Yard, the future of which is so uncertain that part of it, at least, may have been pulled down before this book is in print. The entrance is—I hope it may not be necessary to say 'was'—through a little tunnel between Martin's Bank and The Angel Inn. You come first into a very narrow lane, with the houses seemingly slid into place like bricks lining a chimney. The buildings fall away for a space, letting the light in, then close up again—indeed, close *over*, for the two sides of the lane meet overhead in a bridge, with a little house on top of it, approached by stone steps at the side. There are several of these bridge-houses in the course of the Yard, making it look more like a dried-up canal than a street. Here and there, too, in the near neighbourhood of the Yard are old three-or-four-storey wool-warehouses, of fine proportions and presence. And walls, houses, arches, warehouses are all of grey limestone, furred over with that black, mottled moss that makes part of Kendal look as if it had been upholstered in cat-skin. New Bank Yard is not elegant, of course. You could hardly call it 'charming' and not, in any circumstances, 'quaint'. Professor Pevsner has little to say about it, and perhaps it contains no single building which is not surpassed in style by others in Kirkby Lonsdale, Appleby, Ulverston, Brampton or even Whitehaven. Yet, taking it as a whole, and taking it with the other yards which have been pulled down, it formed part of an environment of great character and historical interest. To my mind, the destruction of this part of the town has done far more harm to Lakeland than the building of a garage beside Windermere would have done, or of a bungalow in Langdale or any other of the minor blemishes that the National-Park planners fuss about so much.

Yet it is not easy to know where to put the blame for the demolition. The medical authorities said that the Yards were a danger to health, and this I cannot dispute. To have restored them, to have made them wholesome and habitable again, would have cost a great deal of money, and where was a town of less than 20,000 people to find that money? And, if it comes to that, who was going to live in them when they had been restored? Of course, if these Yards had been in the centre of London, they could have been renovated and modernised and let at high rents to young, affluent, childless couples wanting to live near to the West-End night-life. But there are not many couples of that kind in Kendal, nor much night-life either. The Yards were neither pretty enough nor picturesque enough to attract tourist crowds like the Rows at Chester or Stonegate at York, and there could never have been enough gift-shops or cafés or house-agents' offices to occupy more than about one-tenth of them. Commercially, in fact, they were a dead loss.

I do not want to imply that the people of Kendal are entirely unconcerned with what happens to the old town. There is an active Civic Society which planned the admirable wash-and brush-up in the Market Place, hopes to do the same for Finkle Street, and, at the time of my writing this, is putting up a vigorous defence of New Bank Yard. Another splendid act of local enterprise has been the restoration of Abbot Hall, built in 1759 by Carr of York for yet another member of the Dallam Tower Wilsons, who, however, left it after ten years. The house was bought by the Kendal Corporation at the end of the last century but remained uninhabited and began to fall into serious disrepair. Since the last war, however, it has been most imaginatively renovated, and, under the stimulus of continual re-charging from its electric director, Helen Kapp (now, alas, retired), it has become both an adventurous art gallery and a very lively local centre.

Yet I still feel that, in the case of the Yards, the decision between restoration and destruction should not have lain with the Kendal people alone. Of course, there are government grants and loans and advice, but these are not enough—the responsibility still weighs too heavily on a community as small as that of Kendal. It should certainly be made at least as difficult to pull down old buildings as interesting as these as to put up unsightly new ones in Easedale or Little Langdale.

Let us hope that the county council, the Lake District National Park, the National Trust and everyone else who is interested will co-operate to save those Yards which are still left. And let us hope that the most imaginative and enterprising planning and designing will go to the rebuilding of the devastated areas*. It will be a poor justification for pulling down if we only build worse.

One other building must be mentioned, the parish church next door to Abbot Hall. This is an enormous church, the kind that the Victorians used to call a 'sacred edifice'. It is completely rectangular and so wide that inside it looks almost square. No part of the church, except the nineteenth-century porch, protrudes from the rectangle, the chancel being merely the eastern end of the central aisle. Even the tower is built over its western end. Much of the building was restored in the nineteenth century, but such matters can be left to architects and church historians. What immediately strikes you on entering at the west end of the southern aisle is that you have come into a vast, forest-like landscape of verticals and spaces. The church has five aisles, which means that it has four arcades and four rows of pillars, the appearance and spacing of which change at every step you take. The whole is so large that the outer corners seem not only to be out of earshot of the pulpit but almost out of memory of the congregation. You go into the south-west corner, for instance, as if you were going into another building, another part of the forest. An imposing church, certainly, but a solemn-faced church, and one, I feel, that must look half-empty even when it is full.

* What I have seen on my most recent visit to Kendal (summer 1968) does not, in fact give rise to much hope

CHAPTER SEVEN

MORECAMBE BAY

THE official Ordnance Survey 'tourist' map of the Lakes almost entirely severs the district from the sea. On the west it touches the coast only near Bootle; on the south, it cuts out Morecambe Bay altogether, except for the apex of the Kent Estuary opposite Heversham. From this map you would scarcely guess that Cumberland and Lancashire are essentially maritime counties and that the whole of western and southern Lakeland is within sound or smell of the high tide and has the mark of the sea worn into its history.

In Cumberland the coast faces open sea, and you can draw a clear line between sea and land. In North Lancashire and the Sandside-Arnside corner of Westmorland, the land looks out on a huge estuarine system, and it is hard to say where the land ends and the sea begins. This is quite unlike a fjord coast, that of Norway or Scotland where the sea has flooded the sunken valleys. In Morecambe Bay we have a coast line which has lifted itself *away* from the sea. So that instead of a between-tide margin, 200 or 300 yards in width, we have a vast area which, at one time of the day, is an arm of the sea, half as broad as the English Channel, and, six hours later, is a sub-county of sand-banks, skears, mud-flats, saltings and marsh. Above Greenodd at the meeting of the Leven and the Crake, and along Rusland Pool, the Eea, the Gilpin, the Kent and the Bela, the high tides push so far among the mosses and meadows, that the seabirds can be seen feeding only a few yards from the chickens in the damson orchards. Conversely, the fells are encroaching on the sea, for the sands and banks of the estuaries are made up largely of silt washed down from the eroded rocks of the fells. Look at Morecambe Bay when the tide is out, and you are looking at the mountains and hills brought low.

The bay has played an enormously important part in the human history of southern Lakeland. First of all it was a barrier, dividing the area from the rest of England. Then it was a line of approach, especially for the Vikings. Finally, it was a line of communication, a highway, linking Lancashire to West Cumberland and the Lakes.

It is this latter aspect which means most to me, for my grandfather came from Cartmel beside the Eea, my grandmother, from Milnthorpe beside the Bela, and both settled at Millom beside the Duddon—which, though it is not on the bay, is just beyond the northern tip of it, and shares the same weather, the same limestone and the same industrial history. It was the bay which brought them together, brought them to Millom and brought me into being.

From early times the cross-bay route was a matter of both profit and danger. In 1322 the Scots, under Robert Bruce, came down the Cumberland coast, crossed the Leven Sands to Cartmel —where they spared the Priory but stole cattle and burnt farms— and finally crossed the Kent Sands to Lancaster, where they sacked the town and castle. Other travellers often spent the night between tides at Cartmel Priory, where the Austin Canons were responsible for maintaining guides across the Kent, just as the lesser religious house of Conishead, near Ulverston, had a similar responsibility for the Leven. (The guides, who are called 'Carters' after the first family to hold the office, still carry out their duties from Kents Bank and Canal Foot, Ulverston. They are appointed by the Duchy of Lancaster, and draw their salary of £15 a year from a charity trust, which, however, is finding it difficult to raise the money to pay the guides and maintain the guide houses provided for them.) According to West's *Antiquities of Furness*, the Conishead monks used to say mass for travellers on Chapel Island, a small rocky knoll in the Ulverston Sands, about a mile from the Bardsea shore, but the tradition has little evidence behind it, and the building which you can see from the railway viaduct is that of a mock ruin set up by Colonel Braddyll who built the Gothic-revival Conishead Priory in the early nineteenth century.

Even before Braddyll's time the bay route had become the main line of approach to the booming industrial area of West Cumberland. The Whitehaven-bound travellers, having reached Ulverston, went through Low Furness to the Cumberland coast, crossing the Duddon from Askam to Millom and the combined estuaries of the Esk, Mite and Irt at Ravenglass. It was an adventurous journey and had to be timed carefully if the traveller was not to be held up by the tides. At Holborn Hill, the village which has grown into the town of Millom, there used to be an inn called The Pilot, where you could hire a guide, and, though the inn itself has been pulled down, the rhyme announcing this service can still be seen carved on a stone let into the wall of a house built on the same site:

William and Ann
Barren live here
Who also sell
Good ale and beer

You that intend
To cross ye sand
Call here a gide
Att your command.

The shape of the bay is roughly that of a capital 'M', the dip in the middle, made by the second and third strokes of the letter, being the Cartmel Peninsula. Travellers coming from the south used to embark at Hest Bank, a few miles north of Morecambe, fording the channels of the Keer and the Kent and touching solid ground again at Kent's Bank near the present-day Grange-over-Sands. There they often rested between tides, perhaps spending a night at an inn in Allithwaite, Flookburgh or Cartmel, or at Holker Hall, if they had friends who could give them an introduction to the Cavendish family. The dangers of the journey may have been exaggerated, but the parish registers of Cartmel Priory and other bay-side churches are full of records of coaches over-turned, small carriages stuck in quicksands, horsemen washed away, foot-travellers, fishermen and cocklers caught by the tide. Yet, throughout the eighteenth century and right up to the middle of the nineteenth, there was a regular service of public coaches from The King's Arms, Lancaster, to The Sun Inn, Ulverston, the northbound crossing being made on Monday, Wednesday and Friday, and the return journey on Tuesday, Thursday and Saturday. In fact, the cross-sands route continued to be used long after the making, in 1820, of the turnpike road from Carnforth to Ulverston, via Levens Bridge and Greenodd—in fact the public coaches do not seem to have used the new road at all. What finished the coaches was not the turnpike but the opening of the Ulverston and Lancaster railway in 1857, which also finished most of the bay's shipping.

Before this time, however, Furness and Cartmel had carried on much of their trade by sea. General supplies and stores were brought in by small vessels and unloaded wherever a landing-place could be found. The two main ports in earlier days were Lancaster and Piel Island, near Barrow, which had been used for at least five centuries. There are records also of landing places at Hest Bank, Carnforth, Arnside, Milnthorpe, Cark, Greenodd, Conishead, Bardsea, Baycliffe, Barrow and several spots in the Duddon Estuary, including Borwick Rails, which became the port of Millom Ironworks. By the late eighteenth century a good deal of iron-ore and slate was being shipped from the Furness ports, and in 1796 the mile-long and dead-straight Ulverston Canal was cut to connect the town with the sea. The canal has been closed for many years, but if you stand at Canal Foot at low tide and look at the narrow trench of muddy water that wriggles out to the Leven-Crake Channel, you will get some idea of the skill needed by the Morecambe Bay mariners. There are few spots in the bay which bring together so much of past and present. You look across the yellow-silvery pools and mud-slides, with the railway viaduct on one side and Chapel Island on the other, and the woods of Holker and the bracken hills of Bigland over the water, with a new aluminium silo near Cark shining out like some modernistic limekiln. Immediately around you is the amiable muddle of the old landing-stage—the rotting canal sluice-gates, the coaching inn, the Carter's House, a bungalow or two, with anglers and courting fifth-formers and acrobatic boy cyclists giving a surface stir to the otherwise lethargic scene. And behind is the new penicillin factory, built on the site of the old Ulverston Ironworks, themselves built on the site of tanneries and bloomeries and early industrial workings that go back for centuries. It was not far from this spot, in 1794, that Wordsworth heard of the death of Robespierre*.

After the opening of the canal, Ulverston became the chief

* See *The Prelude*, Book X, lines 553-75 (1850)

port for Furness ore and iron until the rise of Barrow. It also became a small ship-building centre, so following an old Bay tradition, for the building of ships had gone on for many years at Lancaster, Carnforth, Arnside, Greenodd and around Piel Island. In 1772, Thomas Pennant, one of the discoverers of 'picturesque' England, even reported the trade at Penny Bridge, well upstream on the Crake, which, if it is true, shows how the seafaring and shore-faring life of the bay pushed its way high into the Lakeland dales.

Today, of course, shipbuilding is confined to the great yards of Barrow, but it went on at Millom right until the beginning of the twentieth century, and my father could remember the launching of *The Happy Harry* and other coasting vessels at Borwick Rails round about that time.

The routes across the sands are now recognised as rights of way and marked on the new Ordnance Survey maps, though they are little used, and the bay walk survives largely as an organised outing held several times a year for the energetic young. I am neither young enough nor energetic enough to hope to join it, but many hours spent well off-shore at Bardsea, Baycliff and Silverdale and, above all, on the sands of the Duddon, have given me some idea of the emotions of the eighteenth-century travellers* at this tremendous curtain-raiser to their tour of the Lakes. For out in the bay all their preconceived notions of Lake scenery were swilled away. The shore, with the line of cliffs, seems no taller than a bed of shingle, and even the fells themselves are dwarfed by the enormous flatness of the sands. It is a melancholy landscape. Here and there, skears and boulders and inexplicable old posts jut out of the sand, black with weed and fortified with a whole Maginot Line of mussels and barnacles. There is an empty hollowness about the air, so that the clangings and pipings of the seabirds seem to echo one off another, having nothing else to echo off. In summer, when there is a hot sun, a haze can steam up from the sands, making the shore less definite than ever. And when there is mist all landmarks vanish, so that if you turn round twice you don't know where you are. Fishermen on the Duddon Estuary tell me that, when the mist comes down suddenly, they

* For more about the early tourists and the Bay crossing see N. Nicholson: *The Lakers* (R. Hale)

sometimes have to wait for the sound of a train in one of the sand-side stations before they can be sure which is their way back to the shore.

In the days of the cross-bay travellers the sands were, for an hour or so each day, a place of lively bustle and traffic. Today they are one of the loneliest places in the Lakes. The tide flows and ebbs, the wind veers, the weather varies, the geese come to the saltings in autumn, the shelducks fly off to the hills in spring, everything goes on and on. Nothing really changes. In fact, the landscape of the sands is probably the least changed landscape in the whole of the Lakes.

It is somewhat ironical, then, to find that one of the best ways of seeing the changelessness of the bay is from the biggest change that man has yet managed to make—the railway line from Carnforth to Barrow. For by rail you pass much closer than by road to the old cross sands route, and it is a journey you can take in any weather. After riding up and down this line many times at all seasons of the year, certain views stay in my memory: the full tide pouring under the Leven Viaduct and turning the upper estuary into a Scottish firth; Holker Mosses in winter dusk, with the swamp-mist clogged about the birches, the yews glooming up blackly on the limestone cliffs, and the sheep, on the salt marshes, eating their way steadily into the night; gales and driving rain slashing at Humphrey Head on the Kent Bank shore, till the ebb-tide sands seem as flooded and frothy and turbulent as at high tide; the Meathop Sands, between Grange and Arnside, in the dead grey of winter, with the creeks and pans frozen, the mud dirtied with white, and the smashed glass of ice-floes piled up at the edge of the tide. Take away the railway and Agricola might have looked on the same scene if he marched his legions this way, nearly 2,000 years ago—which he probably didn't.

One further way of crossing the bay must now be thought of. As long ago as 1836, George Stephenson put forward plans to carry the main railway to Scotland across Morecambe Bay and along the Cumberland coast. And now, in the 1960s, the late Dr E. L. Leeming and others have been advocating the building of a dam from Hest Bank to Bardsea, turning the bay into a freshwater lake with a new road and railway from Carnforth to Barrow. The dam, if it were built, would provide enormous extra water storage for Manchester and industrial Lancashire, while the road would give the line of easy communication so urgently needed by Barrow and West Cumberland. This joint aim of both saving the Lakes from further waterworks and floodings and of helping to revitalise Barrow and the West Coast has gained for the scheme the overwhelming support of most people in Furness and Cumberland, including the present writer. One must admit, sadly and regretfully, that it would undoubtedly change the character of the bay. One must also admit that, so far, the plan has aroused no great enthusiasm outside the North-west, though a large-scale feasibility study is now being carried out. But just in case the scheme is approved and the dam eventually built, let us take a look at the shores of the bay as they still are.

On a map Morecambe Bay appears to swing right round from Walney Island to Heysham Harbour, but the southern shore from Heysham to Bare no longer belongs to Greater Lakeland. Industrial Lancashire and Yorkshire have taken it over. The name derives from the 'Moricambe' estuary mentioned by Ptolemy and geographers of antiquity as being near the mouth of the River Eden, though the exact location is uncertain and our area has a second Moricambe on the Solway. (In either case, the name means 'sea-bend'.) Until the beginning of the nineteenth century there was, in fact, no such place as 'Morecambe', but only a group of villages: Heysham, Torrisholme, Poulton-le-Sands and Bare. Then, when sea-bathing became popular in the mid-nineteenth century, the village of Poulton began to grow, and soon annexed the name of the bay and adopted it officially in 1870. And by this time the town was linked to the West Riding by train and had become such a favourite with Yorkshiremen that it was sometimes called 'Bradford-by-the-Sea'.

This, however, is comparatively recent history, and, before Yorkshire took it over, the pre-Norman, ninth-century or even earlier chapel of St Patrick on Heysham Head might have been called the 'holiest' spot in Greater Lakeland. One has to put the word in inverted commas, especially in a place which is now almost overhung by the strident tinsel of a modern pleasure dome. But this chapel, and the six coffins nearby, hewn out of the solid rock, belong to the time of the early Celtic Church, when the

Morecambe Bay, Arnside

word 'holy' really meant something. (Incidentally, the tenth-century St Patrick's Church, which still stands in a dell just below the headland, is almost equally interesting, and contains a pre-Christian, Anglian hog's back, the 'crack of Doom' stone, which is said to be one of the best preserved examples of its kind anywhere in the world.)

Present-day Morecambe has surely the most magnificent site of any seaside town in the North of England. Yet, in its own appearance, it is about as aesthetically distinguished as a stick of Brussels sprouts. There are other places in Greater Lakeland where one feels sad that people have to live and work in such surroundings. But nobody has to live at Morecambe. The sad thing here is that people like it as it is.

Not far to the north of Morecambe, however, you come upon the Lake limestone which first shows itself in garden walls and rockeries. This is pensioner's land, stocked and stacked with villas and bungalows, small and safe as annuities. But at Bolton-le-Sands, if you push up the hill away from the main road, you will find the agreeable remains of the old bay-side village. The church has a square tower like a watch-tower, a low arcade, and, in the chancel, a memorial to a former vicar on which the stone mason has tried to save words by bracketing together the man's age and the years of his incumbency.

At Carnforth the limestone suddenly reveals its sleezy side—half of Warton Crag is quarried away for blast furnaces or road-building, while the old slagbanks lie about like uncollected rubbish at the mouth of the River Keer. It is not until you cross this river and reach the southern tip of the Silverdale Peninsula that you arrive at the true boundary of Greater Lakeland.

Silverdale is not really a peninsula but a bow-shaped protuberance bulging out into the bay, yet the Leighton Marshes and Silverdale Moss so divide it from what you might call the mainland that it has all the characteristics of a peninsula. 'Silver' means what it says; the whole area is, in fact, one huge cat's paw of silvery limestone, clawing at the estuary. If you approach from the south, by the sands or, as is more likely, by the train, you see the limestone first in its more commercial shape, as the old kiln and chimney near Jenny Brown's Point. Continue in the same

Morecambe Bay, Canal Foot, Ulverston

train as far as Arnside, and you will pass close to one of the few remaining working quarries, tucked away in a wood, where, all the year round, the trees are hoary with a rime of lime-dust. Apart from this, the rock is now less practical-looking, more ornamental, more delicately coloured and moulded than almost any around the bay. If we must say that it is carved, then the carving seems to be carried out in a softer material than stone—in ivory, for instance, for it is more of a white dale than a silver dale and is often yellowed by lichen and peat-stain until it is the colour of the keys of a rarely played piano.

Silverdale is an exceptionally pretty village—about as pretty as I can stand without finding it too painful. But behind the houses, and linking the outlying parts of the village, are little 'back lanes', running beside high garden walls as conspiratorially as the secret alleys of a medieval town. There is one right of way which leads from the cross-roads at the Arnside end of the village to the part of the shore called The Cove, where it is hard to convince a stranger that he is not trespassing in private gardens and entrances. It is sometimes hard to convince the dogs, too.

The Cove itself is one of the most engagingly melancholy spots in the whole bay. When the tide is out—and it seems to be out for roughly twenty-three hours of the day—the salt-marsh stretches so far that not only can you not see the sea, you can't even see the sand. The cliffs drop down aimlessly to miles of salt mud, scored by tractors, split and scooped by sun and water. The sour leavings of each tide are dried by the sun, and the dubs smell like a rotting cockle. Sheep, with yards of blackberry trailers tangled in their wool, graze so far out that the tide can surround them in the gulleys without their knowing anything about it, for only when the water actually covers the grass will they lift their heads. The cliffs themselves are caved and quarried, and draped like the Hanging Gardens of Babylon with flowers that take to the lime: rock roses, horse-shoe vetch and broomrape, as well as hawthorns that bend over downwards, with their heads below their feet, as if the wind were trying to give them first aid after a nasty knock in the crotch.

Arnside is further up the estuary than Silverdale and is quite out of sight of open sea, yet, oddly enough, it is by far the more maritime of the two villages. Most of the day, admittedly, the little promenade and the huge, upholstered cliffs overlook wet sands and the placid channel of the Kent. But when the tide does come in, it comes in with a rush and a bore, knocking the boats together and flushing pounds and pounds of fresh salmon under the arches of the railway viaduct. Arnside is in Westmorland, though it is almost entirely surrounded by sea and Lancashire, and is connected to the rest of its county only by a small neck of land around Sandside and Beetham. The village looks its best from the train on the other side of the Kent channel, where, in the grey winter dusk, you can see the orange and red lights of shops and inns flashing and swaying on the water like the Morecambe illuminations seen from a merciful twenty miles away. Because the promenade is pinched in between the railway and the cliff-bulge, it has not had space to spread sideways, so that nearly all the new building of the last few years has gone on at the back of the village, on the slopes of Arnside Knott, where it is so hidden and camouflaged by birch and bracken that much of it is scarcely noticed. Along the sea front there is no new building at all. Scarcely a house that is not of old-fashioned, native limestone and slate. Even the cafés look as if they are only obliging the visitors for the season and will change back into parlours and pot shops when everyone has gone home. Arnside, in fact, is a rare case of a seaside town which has been able to turn itself into a holiday resort without selling out to the devil.

Charming as the village is, however, it bows into modest insignificance beside the hill it has given its name to*. Arnside Knott is only just over 500 feet high, but it is one of the best look-out towers on Morecambe Bay. It is also a most lovely lump of rock—solid, bumpy, cliffed and quarried on the inland side, with slivers and slithers of cream-cheese scree; while, on the seaward side, it is padded from boot to collar in trees. These woods, like those of King William's Hill on the Silverdale border of the parish, are thick and dark, spiky with bluebells in spring, but clouted up with the musty greens of ferns and dog mercury in summer. Out on the fellside everything is bare to the sun, and you feel that you are at least 1,000 feet higher. Here the yellows come into the scene again—gorse, broom, tormentil, hawk-weeds beyond number and, so far as I am concerned, beyond identi-

* Or, more properly, a Viking called, perhaps, *Arni* gave his name to both

fication, and the ploughman's spikenard, which is common enough round here but so rare in Cumberland that I may be one of the first to have recorded it there. You will find clints and limestone pavings, moulded and hollowed and fretted into the shapes of the most frivolous pottery—brackets and cups and candle-holders—and solid stone cloches with fissures that you can put your foot through up to the knee. And right in the dip between the Knott and the other hill stands the old pele of Arnside Tower, so sited against the western sky that from the train, in the evening, it gathers to itself the whole romantic back-drop of the sunset.

The Cartmel* Peninsula, which has the shape of a map of India, is, paradoxically, a valley—the valley of the small river Eea or Ea, a name derived from the Old Norse *ā* or the Old English *ea*, both meaning river, and both derived in *their* case from a language of still greater antiquity, as with the French *eau*. The name of Eea, in fact, may be a distant memory of mankind's most primitive word for water. The river, which, in any case, is far older than any form of its name, flows in a valley between two low ridges, Bigland Heights on the west, and Hampsfield Fell on the east; and as the Bigland hills are a continuation of the Silurian slates of Rusland and Windermere, while Hampsfield is of the limestone of Humphrey Head, the valley of the Eea shows in miniature the same geological two-tone pattern as that of the Winster.

You have no reason, however, to suspect the nearness of slate as you approach Grange-over-Sands in the train, from which you get a far better view of this central segment than you do from the road. The railway passes close to the scar of the old Meathop Quarry, and then crosses the Winster Marshes, which, thanks partly to the railway embankment, are now no longer marshes but what is surely the flattest golf course in the north of England. Here, the Winster, having forgotten the crochety petulance of its upper reaches, gives itself up to the sea as tamely as a fenland cut. Thanks again to the railway, Holme Island is now no longer an island, since John Brogden, one of the promoters of both the Furness and the Ulverston and Lancaster Railways, constructed a

* 'Mel' is Old Norse *melr*, a sand-bank; 'cart' may be Old English *ceart*, rocky, rough

causeway and built a house there. Today the breakwaters which keep back the tide are less obtrusive than the notices which keep keep out the picnickers, and anyone who has good reason or excuse to get on to the island will find it, at most times, stranded like a whale in acres of sad sand.

Grange is something of an oddity. It was meant to be a rather sedate, old-lady-like, Victorian watering place, but, being built of the chubby, almost frivolous limestone from local quarries, it cannot have looked very sedate even at the start. It has an artificial lake of almost excruciating prettiness, with islands, weeping willows, twining paths and a whole Wildfowl Trust of tame ducks, though I cannot understand why anyone should want to look at 200 yards of ornamental plumbing when there are the twenty miles of Morecambe Bay on the other side of the railway. In summer Grange seems to be the place where campers and caravanners come when it is wet. In late autumn and in winter, on the other hand, it has a rather batty, self-indulgent charm, when the boarding houses are closed, the bathing pool is drained empty, the trees are withered to sodden yellows and browns and the incorrigible local stone pushes up its nose from every wall and rockery. It also has the distinction of being surely the only holiday resort on the north-west coast that faces almost due east. All sight of the west and of the Irish Sea is, in fact, blocked off by Humphrey Head, one of the several places where, according to legend, the last wolf in England was killed. According to fact, it is one of the only two major headlands on the whole of the Greater Lakeland coast—St Bees is, of course, the other—and one of the very few places between Wales and Scotland where true rock defies the sea, though, most of the time, it is defying a sea that isn't there.

The Cartmel Valley is surprisingly unspoiled. Surprisingly, that is to say, when you think how close it is to Windermere, but not so surprisingly when you remember the history of these parts. For the travellers over the sands touched only the southern tip of the peninsula, though some would turn aside to visit Cartmel and the priory, especially in mediaeval times. Travellers by land kept even further away, for in the days before metalled roads the great obstacle to travel was mud—Cumberland roads of the seventeenth century were actually praised because they were hilly and stony. The main land route into Furness avoided the marshes of the upper estuaries and ran by Kendal and over Gummer's How to the foot of Windermere. Even when the turnpike was opened in 1820 it ran along the lower slopes of the Newton Fells, keeping well above the Cartmel Valley. The modern road follows the turnpike, the railway follows roughly the cross-sands route, so that the valley remains remarkably free from traffic—neither remote, nor wild, nor spectacular, yet as typically Cumbrian as any part of Lancashire can be.

At a first glance it may not look typical. The River Eea, with no effort of its own, has inherited the lower part of the valley of the prehistoric river which, before the Ice Age, flowed where Windermere stands today. It is shallow, wide, much plastered with glacial clay and quite different from a beck-carved, Lake-District dale. But, at bottom, all is of the same rock—whether the limestone of the middle valley, with its more than usually comfortable farms and manor houses, or the slate of the Bigland Hills. In fact, the road from Cartmel racecourse past Bigland Hall to Haverthwaite runs through some of the most captivatingly scruffy, scrubby, broken and brackenny country in the whole of Lake Lancashire.

I have a right to be proud of Cartmel as the home of my ancestors. Family pride apart, it is still a place of great presence. Often it is classed with Hawkshead as one of the two most beautiful villages in Lancashire, and it has something of the same look of rough, rural antiquity, though it would be sheer impertinence to call it 'quaint'. I would not even call it pretty. And though it has often won prizes as one of the best-kept villages in the country, it has done so by being neat and tidy, not by tarting itself up with window boxes or little trees in tubs.

What is unexpected is that, though it is at the hub of a valley of glittering white limestone, that stone is scarcely to be seen in the centre of the village. The two honest-faced inns and the unlicensed Priory Hotel in the little square are rough-cast and painted; the pillared and porched shops and the priory gatehouse are built of mixed stone, much of it red and brown and slaty rubble. But if you go to the bridge over the Eea, and look upstream, you can see limestone walls holding back the water and limestone steps going down to it. There is a legend saying that the Austin Canons who founded Cartmel Priory heard a voice telling them to search for a spit of land between two streams which flowed in opposite directions. But unless they came when the Eea was in spate, they must have found it hard to decide which way it *was* flowing. For in ordinary weather the water lies as still as in a canal, though much clearer, so that in winter you can see bright green weeds fanning out like sea-anemones on the river-floor, while in early summer the surface is half-hidden with white water-buttercup and speckled with dropped apple-blossom.

Cartmel is fortunate in having no popular literary or romantic associations to draw the crowds. It has associations with Wordsworth, nevertheless, for 'an honoured teacher' of his youth was buried here, with a tombstone, which can still be found on the south side of the church, inscribed with 'lines from the churchyard elegy of Gray'*. It happens, that an honoured teacher of *my* youth, Canon Samuel Taylor, is also buried at Cartmel, in the new cemetery near the racecourse, and it was he who, in his retirement, wrote the admirable book on *Cartmel People and Priory*, in which he tells, with much charm, almost all that anyone will want to know of the history of the village. It was he, too, who discovered the entry in the parish register recording the marriage of my grandparents.

If the Lake District were a separate diocese then surely Cartmel Priory would be its cathedral, for it is a true church of the dales, rock-built rather than just stone-built, and having that piled-together, unconcernedly uncouth look of a dale barn. From a distance and from all approaches except that from Cark, it is seen as rather low-lying, like an angular water-lily at the bottom of a dried-up pond. The whole church, in fact, is bunched up and cubical rather than spreading and spired in the usual English cathedral manner. This is partly because of the shortness of the nave, added in the fifteenth century and built more roughly than the rest of the church. But it is still more because of the oddness of the tower. Originally the church had only the squat, square tower, not much higher than the roof, which still stands over the crossing, but in the fifteenth century there was added a smaller belfry tower, set diagonally inside the first. One feels that, logically, there should have been another smaller tower set

* See *The Prelude*, Book X, lines 523-52

diagonally inside the second, and another inside that, until the whole structure tapered up like a stone wedding cake or the whole building collapsed under the weight. Yet, clumsy as this double-tower is, it seems, as Canon Taylor says, to harmonise with the rest of the church, having much of the familiar angular awkwardness with which pieces of rock normally lie about the fellside.

The Piper choir, the windows, the tombs, the first edition of *The Faerie Queen* (which was stolen from the church and returned from an antiquarian bookshop in London) and the rest of the interior I can leave to Canon Taylor and the loyal helpers who show visitors round the church in summer. Except, that is, for the woodwork. When Cartmel Priory was dissolved in 1536 the roof was torn off the nave and chancel, and the misericords of the choir were allowed to rot in the rain. A small portion of the church, however, now known as The Town Choir, was preserved for use as a parish church, and by 1618 the village had so grown in wealth and population that the parishioners were able to repair and re-roof the old chancel. Almost miraculously the fifteenth-century misericords had stood up to eighty years of Cartmel weather with little sign of damage and are, in fact, excellent and most entertaining examples of that kind of work. But medieval misericords can be seen in many churches; the woodwork which was installed about 1620 cannot. For at that time George Preston of Holker* Hall, whose family had taken over most of the priory estates—another branch of the family had acquired those of Furness Abbey—gave to the church the carved screen and the pillared canopies above the old canons' stalls. It is said that Preston imported Flemish workers for the job, in which case they may also have helped to embellish that part of Holker Hall which was burned down in the nineteenth century. Whether or not this is true, the screen and canopies, with their pierced panels and pillars, entwined with vine leaves and symbols of the Passion, remain one of the loveliest works of art still to be seen in Greater Lakeland.

Cartmel has very little touch or tang of the sea about it, yet such wealth as the Augustinians had probably came as much from the sea as from the land—from fishing and wild-fowling and all the petty scavenging which in the Middle Ages made marshes

* Pronounced Hooker

almost as profitable as cultivated land. And the two villages most closely bound to Cartmel both belong to the shore: Cark, where boats used to unload at the mouth of the Eea; and Flookburgh, which is still the main centre for Morecambe-Bay shrimps.

My last memory of Cartmel, therefore, shall be one of the shore. The road along the Holker Mosses is much favoured in March and April because the Bigland hills hold off the east winds, the wooded slopes are full of celandines and wild arum and all the spiky greenness of early spring. If you turn off this road about a mile above Cark and follow the signpost to Old Park, you will come, first, to one of the most cleverly-chosen caravan sites in the Lakes, and, beyond that, to the Leven Estuary, just inside the Ulverston railway viaduct. This is, of all spots on the bay, the one where the tide pushes highest among the rocks. Across the river are the slates of Greenodd, with Grizedale Forest heaving and billowing in the middle distance, and the Coniston fells behind them. But on the Holker side you are still among the limestone, and, if you walk along the shore around Park Head, you will find yourself in a desolate equilateral triangle of saltmarsh that looks as if it had been washed up on a prodigious high tide and left stranded between the railway embankment and the cliffs of what once used to be the coastline. The marsh here so seldom feels the moistening of the sea that, except in wet weather, it is as dry as putty. Sea-milkwort is practically the only flowering plant, and the cliffs are almost as bare as slag. The tide is blocked off from sight by the railway, but if you wander out to the sands which make up the third side of the trangle, the salty runnels, the shelducks, curlews and sandpipers leave you in no doubt that, though you are only four miles away from England's largest fresh-water lake, you are nevertheless at the edge of the Atlantic.

The Furness* District of Lancashire is bigger than most people think, covering all the land between the Duddon and Windermere, and, together with Cartmel, making up the whole of North Lonsdale. But High Furness, which lies entirely within the National Park, seems not anxious to associate itself with its neighbour below the boundary. You don't hear of Coniston-in-Furness or Hawkshead-in-Furness, though 'in Furness' they

* Accent on the first syllable

certainly are. But once you get south of the park boundary, which runs along the line of the Duddon Bridge-Greenodd main road, you will find Broughton-in-Furness, Askam-in-Furness, Dalton-in-Furness, Barrow-in-Furness, Furness Abbey, Furness Railway and the Furness Cricket Club. People, here, are obviously proud of belonging to Furness, and so they should be.

On the map Low Furness looks compact and very much of a whole; in fact, it is quite the opposite and it is this which makes it one of the most interesting of all the outlying parts of Greater Lakeland. For it is a peninsula of contradictions. The hill-lands bordering High Furness are full of place-names of Viking origin; but along the coast and in the lower valleys there are many names which show that the Angles settled there:—Broughton (brook *tun*), Dalton (dale *tun*), Pennington (penny *tun*), Aldingham (the *ham* of the descendants of Alda), Leece (leas, pastures), all of which are mentioned in the Domesday Book. And while the people of these two races were settling down together, Low Furness belonged neither to Scotland nor England. Cumbria ended at the Duddon, if it can be said to have ended anywhere, but, though Low Furness was included in the Domesday Survey of 1086 (together with Millom at the extreme south of Cumberland), it was still regarded as a borderland, a buffer county, rather than a true part of England. Annexation by the English crown did not really begin until the next century. Then, in 1111, or a little earlier, Henry I granted a large tract along Morecambe Bay to Michael le Fleming, and in 1127 Stephen gave his patronage to the founding of Furness Abbey. Le Fleming came as the military overlord, ready to put down any opposition there might be. He set up his castle—a Norman motte and bailey on Mote Hill at Aldingham—began the building of the church which still stands in the village, and left the name of Fleming written into the history of Aldingham, Allithwaite, Coniston, Grasmere and elsewhere, and the name of Michael on the map of Furness in the Manor of Muchland, a corruption of 'Michael's land'. The monks came as the civilising influence, and organised and revitalised the economy—agriculture, fishing, mining—of the whole of Furness. Inevitably, with these strong Norman-French influences at work in the district, it began to look to the south rather than the north. Lancaster Castle established itself as the headquarters of the law, where Furness people now had the privilege of being hanged, while the cross-sands route became their main link with the rest of the world.

Geologically, much of Low Furness seems to belong to west or north Cumberland rather than to the southern Lakes. The iron-bearing limestone of Dalton and Askam anticipates the landscape of the Ennerdale mines; the sandstone of Furness Abbey, that of the Carlisle Plain. The eastern coast of Furness, however, belongs entirely to the bay, and if the barrage is built, it may be the only stretch of the shore left comparatively unchanged. From Bardsea to about Roosebeck this is still a limestone shore, as at Silverdale, but here it is less cliff-like, and the rock does not bare its teeth nearly so much. For all that, sea and rock come up sharply one against the other, for there is scarcely any half-and-half of saltmarsh along this coast until you get nearly to Rampside, while the sand, though still rather sticky under heel, looks more like sand and less like mud. The tide, when it comes in, rolls right up to banks of white shingle, overhung, in places, by woods. Near Bardsea you can sit in the shade of oaks and throw stones into the sea.

The Bardsea shore, however, is on the Barrow-Ulverston coast road, and Aldingham is just off it. I do not much like this road. I agree that it gives eye-swivelling views of the bay and makes it easy for people to get down to the sea. But it is one of those wide, sweeping motor-roads, with concrete curbs and grass verges like billiard tables, and makes me feel I am in a housing estate rather than the country. I know that not everyone agrees with this. Some people even choose to picnic in a lay-by, with the passing cars blowing petrol fumes over their sandwiches, though perhaps they do not notice the cars, just as moorland sheep reared beside an unfenced road seem not to. But there is one stretch, from a little south of Bardsea as far as Aldingham, where the coast road swings inland for about a couple of miles, leaving the shore quiet and unspoiled. You can reach it either down the very narrow road from Baycliff or by walking from Aldingham or Bardsea. And you won't have to walk very far. For this road shows how incurably gregarious town people have become. At Bardsea on a summer afternoon you will find hundreds of cars parked among the cobbles and gorse bushes. Buses tip off their loads; schoolboys ride up on bikes, girls on ponies. For about half a mile, the strip of turf between road and sea is as busy as an ant-hill. Then the road turns away from the shore, through a wood, and if you walk even a hundred yards along the shingle, you will find that the crowds have been left behind. The beach is so wide and silent that the sound of the waves seems like an intrusion. Not even the courting couples come here. Not even the bathers, feeling perhaps that there is something slightly improper in undressing where nobody can see them.

Bardsea Village stands away from both the shore and the road, and has a white-iced gateau of a church, and an inn, *The Braddyll Arms*, named after the family of Conishead Priory. A little way behind the village is a golf-course, one of the few in the area to lie on limestone, where, I should think, any exposed clints or rock-pavements must make agreeably exasperating bunkers. Above the golf-course the rock breaks out more aggressively in the round pate of Birkrigg Common, a bald version of Arnside Knott's Beatle-cut fringe, which is the highest point of the ridge dividing the coast from the little valley of Urswick. This is the Cotswolds of the Lakes, bare on the heights, but prosperously cultivated in the valley, with aluminium silos like huge money-boxes and a complexity of walls and little roads. There are six or seven villages here—Great and Little Urswick, Scales, Gleaston, Stainton, Dendron, Leece—which, if they were near London or Manchester, would be renting out rabbit-hutches at £1,000 a year. As it is, they are among the least self-conscious spots in Greater Lakeland—cottages of limestone, often rough-cast and lime-washed, or, towards Rampside, of red sandstone, pigging in quite unconcernedly among the new bungalows and garages.

'Uzzick'*, as it once used to be pronounced, was the site of the Bronze-Age capital of Furness, with an important settlement at the place now called Urswick Stone Walls. Even today an extra-ordinary number of roads converge on the village, the best, for the new-coming visitor, probably being the very narrow one from the coast, near Bardsea, past Sunbrick†, from whence you can see a large Bronze Age burial circle only about one hundred

* Urswick: The second part of the name is from Old English *wic*, 'village, dairyfarm'; the first is probably 'bison lake', the old name for the tarn

† An intriguingly modern-sounding corruption of Old Norse *svin-brekka*, 'slope where swine are kept'

yards from the road. You pass over a ridge that rears nothing but stones and sheep, turn left at the cross-roads and then dip down a sharp twisting hill to Urswick Tarn. The name is deceptive. This quarter of a mile long pool has little in common with the tarns of the fells, apart from being wet. It is like a small Norfolk Broad pumped into Lancashire. It is green as watercress, feathery with reeds and infested with swans and moorhens. After the grey bareness of the hills the whole village seems awash with leaf, and there are copper beeches in the gardens almost big enough to fill the tarn. The houses more than half-surround the tarn, in a horse-shoe, but mostly turn their backs to the water, rather as if they were waiting for sun to dry it up. The old church has a massive tower and a leper's squint, and some local woodcarver has equipped the choir stalls with a whole celestial orchestra, including a barrel organ and its monkey.

Ulverston, the modern capital of Furness—in medieval times Dalton held that honour—is a place of considerable distinction, though you can hardly tell this from the new trunk road which bull-dozes its way through the centre of the town. The best of Ulverston (Princes Street and the Market Cross end of King Street) belongs, as might be expected, to the eighteenth century, but it has little of the 'county' snootiness that you often find in a Georgian country town. I think this is due to the fact that towards the end of the eighteenth century, Ulverston realised that it could not go on being just a place of merchants and lawyers and doctors, a place where the gentry of the district came in to visit the theatre and attend balls. So it developed its canal and entered the new century as the port of industrial Furness. And this time of looking both ways, to the country and to the town, is beautifully captured for us by John Soulby, father and son, jobbing printers of Ulverston between about 1790 and 1830, collections of whose work can be seen at Barrow Public Library and also at the Museum of English Rural Life in the University of Reading*. Among their work you will find notices of sales of hay, wheat, clover, turnip-seed, farms, coppices, and dwelling-houses:

> Shop, Barn, Stable, Warehouse and other Outbuildings, Orchard and Garden, and *4* Inclosures of Land (in good

* See *John Soulby, Printer, Ulverston,* printed by the University of Reading as a catalogue to their exhibition of 1966

cultivation) containing together, by admeasurement, twelve Acre, Statute measure, or thereabouts, together with

1 PEW IN LOWICK CHAPEL

contains 7 sittings

And a parcel of peat Moss, about one customary Acre (of freehold tenure) upon Roam Moss in the Parish of Colton in the said County.

And side by side with these, you will see signs of the new Ulverston: the sale of the hull of the Sloop *Tom*, the sale of the wreck of the Schooner *Sally*, and advertisements for carters for the 'Gothwaite' (Gawthwaite) Quarries and for 'Twenty Men who have been accustomed to work in IRON MINES' for Lindal.

Later on Ulverston had its own blast-furnaces and foundry, and though the one has now been pulled down and the other was transferred to Millom, the town has not lost its practical, workaday look, which delights me, though it may discourage some people from exploring anything more than the obviously Georgian centre. This is a pity, for Theatre Street, opening off Princes Street, and a little warren of alleys off King Street, are full of twists and double-backs, while the houses round the Gill, now a parking-place, have the unsmiling, straight-backed rectitude of the villages of Galloway. Then there is the lighthouse-shaped memorial on the Hoad to the man* who wrote *The Mutiny on the Bounty*, though that is not what they remember him for. And at Swarthmoor, just outside the town, there is a fine Elizabethan manor-house, once the home of Margaret Fell whose second husband was George Fox, so that Swarthmoor Hall has become a place of Quaker pilgrimage, while the meeting house, not far away, has a simplicity and severity that is almost romantic to present-day eyes.

To me, however, the main attraction of Ulverston comes from the fact that it lies, like Kendal, at the junction of the limestone with the slate. On one side the town eases itself out into the suburbs and gardens towards the limestone of Birkrigg and Bardsea. On the other, the terraces slant dourly up the steep lower slopes of Kirkby Moors—the most westerly outcrop of the

* Sir John Barrow (1764-1848), born at Dragley Beck, became Secretary to the Admiralty and did much to encourage Arctic exploration

Silurian slates which make up, together with the limestone, the whole of southern Lakeland. It is, in fact, the last we shall see of these slates for a long time, since, apart from a small patch at Millom, they do not occur in Cumberland at all. As it happens, the triangle of country bounded by the Ulverston-Gawthwaite-Greenodd-Ulverston main roads (Newland Bottom, Broughton Beck and west of Penny Bridge) is very typical of this rock—full of scars, steeps, becks and gills, all on a smallish scale, continually secretive and continually surprising. There is a whole Minotaur maze of roads here, some of them unfenced and gated, which offer hours of unravelling to those who want to escape the queues of Windermere.

But the Kirkby Moors themselves are quite different. They are bare to the point of being indecent. They have no shape, except in the way a stretched-out pig has shape. They only just top the 1,000-foot contour, yet they raise themselves into such a cold air that the snow often lies thick on them when Black Combe, twice their height, is quite clear. They are of all the hills west of the Kent, quite the dullest to look at from a distance, yet, once you are among them, they have a powerful, almost hypnotic attraction. I like country like this—country that takes no notice of man, that is stripped of all prettiness and never condescends to order itself into a view. The views are what you see *from* it.

You can approach Kirkby Moor from the south by roads from Ulverston, Pennington and Marton*, all of which converge at the farm called Horrace. This was once the home, in retirement, of a forgotten poet, Edmund Casson, who endeared himself to me, twenty-five years ago, by telling a friend that he had heard there was a young man, just over the Duddon, who was writing rather well. At Horrace there are immense views backwards, across the bay and down the line of the peninsula to Piel Island and Walney. And then, beyond Horrace, you dip into the heart of the hills, where there are no views at all. All distances are blocked from sight by the shapeless heavings of moor, black and ochre, most of the year, but in August suddenly smouldering up to one of the greatest conflagrations of heather I have ever seen. It is also one of the best places for bilberries. The peat, sometimes cut and stacked, swells up about you like a half-solidified, oily sea. There

* Or Martin. Neither the maps nor the signposts can agree about the spelling

are sumps and squelchy patches, with lousewort and bog asphodel growing there; and if you drive slowly in a car, a brown grouse may cock its red eyebrow at you. And beside the small beck which drains this upland valley, there is a track which leads along the moor tops to the Burlington* slate quarries of Kirkby. (Its real name is Kirkby Ireleth, to distinguish it from all the other Kirkbies, but in practice the name of 'Ireleth' is kept for a village on the hill above Askam.) In the nineteenth century, Burlington Quarries roofed many of the factory towns of the North-west with slates known as 'Kirkby Roundheads', so that I grew up believing that Cromwell had recruited most of his army in this part of Furness.

When you move out of the dip of the moor on to the northern slopes, you look down on the Duddon Estuary and what, to me, is the greatest view of Greater Lakeland: Black Combe, Dunnerdale, the Scafell and Coniston ranges, the sands, Millom and the sea; Skiddaw slate, Borrowdale volcanics, Kirkby Moor flags, limestone; fell, valley, farmland, marsh, blast furnaces and the mines. I could write a whole chapter on this view. I could write a whole book on this estuary. I *have* written a book† on the town. So at present I'll say only two things. First, about the marshes.

On the Cumberland side of the estuary, near the Green, there has recently been an interesting attempt to bring back the greylag goose, which, 200 years ago, used to nest regularly in the Lakes. The birds have always come to the area during the winter, of course, and now it has been possible to bring eggs from Scotland and have them hatched under Cumbrian hens, in the hope that the fledgelings will stay and nest here. Some, at least, are already doing so, though it is not possible, as yet, to say if the experiment will be more than temporarily successful.

Secondly, about the town. It has pleased some people to sneer at Millom. When the Millom Council decided to subscribe to a tourist organisation, a Barrow paper printed a comic cartoon about it, forgetting that the area served by the council included the Scafells, the shore of Wastwater, Eskdale, Devokewater, Ravenglass and Silecroft—places which, as tourist attractions, compare

* William Cavendish (1809-91), Earl of Burlington and later the seventh Duke of Devonshire, was one of the two chief landowners in Low Furness—the other was the Duke of Buccleugh—and one of the pioneers of the Furness Railway

† *Provincial Pleasures* (Robert Hale, 1959)

favourably with Barrow Town Hall. But Millom, as I said earlier, has one distinction not shared by any other of the industrial towns of the area. It is built of true Lake-District slate. The Furness iron towns are built mostly of limestone: the west Cumberland towns, of sandstone. The iron-ore mines of Millom are sunk in the limestone, of course, but the town itself is built upon and out of the Coniston flags and grits which lie along the Cumberland side of the Duddon Estuary. Small, drab, out-of-date you may call it if you want to, but it is as much a part of the Lake District as Hawkshead or the islands of Windermere.

Mention of Millom brings us to the haematite iron-ore fields of Low Furness, of which the Hodbarrow Mines of Millom are an out-lier—in fact, many of the old miners believe that there must be untapped resources of ore beneath the sands of the Duddon itself, though borings have not confirmed their belief. I have written much about Hodbarrow, which, in its time, was one of the most famous mines in the world and now offers a romantic landscape of caved-in shafts, subsidences, abandoned railway lines, broken-down chimneys and pit-gear, with acres and acres of dune and willow marsh, wild orchids, sea holly, partridges, plovers and terns. A poet to whom I showed Hodbarrow said that, though much of it is below sea-level, it was for her the high-spot of the Lakes. That was in the summer of 1967. But in March 1968 the mines were finally closed, the pumps stopped working, and water from the sea and from underground has already begun to seep into the hollow, and by the time this book is published will have begun to form a new landscape which I cannot yet clearly imagine.

Hodbarrow, however, is protected from the holiday public by a hinterland of slagbanks, factories and the nineteenth-century working-class town. Whatever I may say about it, not many people will take the trouble to go there. The Furness iron field, on the other hand, is far more accessible, and you can hardly approach Barrow from any direction without touching the edges of it. Again, all the Furness mines have been closed down for at least a quarter of a century, and most of them for much longer. Nature has had more time to re-colonise the land, and Lindal, one of the three chief mining centres, has already learned how to act the part of the old-world rural, with its church and terraced cottages standing round a convincing copy of a village green.

Mining in Furness, moreover, has a longer history than mining at Millom. Many of the pits were working in the eighteenth century, supplying ore to the charcoal furnaces of Backbarrow and nearby valleys, though it was the opening of the Furness Railway in 1846 which really started the boom. To begin with the railway was as local as the Eskdale 'Ratty'. The first section ran merely from Dalton to Barrow, with links to Kirkby and Concle on the Walney Channel, but soon afterwards the small Roa Island was connected by causeway to 'the neighbouring island of Great Britain' so that the railway could reach a deep-water pier. In 1847 the line was extended to Broughton, and in 1854 to Ulverston, but it was not until 1857 that it was prolonged across the bay to meet the main Lancashire system at Carnforth. Before that time, almost the main purpose of the railway was to carry ore to the port of Barrow for export to South Wales and elsewhere, though there was also a passenger service, with connections by steamer, across the bay, bringing tourists from Fleetwood to spend the day at Furness Abbey. Even rolling-stock and locomotives had to be brought by sea—one of the latter, known to everyone as 'Copperknob', stood for many years just outside Barrow Station, like an antique clock in a glass case.

Before the boom, mining was centred on Dalton and Lindal, and it was the coming of Henry William Schneider, an iron merchant and industrialist of Swiss descent, which changed this as it changed so much of the face of Furness. It is said* that Schneider was on a visit to the Lake District in 1839 when he was shown a small iron mine near Askam. The following year he took out a lease of the mining rights at Park, near the shores of the Duddon Estuary, in the royalty of the Earl of Burlington. With three other partners, he founded the Furness Company and built a jetty at Barrow to ship the ore. For ten years they had next to no success at Askam, though they did fairly well from an older mine at Whitriggs near Lindal, Then in 1850, when hope had almost been given up, the company decided to prospect once more at a site which had already been tried and abandoned. And so, in October 1850, there was made the greatest discovery of haematite iron-ore then known to British mining history—a

* See J. D. Marshall, *Furness and the Industrial Revolution* (Barrow, 1958)

continuous mass, 200 yards by 300, of between 8 and 9 million tons of finest quality ore. A few years later even this was surpassed by the finds at Hodbarrow, but by that time the Furness annual output of ore was already greater than that of all West Cumberland, and Barrow was at the beginning of its long career in iron and steel.

The story of the rise, prosperity and decline of the Furness iron industry is full of over-life-size Victorian personalities, stiff, ruthless, yet, in their own way, benevolent and far-seeing. It is as if the statues had stepped down from their plinths in the Barrow streets and were striding about a still empty countryside, casting around them mining-shafts, quarries, blast furnaces, railway stations, workers' houses, schools, churches and even town halls.

For the moment, however, I will ignore the townscape which they designed and look, instead, at the marks they made on the countryside. You can inspect this, quite comfortably, by way of three easy excursions. The first is by the road that leads from the centre of Dalton, past 'The Black Dog', to Ireleth. You climb out of the town between high-ish limestone walls—looking back, there is a pleasing view of huddled roofs and chimneys, where the smoke blurs with the mist on a moistly-sunny autumn afternoon. Then suddenly, for 200 or 300 yards, the road twists among the old workings—the ground scratched and scuffled as if by gigantic claws; quarryings, blastings and scoops, flooded to the over-flow pipe with rain water; red screes of rubble tips; white walls of collapsed huts. And, everywhere, grass, weed, scrub and tree are growing a new skin over the old sores. In autumn the willows are as rusty as the cobbles of ore still lying about the ground, and in spring the may is nearly as white as the limestone.

It is all on a small scale, for most of the mines of Furness *are* on a small scale. From the second excursion, however, by train from Barrow to Askam, you can see mining almost of the scope of Hodbarrow. The train leaves Barrow Station as if the town were not there at all—only sidings and waste ground and allotments, with yellow wild parsnip growing in the cinders and yellowish elder by the side of the lines. For a while the seaward side is blocked off by an enormous slagbank, weathered and half-greened over, and scored by tracks like the sheep-trods along Wastwater Screes. Then the slag falls away, and you find yourself looking across the channel to the north end of Walney Island—so seemingly close, yet really one of the loneliest spots in Lancashire, approachable only by a trudge along miles of slithering sandhills. Almost immediately, you pass from the old industry to the new—a cellophane factory beside the dunes of Sandscale. The train runs through what is left of Sowerby Woods, bends sharply left and meets the loop-line from Dalton at a point where a quarter of a mile of ponds and flashes lie at the foot of the raw-white, dynamited crags of the Goldmire Quarry. A minute more and you are in an heroic landscape—a man-made lake, the size of Loughrigg Tarn, with quarried sides dropping sheer into the water, and a parson's collar of limestone with thorn trees twisting out of splinters of rock. In spring the broken stone and scruffy ore-red soil are littered with wood anemones, the bright-green onion-smelling leaves of ramson, primroses and the cowslips which are not to be found at all on the other side of the Duddon. The train now moves into Askam, a town which seems to have died of starvation when the mines gave out. Once it had an iron-works, and the old slagbank still juts out into the estuary like a jetty. The terraces straddle about, awkward-angled and disconnected, among greenhouses, hen-runs and scrapings of cindery sand. To anyone brought up in the new suburbs of the South, this old part of Askam must seem as ugly an example of industrial mal-housing as any in England. Yet, particularly on a late summer evening, when a low tide of light floods the eastern shore of the Duddon, there is a forlorn beauty about the little town, stranded on the frayed edge of an era. The children can step just ten or fifty yards down the crabbed, un-made-up back streets on to miles and miles of sand. Or the men can lounge on the old slag-bank, throwing out a line for flooks or mackerel. (An Askam fisherman, incidently, is one of the three who are allowed to hold the £70 a year license for salmon-drawing in the Duddon Estuary. This is the method in which a man in a boat rows in a circle or horseshoe across the flow of the tide, slowly letting out a net, seventy yards long and of four-inch mesh, the other end of which is held by a colleague on the bank. When the boat has returned to the shore, the net is hauled in, until, with the last few yards, a wrestling mass of fish is tipped out on the sand. The salmon, of which there may be only one or two of over a hundred pounds' weight, according to the luck of the tide, heave and contort themselves a foot or more into the air, trying to bounce back into the water. The flooks wriggle into suffocation in the sand. I have watched the fishermen at Borwick Rails, on the Millom side of the Duddon, and, as soon as they had finished hauling, the little girls of the near-by ironworks houses picked up the flooks, washed them in the tide, and put them in baskets to take home for tea. The permitted season is from February to mid-August; the time of drawing must be exactly seven hours after high tide, which, in this part of the estuary is the moment when the tide begins to turn; and no fishing is allowed on Sundays.)

We must make one more excursion, before we leave industrial Furness, to the Duddon shore near Roanhead. You reach this either through Sowerby Woods, from Barrow or, from Dalton, over St Helen's level crossing. The signs of mining are not obtrusive: an old quarry-tarn, red dribbles in the sand, and a short block of houses looking as if it had been snapped off the main stick like a piece of Blackpool rock. But, here, as at Hodbarrow, the mines run right out to the coast, though you are not so aware of the open sea. Instead, you look inwards to the finest of all sand-level views of the Duddon Estuary—the rounded Black Combe and all the spikes of the central mountains, from the Scafell trio, with Esk Pike, Bowfell and Crinkle Crags, round to the Coniston group.

Once you pass through the heaped embankment of sand-dunes, the mining scene seems to become oddly distant, and if you walk along the side of the little Sandscale promontory, towards the mouth of the Duddon, you reach a place where the estuary is so narrow that you will be about the same distance from Millom's Hodbarrow Point as I am at this moment, writing here in the town. This is presumably where they will build the dam across the Duddon, if they ever do build it, so reducing the road journey from Millom to Barrow from fifty minutes to about fifteen. Looking back, you will see that the Askam slagbank has dwindled and the limestone rock of Dunnerholme has come into view. (Incidently, Dunnerholme, though a bit difficult to get to, is the best picnic spot on the whole of the estuary.) The Lake District Naturalists Trust has taken a special care of Sandscale and arranged with the tenants to keep the area free from grazing in order to preserve the very interesting flowers of the haws or turfed-over inner dunes. The outer shore dunes, too, are full of the flowers that are so familiar all along the coast but are mostly quite unknown even a quarter of a mile away from it: sea-holly, bloody cranesbill, burnet rose, the milky sea-spurge, and, from early spring to the very end of autumn, the tiny, companionable, pansy-like heart's-ease. Once I found its much rarer relative, the yellow dune pansy. All these flowers can be found on other coasts, however. What gives to Roanhead its peculiar personality is the fact that here they are growing close to an area devastated by industry, cracked open like a nut and robbed of its kernel. In the morning, with the sun from behind the dunes falling full on the fells, it can be a most exhilarating scene; but in the evening, when the estuary is awash with dazzle and every hillock in the dunes or hollow in the mines is exaggerated with shadow, it becomes as poignant as an old battlefield.

As the mines were exhausted and the blast furnaces were closed down at Askam and Ulverston, Furness industry concentrated more and more on Barrow. Yet before the Industrial Revolution Barrow did not exist. Its one antiquity, the magnificent Furness Abbey, really belongs, historically, to Dalton, though it is now almost enclosed in Barrow suburbs. So much has been written about these ruins, the finest ecclesiastical ruins west of the Pennines, that I will add no more now. Except to say that Wordsworth wrote twice about them: the first time, memorably, in *The Prelude**; and the second, in 1845, in an indignant sonnet written when he came across the navvies of the Furness Railway taking their 'noon-tide rest' among the ruins!

Apart from the Abbey, Barrow, as a town, is almost without history. It has no church, no hall, scarcely a house older than the nineteenth century. Its streets do not follow the lines of any earlier village, as in so many towns, where the traffic of today is held up at the corners of the Middle Ages. Its name, in fact, was originally given to what is now known as Barrow Island, the second syllable being derived from the Scandinavian *ey*, an

* *The Prelude*, Book II, lines 102-31

'island', as in Barra in the Hebrides or Hinnøy in the Lofotens. At the beginning of the eighteenth century Barrow was still an insignificant hamlet; and even as late as 1845 it was no more than a village of thirty houses. The next year, however, the Furness Railway was opened and Barrow started to develop as a port; in 1857, H. W. Schneider and his partner Robert Hannay began to manufacture iron at Hindpool; and in 1870, the Barrow Inn Shipbuilding Company was founded, and a yard set up on Barrow Island in the Walney Channel.

For about ten years Barrow was the boom town of England, and the men behind the boom—Schneider, Hannay, the Duke of Devonshire, Sir James Ramsden—dreamed of a great new centre of world trade, and set to work to plan a town worthy of that dream. And because there was nothing there to begin with they were able to start from scratch. Of course, the mid-nineteenth century was not a great period for town architecture, though, to judge from photographs, the old Flax and Jute Works and other public buildings of the Ramsden era had a dour no-nonsense dignity which the structures that have replaced them most certainly lack. The planners had their own kind of vision—solid, square, down-to-earth and down-to-pocket as it was. So they built the town on the pattern of a grid. It was not, heaven knows, a very imaginative pattern, but it meant that what were to be the main streets stood wide and straight and right-angled one to another. There is nearly everywhere in the business part of Barrow this sense of openness, squareness, of having nothing to hide, nothing up the sleeve. There are no alleys, no courts, no archways, under-ways or tunnels—nothing with the least look of furtiveness or secrecy, scarcely even of privacy. Barrow must have been the least Dickensian city of Victorian England.

But for all the bluff openness and confidence of their streets, the men who planned Barrow must have had, from the middle 'seventies onward, a secret fear that their dream would not come true. In 1872 the citizens of Barrow erected a statue to the honour of James Ramsden without waiting for him to die. Thousands of people watched the unveiling and cheered Ramsden in the square named after him, while the Bishop of Carlisle, sanctifying the occasion, spoke of Barrow as:

> this wonderful town (which) strikes me as being one of the miracles of our time, and I look upon it with the same sort of ignorant wonder with which some people regard the pyramids—how on earth it has been built, is being extended, and what is to become of it if it continues to go on as it is doing at present*.

But it did not continue to go on. Ship-building and steel prospered, and the town went on growing, but it failed to become the great port and manufacturing centre which Ramsden's statue, if not Ramsden himself, was expected to see. Since 1920, in spite of attempts at diversification, Barrow has become far too dependent on its two main industries, and today even steel is in retreat. An order for a tanker or a submarine can bring work to thousands for eighteen months or two years, but after that time anxiety returns until the next order comes along. Barrow, it has been said, is out on a limb, on a 'far ness', and is no longer an economic proposition for the country. It should be written off as a non-going concern, said a notorious article in a financial paper, and allowed to decline and decay. Yet, if Barrow could prosper in the days of the steam engine, it seems absurd to argue that it is too remote in the days of the motorway and the aeroplane. A barrage across Morecambe Bay, or even a good link road to the M6, would solve most of Barrow's problems of communication. It has a beautifully sheltered harbour, which could be made to accommodate very large ships. It has labour to spare and plenty of space for new factories and new houses.

Above all, it has a wonderfully pleasant situation. The long Abbey Road—three miles of sweeping tarmac, with trees lining the route like policemen—is surely about the finest approach to any industrial town of the north. The main streets may look rather stiffly pompous, yet in Duke Street and Abbey Road and the residential streets which run off the latter there is always the feeling that, just round the corner or just over the brow of the hill, there will be open sea and open sky. In fact, at high tide the sea is round three sides of Barrow, and at all tides the winds blow in clean air from any direction. And even in the narrowest streets you can often look up to the giant cranes of the shipyard, riding in a rooks'-nest world among the mists and the sunsets.

* Quoted from J. D. Marshall, *Furness and the Industrial Revolution* (Barrow, 1958)

Duddon Estuary with Black Combe

(overleaf) *Sand-dunes, Eskmeals*
Lighthouse, St Bees

SOLWAY HOTEL
SOLWAY HOTEL

J. ROUTLEDGE

Like Kendal and Whitehaven, Barrow is one of the towns which hold the key to the future of Greater Lakeland. It is not written into the history of the district, as they are, but, like them, it brings work and money to a large part of the Lake population. The central fells and dales are coming to depend, very largely, on the tourist; but Low Furness, the northern shore of Morecambe Bay and the villages between the Duddon and the Crake depend to a considerable extent to Barrow. If Barrow declines, yet another part of the Lake District will have to live on taking in other people's washing.

The same Norse element *ey* (or Old English *eg*) which is found in the second syllable of Barrow is also to be seen in the names of nearly all the islands of the Walney Channel: Walney* itself; Ramsey (now built into Ramsden Dock, though the resemblance between the names is mere coincidence); Roa and Foulney (bird island), both joined to the main shore by a causeway; and Fouldrey, the old name for Piel. These 'Channel Islands' of Lancashire are the product of the Ice Age, when the coastal glaciers blocked up the waters of the Duddon Estuary, forming a lake. As the ice slowly melted from the south, the waters found various escape routes from time to time, one such being now annexed, part of the way, by the railway line from Dalton to Barrow, through the Vale of Nightshade, past Furness Abbey and on to Roose. The present Walney Channel probably marks the last of these escape routes carved out by the Duddon waters before the river finally broke through to the open sea between Sandscale and Hodbarrow Point.

What we can see of Walney and the other islands consists, in fact, almost entirely of boulder clay, sand and the like, deposited by the glaciers, and of alluvium, deposited still more recently by the tides. Walney itself has the look of one enormous heap of gravel. Scratch the soil anywhere and the stones show through—in the shingle-banks along the shore, in the pebbles in the ruts of cart-tracks, and in the old field-walls made of layers of huge cobbles separated by thin spreads of roofing-slates and mortar. The island is of about the same length as Windermere and has something of the same general shape. Turn it upside down, south

* Possibly from Old Norse *vogn*, a grampus. See E. Ekwall, *Place Names of Lancashire*

Criffel Street, Silloth
Market Place, Whitehaven

to north, and it would fit into the lake-basin like a badly made piece of jigsaw. It is never much more than a mile broad and barely a quarter of a mile at its narrowest. One day it may be even less, for the tides of the channel are gradually eating into the western shore at several points, and dropping the silt two or three miles away at the southern end. Unless the borough council does better than Canute, Walney may become two islands or three, as, indeed, it probably was when the coastline was lower than it is today.

The island is not quite as straight as it appears to be, since at either end a long spit of sand or shingle bends back away from the sea. The vast dunes of the North End almost meet those of Lowsy Point, in the Duddon Estuary—from the Millom side it is not easy to spot the opening of the channel; and at the South End, the gravel banks stretch out towards Piel and Roa. From the top of Black Combe, the curve of the two ends is so distorted by the angle of vision that the whole island looks like an arrowhead attached to the shaft of Furness. Nevertheless, it is the straightness and narrowness that gives the island much of its character. On the seaward side you have eight miles or so without cove or creek, though the little bends north of the West Shore are more like bays than you would expect from their apparent shallowness on a map. Next to Silecroft, this is the finest beach in Greater Lakeland and the one where you are most conscious of looking out to sea. Today the central sector of this stretch has become the summer playground for the people of Barrow, and there has been some attempt to develop it into a pleasure beach, with a putting-green, a kiosk or two and a paddling pool, which, however, seems often to be bone-dry owing to difficulties with water supply! A couple of miles further north, at Earnsey Point, there is a large caravan site, but this is all, and the other five miles are completely unspoiled and, for most of the year, as empty as the South Arabian Desert.

Human settlement on Walney has so far been concentrated on the landward side. The two pre-industrial villages of North Scale and Biggar both stand on the shores of the channel, and when Walney grew into a Barrow suburb, towards the end of the last century, the new houses sprang up on the line between the two villages. There were great hopes for this new development, named Vickerstown after the shipbuilding firm which owned most of the land. True to the spirit of the age, the new suburb did not hide its face from industry but proudly looked back to the shipyard and the steelworks. A handsome promenade was laid out along the channel shore, and the people began to talk of a new 'marine garden city'. Even today the site must be one of the most pleasant of any northern industrial suburb, with self-respecting, bay-windowed, late nineteenth-century or Edwardian terraces, many of them exotically named after ships launched at Barrow.

Walney was reached from the mainland first by a ferry, and then, after 1908, by the present bridge—a toll bridge to begin with, but freed in 1935*. This may seem to have de-insulated Walney which is perhaps the reason why few people remember to count it among the islands of England. Yet a great deal of the old island character still remains. During the early 'fifties I made many visits to the old vicarage, now standing empty and boarded-up on a bank above the promenade. It was a haphazard warren of a building, with tiled or slate-paved tunnels communicating between rooms so distant one from another that it was only after you had been in the house for several days that you were sure how many people lived there. My room was a kind of attic, called 'The Tent' because the roof sloped in all directions and was supported by one upright central pole. To make me sleep better, my hosts told me that the upstairs rooms were haunted. When I did manage to stay awake, however, I could look right across to England—to the slagbanks of the steel-works and the roofs and chimneys of Barrow Island and the town hall clock on the mainland beyond. At high tide, the channel was a shoal of small boats, knocking one against another or wriggling their way under the bridge and down to Roa or Piel. At low tide there was only a pool, a few feet wide, in acres of black mud broken by barnacled jetties and water-pipes. Yet that twice-daily incursion of the tide was enough to leave me in no doubt that I was on an island. Jim Eckersley, the vicar, used to describe himself as missioner of the Church overseas, not forgetting that, apart from Furness Abbey, his church† was the oldest religious foundation in Barrow. But Christianity has always flourished on islands.

North Scale, about three-quarters of a mile north of the bridge,

* See F. Barnes, *Barrow and District* (Barrow-in-Furness, 1951)

† Not, of course, the present building which belongs entirely to this century

still holds on to the look of an old village, though it is now swamped all round by new housing estates. As a settlement it has a longer history than Barrow, and, in the thirteenth century, was one of the 'granges' cultivated by lay-brothers for the Abbot of Furness. North of the village, much of the land is taken up by the wartime airfield, still used to bring royalty and brass-hats to naval launchings. Beyond this are the North End Haws, or sand-dunes, which were the site of one of the largest neolithic flint 'factories' in the district, where many arrowheads and scrapers have been found. Miles of slithering sand discourage even the hardiest walkers and make this perhaps the least accessible spot in all Lancashire.

Biggar Village, a mile and a half to the south of the bridge, has been far more fortunate than North Scale. A few houses have been modernised, but the tide of building has not so far flowed in this direction. It is one of those hamlets built on a little mound with all the houses looking inwards, one towards another, presumably for shelter, though I have heard it somewhat romantically described as a wrecker's haunt, where all the lights were obscured to misguide mariners. Today, the two inns are becoming well known to eaters-out.

South of Biggar the island gets meaner and more moth-ridden. Cattle work hard for their grass in the cobble-cluttered fields. Off shore, the miserable Sheep Island humps up from the sea—I'm told there was once a smallpox hospital on it where, surely, no one could have the heart to want to recover. There is not a tree to be seen, and I've often wondered where Jim Eckersley's bees got the honey to give them the strength to sting the vicarage dog and, sometimes, the vicarage children. The road runs, at low tide, beside treacly marshes where mud-weeds drip and slaver with brown ooze. At high tide it runs actually under the water, though you are now allowed to use the farmer's private track, so that you need not find yourself marooned on the South End until the tide goes down.

Beyond the point where the road returns to dry land you cannot pass without a permit issued by the Warden of the South End Walney Nature Reserve*. For you are now approaching the north-western equivalent of Northumberland's Farne Islands.

* The address may be obtained from Barrow Town Hall

Here too, or at the nearby reserve of Foulney Island, you will find eider ducks, the St Cuthbert's chickens of the Farnes, and here is the only place in England where all five species of tern are known to breed. There is also a breeding site of lesser black-backed and other gulls, almost as interesting as that, twenty-five miles further north, at Drigg.

I have visited South End a number of times but never, as it happens, in the nesting season. Once, accompanying the vicar on his parish rounds, I called at the lighthouse, where the lighthouse-keeper's two daughters, slung out on trestles, were white-washing the walls of the tower. These remarkable young women not only did much of the work of the lighthouse and looked after the bird-sanctuary (as it then was), but also found time to become prize-winning ballroom dancers. One of them stopped her work to show me a nest of young swallows, hatched too late to be strong enough to fly to Africa after their parents. If I understood her rightly, she had plans to pack them in a cardboard box and give them a free lift by aeroplane.

The last time I went to the south of Walney was at the very end of October, when all distances were smudged out in a mellow, yellowish mist. I went first to the gravel pits, disturbing many ducks that I could not hope to identify. The old pits are filled with water, making long, steep-sided tarns; the new ones are still a raw dribble of red screes, with metallic scoops and diggers prodding the sand like gigantic waders. Once the gravel workers lived on the job, and you can still see a row of single-storey cottages, in the style of a Scottish crofter's clay biggin, which unfortunately, have been allowed to crumble into decay.

I left the pits and walked out to the west shore, amusing myself by trying to see how many species of flowers I could find still in bloom at this tag-end of the year. In fact, I found nearly forty, including viper's bugloss, which before then I had seen only at Bamburgh—yet another link between Walney and Northumberland. Out on the sands a huge congregation of oyster-catchers and cormorants shifted about to face the slight offshore wind. I came back, past the lagoon made by the shingle-beds that curl like a pig's tail from the rump of the island. At last I reached the old jetties set up for the boats that once carried Walney sand to the concrete-mixers of Liverpool. No horizon could be seen in any direction. Out at sea, and across what I knew to be Morecambe Bay, the water merged into the mist without join or borderline. Even Barrow Shipyard, only five miles away, was quite invisible. I was as far from England, it seemed, as if I had been in the Outer Hebrides. Yet, in spite of the isolation and the mist, I was still able to enjoy one of the finest views that Lancashire has to offer: Piel Castle from the south.

Piel is less than half a mile from Walney at this point, but to get there, unless you swim, you have to return to Vickerstown, cross the bridge, pass through Barrow and Roose out to Rampside, take the road along the causeway to Roa Island and wait for the ferry—a journey of about fifteen miles. And even then, unless it is a Saturday or Sunday, there is likely to be no ferry.

I first approached Piel from Vickerstown, sailing in a motor-launch up the channel from Walney Bridge. (We sailed too soon, got stuck on a mud-bank, and had to wait for the tide to rise another foot before we could float free.) Other times I have gone by the ferry from Roa. But last summer, arriving midweek in August, I found, to my disappointment, that the ferry was not running and that I must reconcile myself to spending the afternoon at Roa. It is, of course, quite an intriguing spot. Most people would now call it 'Roe', but some of the older ones still pronounce the name to rhyme with 'boa' and I think this must be correct. It ceased to be an island over one hundred years ago, when John Abel Smith built a causeway to carry a railway line. (Another causeway, unpaved and twice as long, branches off to Foulney Island, further out in the Bay, now an important bird sanctuary watched over by the knowledgeable naturalist who writes in *The Barrow Mail* under the name of 'Rowan'.) For a time it seemed that Roa might become a port of some importance. By 1848 daily steamer trips were being made in summer to Fleetwood, and twenty years later there were also passenger services to the Isle of Man and Ireland, but, after the opening of Ramsden Dock in 1882, the point of departure was moved to Walney Channel*. Roa Pier was then pulled down, the railway line was taken up more recently, and the causeway has now become a bus route, yet the island still has its lifeboat station and is extremely popular with yachtsmen and sailors. They nearly had to launch the life-

* See F. Barnes, *op. cit*

boat while I was there, for a fisherman, rowing out to his boat, was overturned by the tide, which runs at up to five knots at this point, and was carried swiftly up the channel. A couple of men standing by seized a dinghy, bounced it down the stone jetty and picked up the swimmer several hundred yards beyond the island. He waded ashore, weighted down by his sogging-wet fisherman's clothes. Had he been wearing rubber waders they would almost certainly have pulled him down to the bottom.

I was feeling sorry for the man, though I appreciated the diversion as a consolation for missing Piel, when I noticed that a brewer's lorry had drawn up and was unloading crates of beer. I made enquiries and found that this was intended for the inn on Piel, and saw that already a boat was putting out from the island to collect the supplies. I waited a few minutes and then asked the landlord of the inn—a genial, bearded buccaneer with the splendid old Lakeland name of Nicholson—to take me back with him.

Even apart from the castle, Piel is a fascinating place. It is so small—smaller, in fact, than Belle Isle in Windermere—that you can walk briskly round it in a quarter of an hour. Yet it is by no means featureless. The cliffs on which the castle stands rise twenty to thirty feet above the shingle, and, at its highest point, the island rears up to forty feet, which looks quite a mountain above the flat sands when the tide is out. The channel between Piel and Roa is fairly deep, and can be rough enough to cut off the island for days at a time. Yet its shores are gentle, the pebbles knitted together by many of the flowers of the shingle—sea-kale, sea-campion and the yellow, horned sea-poppy. Inland, if you can use such a term, there are thickets of gorse and ragwort, and even a bordering of reeds and marsh plants round the little tarn or pond in the centre of the island. It is hard to believe that there can be so many changes and variations of soil and habitat in so small an area.

Yet with all this to look at, you still find your gaze turning continually to the castle ruins. It is not often that I grow enthusiastic about castles, in ruin or not, but Piel is an exception. For one thing, it was never the centre of feudal oppression or military power. It was not the home of a usurping Norman family, nor, indeed, of any family at all. It was built in the mid-fourteenth century by the monks of Furness Abbey to protect the abbot's legal trade in wool and his probably more profitable illegal trade in smuggling. Some people have presumed that it must have been intended as a protection for the abbey against Scottish raiders but it seems hard to see how this could have been so. The huge size of the outer courtyard, however, suggests that, at the time of the raids, it may have been a place where the people of Piel and Walney took refuge with their cattle and other stock until the raiders had moved out of the district.

This outer courtyard, set in the extreme south-east corner of the island, has the shape of a quadrilateral—a square with one side cut short by the angle of the shore. It was once surrounded by a wall, with towers at the four corners and a moat on the two sides away from the shore. The south-east tower and most of the walls on the south and east have been swallowed up by the sea, while the walls on the west and north were left unfinished or, possibly, were filled in with a wooden palisade. Inside the south-east quarter of this outer courtyard is an inner court, again with moat and wall and corner towers, but, this time, with a draw-bridge over the moat leading to a gateway with tower above.

The keep stands in the inner court—a massive three-storey building, divided on each storey into three compartments. It is this internal plan, quite unlike that of the ordinary baronial type of Norman castle, which leads Mr J. Melville (the Barrow antiquary to whom I am indebted for much information about Piel) to believe that this was really a warehouse, a fortified storehouse, occupied only by a small garrison of soldiers, with no resident lord.

Unlike the castles of the Border, Piel's history is largely peaceful, with no known sieges or skirmishes or murders, which may be the reason why it has failed to catch the fancy of the public. In the summer of 1487, however, the rebel forces supporting Lambert Simnel landed on Piel, from Ireland, and the 15-year-old near-simpleton held court on the island, which, for a day or so, must have had a temporary population of about 8,000 men. It is for historians to choose whether to regard this landing, or Paul Jones's raid on Whitehaven Harbour, as the last foreign invasion of England. In either case, that invasion took place in Greater Lakeland.

After the Dissolution of the Monasteries, Piel Castle fell into disrepair, though there was some talk of restoring it during the invasion scares of the reign of Queen Elizabeth. Nothing much was done, however, until 1920, when the Duke of Buccleugh presented the castle to the mayor and corporation of Barrow, who were also able to buy the eight cottages on the north side of the island. A great opportunity was then given to Barrow to make this into an island park, magnificent in its setting and of much historical interest, which would surely have been unique among the industrial towns of England. Today, nearly fifty years later, very little progress has been made. The attractive, old-fashioned inn takes paying guests, but is known, chiefly, for an absurd ceremony, much drenched in beer, by which visitors are dubbed 'Knights of Piel'. One or two of the cottages are in a bad state of repair, and the rest could do with redecoration. The ferry is seasonal and unreliable, and there is no full-time warden responsible for the ruins. The landlord of the inn is enormously appreciative of his island home but cannot be expected to patrol every corner of it. As a result, some fat-heads, not finding a telephone kiosk to smash up, have consoled themselves by knocking lumps out of the ruins. In other parts walls have collapsed under the pummelling of wind and weather or have toppled over the crumbling clay cliffs and fallen into the sea. Fifteen years ago it was possible to climb the walls by the stone staircase and look across Morecambe Bay to Bowland Forest and the cooling towers of Fleetwood. Today there are notices warning you that the ruins are unsafe. Why on earth the whole structure could not have been put into the care of the Ministry of Works, I cannot think. I am sure I have paid half a crown to look round far less interesting ruins in other parts of the country.

CHAPTER EIGHT

THE LAKE COAST

WHEN we cross the Duddon estuary we come to the heart of my Greater Lakeland. I have promised the reader that I will not keep on talking about Millom, but in this autumn of 1968 something has to be said. For in the last few months, with the closing of the mines and the ironworks, Millom has been in the news as never before. One hundred years of continuous production of iron has come suddenly to a stop. Reporters, television cameramen and others flocked to the town like sightseers at an accident, and the picture they gave to the public was one of a dying town on the edge of nowhere, full of disconsolate people trudging along streets of decaying terraced houses. The conscience of the nation was roused but the question that was asked was: 'Can we, in our present-day society, afford any longer to keep up places like Millom?'

Now this is the wrong attitude altogether. The question should be: 'Can we, in our present-day society, afford to lose places like Millom?' In fact we can't, for, after all, Millom is still a very good place to live in. The old part of the town has, no doubt, all the usual faults of nineteenth-century housing, but the present population is moving away from these older houses into new estates on the other side of the railway. Many men who worked at the ironworks and Hodbarrow live, not in dark streets in the shadow of the slagbank, but in new council houses that open straight on to meadows sweeping up to the hills. From their bedroom windows they have views of nearly all the higher peaks of the Lakes, and only a mile away, to the west, are the magnificent sand-dunes of Haverigg and mile after mile of one of the least-spoiled coasts in all England. This is surely the kind of environment that more people are going to demand, in the future, not just for holidays, but for the everyday background to their working life. It is not surprising that the Millom men who now find themselves out of work are reluctant to leave the town.

In any case, the idea that a small town like Millom is of neccessity an economic loss to the nation as a whole is utter nonsense. For if you let Millom die, its 8,000 or 10,000 inhabitants will not die also. Either they have to be supported, unproductively, on the dole, or they must be made to move to other parts of the country, so adding to the present problems of congestion, overcrowding, shortage of houses, shortage of schools and even shortage of water. In Millom there is no shortage of houses; there is a large new comprehesive school that takes all the pupils over the age of 11 and there will soon be two new junior schools for the younger children; there are almost unlimited supplies of water. When South Lancashire is crying out for more water and threatening to dam the valleys of the Lake District in order to get it, it seems preposterous to exterminate a town which has water to spare.

But what matters even more is that Millom—and many more such small towns—is a living and organic community. From the days when the Cornish miners came to Hodbarrow, at the time of the decay of the Cornish tin-mines, Millom has been a closely-knit unit, where everybody feels that he has a share in the health and welfare of the whole. I am not trying to idealise life in a small town. It does not suit everyone. But, at least, it is on a scale that makes it still seem human. Its society is made up, not of impersonal classes and groups and groupings, but of people—liked or disliked, supported or opposed, but still people who are known one to another. In the face of the enormous depersonalisation of the mass city, this human-scaled community is worth keeping. We cannot stop the development of the city society; most people in this country may belong to it before long. But, for heaven's sake, let us hold on to the Milloms of England if only to remind us that the human community takes its perspective from the size of a man not from that of a sky-scraper.

Many visitors to the Lake District are disappointed with the Cumberland coast. It depends, I suppose, on what they expect. They may be looking for cliffs and headlands, but there are no rocky cliffs south of St Bees or Nethertown. Or they may be looking for sea-lochs and estuaries where the tide nudges high among the fells, but the coast from Haverigg to St Bees is a gently bending curve with only the one large inlet at Ravenglass. Most of all, I think, people are disappointed because they find that the mountains do not come down to the sea, but are divided from it by a two-mile-wide strip of rather ordinary-looking farmland.

There are reasons for all this. To begin with, the rock beneath the shore is not one of the slates of the fells, but the red sandstone of the Carlisle Plain, though it shows itself so rarely in the south of the county that it is very hard to credit this. Secondly, the whole shore-line has been shaped and shaved by the glaciers which moved across the Solway during the Ice Age. Before that, the fells must have sloped gently and evenly from summit to sea-level, but after the ice withdrew the western flanks were sliced away almost perpendicularly. Look at Black Combe from Walney Island and you will see that it takes the shape of a bowler hat, with a rounded, flattish crown, and, on the seaward side, a steep drop to the brim.

Yet the ice did not leave the coast planed flat like an ironing board. It dropped huge dollops of sand, clay and gravel, heaped up into ridges that, in places, reach a hundred feet in height. Behind these the natural drainage was blocked and silted up, so that at least five South Cumberland streams—the Ehen, the Irt, the Esk, Annaside Beck and Whicham Beck—shy sideways when they are within smell of the sea, and dawdle about until they find a place to break through the clay ridge.

As a result of this, there is often a swampy dip between the shore and the lower slopes of the hills. To modern road-engineers this would not matter, but in the early days, when most travellers would drive their carriages up Scafell rather than face mud, the roads swung inland, to go bumping over the drier foothills of Black Combe. If, today, South Cumberland remains one of the least exploited stretches of the English coast, this is largely because, thanks to the Ice Age, there is no road running beside the sea.

Haverigg Haws is the Cumberland equivalent of Lancashire's Sandscale or Roanhead, but at Haverigg you are less aware of the sea than of Black Combe. The Combe is, in fact, the wart of the north-west coast, a protuberance that catches the eye from Scotland as far south as Wales. From the south, in particular, it looks as if it were erupting right out into the sea, and, indeed, at high tide it is surrounded by salt water on three sides. And since, on its fourth side, there is only the low, slovenly moorland around Devoke Water, Black Combe looks isolated, left out on its own, an island of a hill joined to the Lake archipelago by the causeway of Birker Moor. It has its own weather, too. When you can see Black Combe, we say in Millom, it's going to rain; when you can't see it, it *is* raining.

'Grim neighbour, huge Black Combe', Wordsworth wrote from Bootle in 1811, to Sir George Beaumont, '. . . In his own storms he hides himself from sight.' Or as the Lancastrian poet of *Sir Gawayne and the Grene Knight* put it 600 years ago:

> The heven was up halt bot ugly ther-under;
> Mist muged on the mor malt on the mountes,
> Ech hille had a hatte a mist-hakel huge*.

In Millom you just can't get away from Black Combe. There are some streets where the view is blocked out at one end by a slag-bank and at the other by the Combe, and on a misty November day there's not much difference between the two. So that to me, as a child, Black Combe was *the* mountain—the others were just names. Then, in my early 'teens, I became worried by the ridiculous notion, still held by some people, that a mountain, to earn the name, has to be 2,000 feet high. And Black Combe was only 1,969. I even thought of going up every month or so and tossing a few more stones on the cairn until it had gained the extra thirty-one feet. Later years have shown me that this is quite unnecessary, for if any hill in the Lakes deserves to be called a mountain, it is Black Combe, and as far as I am concerned, 1,969 feet is as near as dammit.

The Combe is one of the Skiddaw Slate fells and the barest of the lot. Scarcely a tree grows on it anywhere above the 200-foot level. It is not only bare but round as an egg, with, it would seem, hardly a fold or a corrie to break the monotonous smoothness. That, at least, is how it looks from a distance. When you get closer, it begins to reveal its more private character. If you approach from Thwaites or the Duddon Bridge end of Whicham

* The sky was lifted up, but ugly beneath; mist drizzled on the moor, melted on the mountains; each hill had a hat, a huge cloak of cloud

Valley, you will first of all see the flanks of the Combe on your right, public as a shop-window. On the left is the broad, flat bottom of the rift-valley, and across the valley, the ridge of Lowscales*, the most southerly splinter of the Borrowdale volcanics. If you cross the valley (by the little road that passes the amusingly-named Po House† and comes back on the main road near Whicham Church) you will get a close look at the miniature crags and screes, the gorse and heather stair-carpets of this lovely rock; and you will also see that the bluff Black Combe has its own homeliness, its crooks and nooks.

Black Combe is as good a place as any to study all the effects of the Ice-Age glaciers that came down the Cumberland coast from Scotland. Along the westward side of the Combe you can see how the ice has sliced off the lower flanks of the fells, leaving the becks to tumble down the new cliffs and carve out the several gills and chasms which are to be found on either side of Whitbeck village. That carving did not begin until the Ice Age was over, of course. While the ice was still there it held the whole area in a kind of geological paralysis, blocking the lower end of Whicham Valley as it blocked the Duddon Estuary, and turning it into a glacial lake, the waters of which, at one time, found a temporary escape route on the southern side of the hills, and shovelled out the largish watercourse which has now been taken over by the quite insignificant Langthwaite Beck.

Whicham Valley has its own gills—Rallies Gill, Hall Beck Gill and Hall Gill Beck—all of them places where you can step right off the road into a funnel of rock and bracken and falling water. But the most easily accessible of the gills, as well as one of the most impressive, is that called Miller Gill on the coastal side of the Combe.

You turn off the road by Whitbeck Church (where, as my grandmother told me, they bury only the deaf and dumb) and take the rough road behind the farms until you reach the old Whitbeck Mill, where you can get out on to the fell. The best time of the day is early evening, when the sun skims almost horizontally across the sea right into the cupboard of the gill; and the best time of the year is perhaps late summer. August is not

* Pronounced Loskles—the low shieling

† I am told that collectors keep stealing the signpost!

usually regarded as an ideal month in the Lakes because of the drabness of the greens, but there is one week when the ling is in full bloom and the second flowering of the gorse has just started, and down by the beck the rowans are already top-heavy with berry. In the evening sunlight, the purple and lemony yellow and deep orange-red give a Celtic richness of decoration. The fellside leaps up, dizzying in height, though, from here, you can see nothing above the 1,000-foot contour. The waterfalls—so little known that they haven't even got names—face you squarely, one above the other, like receding flights of steps. The water splashes and gurgles in the mosses; kestrels climb and wheel; the light pings off the crags. It is a scene which defiantly refuses to be turned into a beauty spot—as bold, as bare and as exhilaratingly open as any in Cumberland.

Yet it is when you look outwards that the view becomes the most Cumbrian of all, for you look across the down-like swellings of the shore to the sea and across the sea into the past of Cumberland. To the north, disjointed like islands in the distance, are Cairnsmore of Fleet and the prominences of Galloway, and straight across is Man, the Celtic boss of the Irish Sea, Cumberland's Hebridean island. That is where the Celticised Vikings came from—the men who made Cumberland and left their language shouting all around from beck, gill, force, scree and fell. You can hardly find, in the whole of the Lakes, any spot that combines more of the essentials of the county. Yet, 200 yards below, the motorists can be seen speeding along the new level, blithely unaware that there is anything in this stretch of the road worth stopping to look at.

Haverigg is not everybody's idea of a seaside town. It is a small industrial housing estate, set up in the nineteenth century for the iron-ore miners of Hodbarrow. There is still rather an unfinished look about it. Many of the side streets, built of slate or concrete (one has the forbidding name of Concrete Square), seem to have been dumped down on the fields and left there, with the weeds creeping up to the front doors and the sand blowing in at the windows. Again, the village is not on the open sea, but looks across the Duddon Estuary. If the tide is out there are five miles of empty sands, with the old Hodbarrow mines behind the sea-wall on the left and the steelworks of Barrow on the far side. The visitor tilts a supercilious nose and turns away.

Of course, he is quite wrong. For if he will walk just a couple of hundred yards along the beach, past the tennis court and the new caravan site, he will find himself in one of the least cluttered landscapes in all Cumberland. Between him and the sea is a Pennine Chain of sand, with slides and screes and hollows big enough to hide a church. While inland are the Haverigg Haws—a rolling heath-land of turf and sand, with scooped-out bunkers, thickets of gorse and blackberry, and drains and sumps half choked with yellow water ragwort and white water buttercup. I have found field gentians there, and two of our less common lowland ferns, adder's tongue and moonwort, but it is so hard to memorise a position in these dunes that it will only be by an accident if I find them again.

At one time there were acres of sandy pasture open to the public on these Haws, but, during the war much of the land was enclosed to make an R.A.F. aerodrome which has now been converted into one of Her Majesty's prisons, so that you have to burgle a house before you can have the freedom of the dunes. It is still possible, however, to walk along the shore to Silecroft, which has the most popular beach in South Cumberland. Here you really are on the open sea. The beach descends in a series of terraces of shingle, with the stones graded and varied at every step—as big as a football here, and as small as a pea ten yards away. The high tide reaches half-way up the shingle, but low tide exposes 200 or 300 yards of ribbed sand, which the children approach by wading through a swash gulley or by crossing on stepping-stones.

Silecroft, however, can be very crowded at weekends in summer, and you may prefer to walk along the shore to Layriggs which can also be reached by a rough lane from Kirksanton. Layriggs stands on the lateral moraine left by the glaciers. Its name, in fact, means 'muddy ridge', from Old Norse *leirr* (clay), just as Haverigg is the oat (or *hafri*) ridge, and the nearby Whitriggs is the white, possibly wheat, ridge. The clay ridge is backed by one of the most interesting of the coastal swamps, where in early summer you can pick your way among orchids and yellow flags, though later on you will have to kick through a steaming jungle of meadow-sweet, water-dropwort, purple loosestrife and clegs. In winter, on the other hand, these Kirksanton Mosses look as barren as the *tundra*. Go there on a clear evening in mid-February, just after lighting-up time, and you will see the last of the sunset meshed in millions of willow twigs, while the Layriggs farm and outhouses seem no more than black, angular holes snipped out of the green sky.

North of Silecroft, the next point on the coast reached by a metalled road is Bootle Shore, but there are one or two reasonably accessible places in between which are a good deal more rewarding. Gutterby, the first of them, is reached from the same point at Whitbeck where you turn off for Miller Gill. This time, however, you must rouse the keeper at the level crossing and make your way for about a mile to Gutterby Farm. The road is less rough than that at Layriggs, but if you are in a car and the summer is dry, you will travel in your own smoke-screen of dust. At the farm you walk along the lonning to the top of the clay cliffs, and descend by the cleft which looks just like a Dorset chine except that there are no pines. The path slithers down until you come to a small bay, hooped in by the red, oozy cliffs. This, I'm told, is a rare place for crabs. It is certainly a rare place for silence, and you can usually have it to yourself even on a day when people are picnicking by the hundred at Silecroft and Seascale.

Gutterby takes its name from one of its early inhabitants, being the hamlet of Godric. So, too, does Annaside, some two miles further north, which is Einarr's *saetre* (shieling or summer pasture). You take the road from Bootle Village to the Railway Station and turn off just past the old Bootle Workhouse—the building, which still stands, is plain and gaunt but of fine proportions and needs only paint and plaster to make it look like an eighteenth-century country seat. This road is really bad and can be recommended only to those whose sense of history is as great as their curiosity. The sea is hardly in sight. Annaside Beck (wrongly named the River Annas on some maps) gives up trying to find it, and puddles its way behind the clay-ridge like a great, disheartened drain. There are several farms, with barns as big as village halls, all roughly built of cobble-ducks from the shore. By one of the farms the tansy, once cultivated as a herb, has run wild and covers a space the size of a tennis court. It's no good pretending that this is the real back-of-beyond. The farmers' wives shop at Whitehaven; their children attend the comprehensive school at Millom. Yet I know of no place that seems to have kept so much of the solitariness, the dreariness, the defiant independence that must have been found in these coastal communities right up until the middle of the nineteenth century.

Selker Shore, only a mile or so further north, is entirely neighbourly. You start from Bootle Station, go up the lane to Broadwater Farm, then through the gate on the left and across the fields to the shore. Here all the bleakness is gone. Little farms are popped about in every third or fourth field, and good pasture slopes down to the edge of the sea. Cows walk off the grass and stand shin-deep in salt water, and the bull, which I have several times seen with them, seems as placid as they. It is all surprisingly park-like—the land giving way to the sea politely and without a struggle. Except that the Irish Sea looks a bit big, you might be on the shores of Loughrigg Tarn.

For a mile or two north of Bootle the road leaves the shore altogether. The dunes here have been taken over by the War Office as a gun-testing station, though you can still walk along the beach except when the red warning flags are flying. In fact, if it were not for the untidy spilling of red brick huts and bits of machinery, this would be one of the most attractive stretches of that coast, with a fine jagged skyline towards Eskdale and a long ramp of shingle, variegated with many lumps of the Eskdale Granite, in shades from flesh-pink to thunder-cloud blue. Sometimes, from the fells, you can see firing flashes or tracer shells bursting over the sea, and small boys are apt to believe that a new war has broken out.

Immediately beyond the gun range you reach the Esk and South Cumberland's one sizeable estuary. The Esk and the Irt flow roughly parallel down Eskdale and Wasdale, about five or six miles apart, but when they come within a mile of the sea, each is diverted by the coastal ridge, the Esk flowing north and the Irt flowing south, until they meet and force their way into the sea immediately opposite the little in-between River Mite. It is here, on this trident of estuaries, that you find Ravenglass, a port at the time of the Romans, but now known to visitors chiefly as the station for the Eskdale Railway. The Romans made it their supply base for Hardknott Fort in Eskdale, and possibly may have intended it as the invasion port for Ireland. They built a small camp, with home-comforts for the troops in the form of a bath-house, which still stands in the wood near the station and is said to be the highest above ground of any Roman remains in England. For some odd reason it does not catch the fancy of the public, is little visited and looks neglected, though you can still see the holes in the walls where the hot-water pipes ran round the building. In the eighteenth century, when ships from the West Indies could unload spirits, free of duty, at the Isle of Man, Ravenglass was famous as a smuggling port, the contraband being taken by pack-horse over Stye Head and Hardknott. According to tradition Whitbeck Church was one of the places where the liquor was hidden, and the same is also said of Seaton Hall, near Bootle, a farmhouse built on the site of the Benedictine Priory of St Mary of Lekeley, the only nunnery in South Cumberland. The smuggling was suppressed by customs officers with the aid of the military, but, even as late as the middle of the last century, small ships still came into Ravenglass bringing supplies for the local farms.

Today, on a more populated and accessible coast, Ravenglass would probably be a yachting centre, but, in fact, only a few boats lie about on the mud, and the visitors who wander down to the waterside while waiting for the Ratty are sometimes disappointed. One can see why. For Ravenglass stubbornly refuses to look like a conventional seaside village. There is no harbour, no quay; there are no men in jerseys; nothing that you can be photographed standing up against. The houses on one side of the only street turn their backs on the sea, and bolster up their back-yard doors and gardens with cement and sandbags to keep the tide out. For 2,000 years this settlement has been where it is because it is sheltered from the sea, and it is not going to change its habits now.

Yet to me Ravenglass is still the most captivating village on the Lake coast. It is built of the Eskdale granite for one thing, and the houses are all either sparkling grey or rhododendron pink, often timbered and shuttered and gabled in a style which seems to have been caught like a rash from Muncaster Castle—the parish church is, in fact, three miles away, in the Castle grounds. Above all, I like its snugness—its way of positioning itself on the old country principle that you can enjoy the view outside, but, inside, you want comfort. And, for its comfort, Ravenglass depends mainly on those two long spits of dune-land that delay the Esk and the Irt from reaching the sea.

Much of these dunes, however, is closed to the public, at Eskmeals (the name means 'the sandhills by the Esk') by the Gun Range and at Drigg by the bird sanctuary, though you can reach the fine Drigg dunes, where montbretia grows wild as grass, by the road from the Station. (At the time of writing, the inhabitants of Drigg are engaged in a dispute about the right of way along the shore.)

It is estimated that 10,000 pairs of black-headed gulls nest on the Nature Reserve, making this by far England's biggest colony of the species. Most of the English terns have also been known to nest there, including, from time to time, the rare roseate tern. A good deal of ornithological research has been carried out at Drigg, where it has been found that the gull's black head, which it only wears in spring and summer, plays an important part in social behaviour. A bird without a black head is invariably driven off or pecked to death. This habit, no doubt, has helped to preserve a species which has to face enough dangers without that of cross-breeding. Hedgehogs eat the eggs; foxes, weasels, black-backed gulls and carrion crows attack the chicks; and foxes are now known to bury the eggs in springtime and go and dig them up in the lean part of the winter. In earlier years, too, the eggs were gathered by the villagers and often found their way to London restaurants as plovers' eggs. During the war, a local confectioner used hundreds of them in his bakery until customers began to complain that the chocolate cakes tasted fishy. Permission to visit the reserve must be obtained from the Clerk to the Cumberland County Council.

Obviously a bird sanctuary is not a place in which people can be allowed to wander about, but there is one spot on these Esk-Irt dunes where you can still enjoy the emptiness and freedom of this part of the coast, with the sea on one side of you and the fells on the other. Go to the old Eskmeals Station, either from Waberthwaite at low tide, or from Bootle Shore if the road is flooded. When you reach the railway viaduct, look inwards. At high tide this is a sea-loch, and at low a tongue of slithering mud-sand, purple with sea lavender and sea aster. And above the shore, are the granite hills of Muncaster, much spiked with conifer, and the tiny, old, box-pewed church of Hall Waberthwaite, just visible among its sycamores. But turn round, go under the viaduct, and make your way, at right angles to the flow of the river along the side of the fence, and you will cross, first of all, a few hundred yards of rather squelchy saltings and then come to the dunes which are here about half a mile wide, though they seem, when you get among them, to be as vast as the Sahara. The sand is bare and loose, in twenty-foot-high swells and waves scarcely restrained by the marram. The hollows are not turfed over, as at Haverigg, so that these dunes are rather less interesting to the botanist, though I have found sea-buckthorn (*Hippophaë rhamnoides*), which, so far as I know, is not found elsewhere on this coast. Instead of turf, you get flat, saucer-like salt-pans, strewn with cobbles, or dark green in the damp places with sour marsh plants. Through gaps in the ridges you look across the channel to the Drigg Haws, with their almost perpetual umbrella of dipping and screaming gulls. Otherwise you are cut off from the rest of England as if you were on an island. But if you clamber to the top of the dunes, the Wasdale and Eskdale fells bludgeon themselves into your notice, and, above all, the blunt-headed instrument of Black Combe, and you will be reminded that you are in the heart of the Lakes. There is much talk nowadays of the overcrowding of the district but there are still places of solitude for anyone who is ready to walk two miles or even one. How long they will remain solitary depends almost entirely on whether or not we are prepared to keep the road-building in check.

North of Drigg the fells begin to stand further off and the dunes are no longer overawed by Black Combe. Unfortunately, from Drigg to Seascale the land backing on the shore was taken over during the last war as the site for an explosives factory, and though the area is out of view from the beach, it is well visible from the train—an industrial charnel-yard of barbed-wire, underground shelters, dug-outs, concrete huts and weed-cracked tarmac, with the scraped and scarred earth all round. Here and there little volcano-glows of bird's foot trefoil burst out as if from a smouldering resentment below soil. That we should have found it necessary to destroy this part of our own country in order to destroy Hitler was bad enough. That we should have left the destruction unrepaired is surely a disgrace.

Seascale is another place which has changed in the last thirty years, though, in this case, the blame should not be put on the war. To me Seascale is interesting chiefly because it is the first spot along the coast where the sandstone really shows itself. The church, the large hotel and many of the station buildings are of sandstone, and when the tide is out the lower shore looks like an accident case, with dark red splinters and collar-bones of rock, oozy salt trickles and black congealed scabs of sea-weed. At Seascale the coastal ridge lifts itself high above the shore. The hotel, the former girls' school, and the red-brick villas are perched unprotectedly on their sandy cliffs as if the sea they were looking at was the English Channel. Right up to the 1950s Seascale remained, in appearance, stuck in the Edwardian Age, like a little brick model of the Folkestone of Arthur Kipps. But with sixty-mile-an-hour gales hosing the windows with salt spray, Seascale was a healthy place; with neither pier, nor dancehall, nor cinema, nor fair-ground, it was a respectable place; and, tucked away, miles from any bombable area, it seemed, in wartime, to be a safe place. So that, like the rest of this part of the coast, it swarmed with children, both in holidays and in term-time. The cliffs carried the widely-known Calder Girls' School* and a preparatory school for boys, and there was another preparatory school at Gosforth and, of course, the boys' public school at St Bees. The once-forlorn beaches became brisk, invigorating and virginal, and the piping of the oyster-catchers took on a slightly middle-class accent.

The fifties, however, brought a change which the shop-keepers, if not the parents, regarded as a change for the better. The world's first atomic-power station was built just two miles away at Sellafield, and Seascale jumped forward a whole half century in five years. A new, expensive housing estate has mushroomed up between the old village and Gosforth, and nearly all the habitable cottages and country houses within nine or ten miles have been bought up by scientists from Calder Hall. Seascale and district

* Closed down, 1967

now holds the greatest concentration of the highly educated that Greater Lakeland has ever known, while the proportion of B.Sc.s per housing square foot must be one of the highest in England. All this is helping to change West Cumberland society, and its effects can be seen in the music and dramatic societies, in the support given to Rosehill Theatre, and even in the manners of the children at the local schools.

Yet, in spite of all the new money and the new faces, Calder Hall darkens the landscape like a threat. It is not that the buildings themselves are ugly, except for the clutter of car parks and dumps and wire-netting at the periphery. The original towers—now, apparently, already out of date—were slim and elegant, and the new cooling towers, though less pleasing in shape, often turn the coast into a Chinese watercolour with their twisting wraiths of mist. But when there was an atomic leak at the plant in the late fifties, and we, in Millom, had to pour our milk down the drains, we felt as if we were waiting for lightning to strike from a clear sky. There was no recognisable sign of danger, but the air seemed electric. The atom, in fact, is not a comfortable neighbour. Yet atomic fission is now a fact that has to be faced, and at Calder Hall they are facing it and trying to make the best of it. If the splitting of the atom does not put an end to the world, Calder Hall may help to turn it from a menace to a hope.

The atomic age is not the only one to make its mark here, though from Seascale to St Bees the coast is almost entirely free from roads and houses. To begin with, at Seascale, at Braystones and at Nethertown—in fact, more or less wherever a motor-car can worm its way down—there are rows of beach huts, some of them smart with green paint, tiled roofs, and curtains at the little windows, some of them ramshackle cabins, patched together with tarpaulin and corrugated iron, but all of them an eyesore except to the people actually in them.

Then there is the railway. From Seascale to Pow Foot, near St Bees, a single-track line runs, balanced above the shingle on the outermost rim of the fields. The engine drivers pass keys from one to the other, hung on large hoops which they catch through the arm, in order to make sure that two trains do not dispute right of way on the same stretch of track. Every approach to the shore has to be made either across or under the railway, and every view backward from the shore has the railway-line running across the bottom like the edge of a picture-frame. The only place where you can really forget about the railway is in the train itself. There you have an upper-deck view, high enough above the beach huts to ignore them, yet near enough to the shore to feel the spray of the waves at high tide, to see the mauve shingle at low tide or the ginger-bread slabs of sandstone at Nethertown.

Immediately out of Seascale you run beside the golf-course, with Calder Hall like a grotesque hazard for the sliced drive. This is the country of the new science-fiction folklore: how a Lakeland terrier swam across a certain beck and came out of the water completely hairless; and how scientists, having cooked their golf-balls, go round the course in the dark with the aid of a Geiger-counter. The atomic station itself is built near the outlet of the River Calder, where it divides into a gravelly delta. At high tide this is the mouth of the river, but at low tide it is captured in the shingle by the Ehen, which has been flowing almost parallel to the shore for about two miles. Just beyond Sellafield station, you see the old Egremont line, now used to carry only iron-ore, coal and the pupils of Wyndham School.

At about the point where the old line branches off, you can look right up the lower valley of the Ehen and see how the river has cut deeply into the clay ridge, giving it even steeper cliffs on the landward side than on the shore side. The latter, from Sellafield onwards, is much primrosed in spring, and curves in and out so that the train seems to be continually either rounding a little promontory or skirting a little bay. And every time it emerges from a bay, St Bees Head seems to have come one step nearer.

By the time you reach Nethertown, the sandstone has taken over, and the inland villages are built entirely of this stone: Calder Bridge, Coulderton and Beckermet* with its two parish churches, St John's in the village, and St Bridget's, like a spiritual isolation hospital, out in the fields. The narrow road, which manages to run for about five miles within a hundred or so yards of the sea, without ever catching more than a glimpse of it, goes through a red, sandy, high-grassed country, with kettle-holes and ponds

* Accent on the second syllable. The derivation, which has been disputed, is probably from 'hermit's beck'

The Citadel, Carlisle

DALSTON

stuffed like vases with buckbean and waterlilies. To one brought up in the shadow of Black Combe, it seems quite unlike the Lake coast, but the stranger will probably say that St Bees Head is the one feature along the whole shore-line which looks just as he had expected.

Yet St Bees Head has its surprises, too. Thomas Carlyle, remembering it from the Dumfriesshire hills, called it 'that sapphyre promontory', and it is only when you begin to get close to it that it looks red. When you get closer still, you see that it is green almost as much as red, for huge swathes and drapes of turf hang down from the top wherever the cliff eases back. At the bottom, however, the rock is bare as a ship's hull, plated, slabbed and riveted against the sea, with a defensive breakwater of blocks and boulders that the sea itself has piled up. The slabs have been rounded and moulded by the tide, rough to the touch but smooth to the eye, with the ripple of the waves still on them and pools standing in dubs and salt-cellars. At other places the face of the rock is pitted and pock-marked by the spray as if an abstract sculptor had been inventing a design with a blowlamp.

The little bay to the south of the headland used to be one of the most attractive spots on the Cumberland coast, but it now gets so crowded at summer weekends that the council has tidied up the foreshore with stepped concrete kirbs, a car park and a caravan site behind. The result could, in fact, have been worse, but it is enough to tame down the wildness and roughness which once belonged to the bay.

You can still find all this, however, if you climb the cliff-edge path which takes you to the top of the headland. And here you will get your second surprise. For St Bees Head is not one headland but two. The head which Carlyle saw from Dumfriesshire was not the one we have seen from Seascale. The two heads, in fact, are about two miles apart, and half way between them lies the enchanting Fleswick Bay*. I have seen this bay only from above, since it has to be approached by a long descent from Hannah Moor or a sharp scramble from the cliff-top, and, though I could get down easily enough, only a helicopter could get me up again! The cliffs here are almost perpendicular, of beautifully

* Pronounced to rhyme with Keswick, though, in this case, the second syllable derives from Old Norse *vik*, a creek or bay, while the first is *flęsja*, probably a slab or stone

St Mary's, Wreay
Farmhouse at Mealsgate

striated rock, greeny-pink as an under-ripe stawberry, and tufted with thrift and sea campion and the white crochet-work tags of earth-nut and hogweed. But at a point about half a mile beyond Tomlin (the hill overlooking the South Head), the rocks are folded inwards to let a little beck enter the sea, and it is in this indentation that the small sickle of a beach is exposed. The sea-edge is of a dark red rock, worn so smooth that it looks like toffee cooling in a pan, while the beach, seen from the top of the cliffs, seems to be made up of grey-ish glinting shell-sand. The few bathers and fishermen who reach the beach by the long track from Sandwith find themselves in an enormous, eliptical walled garden, one half of which is laid open to the sea. Peeping Toms will have to peep from the Isle of Man. Friends who have descended to the beach tell me that it is the most private and the most paradisal spot of almost any they know.

The cliff-walk goes all the way from St Bees to Whitehaven. It is a clearly-marked path, with stiles between fields and a fence running along the edge, though it is quite easy to step over this if you want to. The whole distance is about four miles, but those who cannot manage the full length of it can come in at the middle by the road which runs from the village of Sandwith to the lighthouse on the North Head. (This is marked 'Private' but rarely seems to be barred.) And it is the stretch between the lighthouse and Fleswick which, for me, makes the climax of the Cumberland coast. For at a point where the cliffs curve like Regent Street, you can look down from your rock balcony and see below you, as if on show in a shop window, sea birds in hundreds and hundreds. In some places the shelves of the rock are thickly plastered with the droppings of year after year. There are guillemots, huddled close as carrier pigeons in a crate, their tails to the sea, beaks to the cliff; kittiwakes, the prettiest of the gulls, which breed nowhere else in the north-west of England; common and herring gulls—the absence of black-headed gulls is noticeable to one who lives near Ravenglass. Nor do you need to be a knowledgeable bird-watcher to be able to spot the birds, for there is usually someone about who will lend you his binoculars and point out the less common species—the razorbill or the black guillemot, of which this is the only breeding place in England, or the puffin, the Manx shearwater or the gannet, all of which are regular visitors. The list of birds which may be glimpsed from these cliffs is, in fact, an exciting one. Before its recent, catastrophic decline, the peregrin falcon used to be seen here, and St Bees was one of the last breeding places in northern England of the Cornish chough.

Of all those rareties, it is the red-billed Celtic crow that I would most like to see back again at St Bees. For as you look out from the North Head you look right into the Celtic past of Cumberland—the Isle of Man, the Mull of Galloway, the Isle of Whithorn, all of which, like Iona and Northumberland's Holy Island and the Farnes and St Patrick's Chapel at Heysham Head, were centres and bridge-heads of the Celtic Church. It seems strange to us that the Faith should have taken root and flourished on such far-away, inaccessible promontories and archipelagoes like some maritime plant washed in by the tide. It seems less strange, however, when you look out from the North Head and realise how the sea, which now divides island from island, was once the easiest means of communication. It is likely that St Bees was yet another of these holy headlands, though the only evidence lies in the legend of St Bega, a princess who fled from Ireland to avoid having to marry a heathen Viking and was wrecked on the coast near St Bees. According to one version, she was granted by the Lord of Egremont as much land as was covered by snow on Midsummer Day, whereupon she founded a nunnery on the acres sanctified by the Cumberland weather. According to another version, she lived at St Bees as an anchorite for some years, and then fled to St Aidan of Lindisfarne, who gave her permission to establish a nunnery at West Hartlepool.

The Synod of Whitby was held in 664, after which it is usually thought that the Roman Church took control in England and the Celtic Church retreated across the Border. It would seem, however, that the Church in Cumberland remained predominantly Celtic long after this. The Irish saints, Patrick, Brigid and Sancton, are commemorated in several church dedications along this coast, and St Bega was held in high honour at St Bees right up to the time of the founding of the Benedictine Priory in the twelfth century. The priory itself, however, was firmly under the control of the new ecclesiastic-social establishment of Norman aristocracy and the Church of Rome. Its spiritual overlord was the Archbishop of York*; its benefactors were the barons of the west coast, from William Meschin of Egremont down to the Hudlestons of Millom. The barons gave generously, making the priory unusually wealthy for its size. Some of its possessions lay as far away as the Isle of Man, and it is said that the prior was entitled to a seat in the Manx Tynwald.

At the Dissolution, the nave and transepts of the priory church became the parish church, the choir was unroofed and allowed to fall into ruin, and the rest of the monastery was pulled down. No doubt many of the stones went to the buidling of farms and houses roundabout, and some, perhaps, to the building of the Elizabethan wing of the grammar school, founded in the late sixteenth century by Archbishop Edmund Grindall, who was born in the district and almost certainly attended the priory school. Centuries later, in 1817, a theological college was set up at St Bees, and the old choir was reroofed and restored, and still remains as a beautiful reconstruction of the Transitional Style, though the college came to an end sixty years ago.

The church itself is surely the finest along all the west coast, bar one†. It is all of the local sandstone—a rich, chocolate pudding of a rock which wears away under the weather, so that the outside of the church is turning into a gallery of accidental, rain-carved ornaments. The recessed rows of dog-teeth on the Norman doorway at the west end, and the figure of the dragon on the lintel above the little courtyard opposite the door, are all being blurred and thumbed into shapes the carver never thought of. He would not have thought of the shapes of Butterfield's new east end, either, nor of the painted iron rood screen, full of twisting leaves that look like diabolical ducks' heads, which admirers of Mr John Betjeman may possibly regard as the finest thing in the church. But I think that the medieval stone-mason would have felt quite at home with the belfry which was added to the tower at the Victorian restoration. It had a squat, slated steeple, very French in appearance, which accommodated itself to the hills around it.

* It should be remembered that St Bees was not included in the diocese of Carlisle until 1856

† i.e. Holy Trinity, Millom. Anyone who feels that my preference is merely a matter of local patriotism should go to see it. It is as unpretentious as a barn on the outside, but, inside, the fourteenth-century Hudleston chapel is one of the loveliest architectural conceptions anywhere in the diocese—the great east window, the windows of the south wall, and the almost unique 'fish' window at the west end

Unfortunately, slates began to slip off, threatening to make martyrs of the churchgoers, so the steeple had to be made smaller still and was surrounded by a wall to catch any further slippings. The result is much less pleasing than the old tower, though the sandstone additions, which looked as raw as freshly cut Cheddar Chesse to begin with, are quickly mellowing into the old port-winey crust.

If Ravenglass half turns its back on the sea, St Bees has the air of not even being aware of it. There is a new housing estate springing up, close to the shore, but this looks, as such estates nearly always do, as if it had got there by mistake. The old village curves up the hill in two rows of dark terraces that shut out all views but that of the road between them. The bottom of the hill takes on dignity from the school, and the one or two large houses built for the students of the Theological College. But the village looks as if it regards even dignity as rather frivolous, though, like some eighteenth-century non-conformist chapels, it achieves dignity without intending to. House by house it sits on the hill-side as if it needed to give no explanation for its presence. The sandstone terraces are seemingly a world away from the heaped-slate villages of the dales, yet, in their own way, they are equally indigenous, coming so obviously from the quarries higher up the fellside—quarries, by the way, which have provided the stone for many of the new churches and church restorations of West Cumberland.

CHAPTER NINE

THE SOLWAY COAST

I COME now to the problem which faces anyone who tries to write about present-day Cumberland: should I include the west coast or just ignore it? If I were writing a history of the country or a social or economic survey, the decision would be simple, for here between Whitehaven and Aspatria is our main concentration of industry and population. But I am writing primarily for the visitor, and visitors come to the Lakes to get away from industry and towns. At Brantwood, near Coniston, where Newcastle University ran holiday courses in the geology, botany, economy, social history and literary associations of the Lake District, students have been known to refuse to join an organised tour of iron-mines and blast-furnaces. Another man I knew, a keen rock-climber, used to dismiss the West coast as 'unfit for human consumption'. For people like this the industrial region of Cumberland is quite literally a blot on the landscape, an intrusion, something which should never have been allowed.

Nothing that I can say is likely to make them change their minds. For twenty years I have been claiming that Hodbarrow Hollow is about the most fascinating spot in all Cumberland, and now it is going to disappear under the water without having been seen except by the local people. Yet, though I cannot and do not even want to make my readers flock to Maryport, Egremont or Dearham, I want at least to persuade them to take a look at West Cumberland, to see it as a part of the whole, as the inevitable result of just those factors and forces (geological, historical, social and so on) which the students were learning about on the shores of Coniston Water.

Let us return to the North Head at St Bees and try to fit West Cumberland into the landscape. First of all, as you look north-west, you see that practically the whole of the horizon is full of Scotland. Further up the coast it is not Skiddaw that dominates the skyline but Criffel in Dumfriesshire. Maryport, in fact, is nearer to Scotland, as the tern flies, than to Keswick, while Workington lies almost precisely at the latitude of Scotland's Land's End, the Mull of Galloway. You could live in Scotland and go north for your holiday to Bassenthwaite, though, admittedly, you would have to live in a lighthouse.

The point is that all along this industrial coast the rest of England is out of sight, blocked off by the backs of the Lake hills and the North Head of St Bees. If, however, you climb to the top of the rise above the cliffs and look inland, you will see how close West Cumberland is to the Lakes. Few visitors realise this. They think of Whitehaven and Workington as being pushed into a dirty corner, well out of the way. Indeed, you can travel by train from Maryport to St Bees without getting the feeling that you are anywhere near the fell country. Yet the distance from Whitehaven to Ennerdale Lake is almost exactly the same as that from Kendal to Windermere or from Ulverston to Newby Bridge, and the little iron towns are even closer to the hills.

Industrial Cumberland lies between the two main regions of the county, the Lakes and the Solway Plain, between the slates of the fells and the sandstone of the farming country. Geologically, it falls into two sectors, each neatly arranged according to age—the older carboniferous limestone lying next to the slates and the younger coal-bearing rocks, next to the sandstone. It was the iron-ore in the curving strip of limestone (like a brim to the fells' trilby hat) which first began to be exploited, since in the Middle Ages coal was thought of merely as a fuel inferior to wood or peat. Iron-ore was worked around Egremont as early as the twelfth century, and the monks of both St Bees and Holme Cultram had an interest in the trade. It remained, however, on a small scale; the 'mines' were probably no more than side-levels and surface scrapings, and it was not until the nineteenth century that iron began to boom. Whitehaven*, in any case, is founded not on iron but on coal.

The true beginning of the town dates from 1630 when the lands of the old St Bees Priory passed into the possession of Sir Christopher Lowther. There is no river at Whitehaven; the

* Early forms of the name, 'Whithofthaven' etc., show that it was originally 'the harbour by the white headland'. The middle element, Old Norse *hofuth* or head, had been lost by the thirteenth century

harbour is open to the sea and depends entirely on the tides. So Sir Christopher built a pier in 1634, but died ten years later, leaving the estate to his son, John, who was then 2 years old. Whitehaven was still only a village of forty or fifty houses and had to wait until the boy grew up before it could itself begin to grow. Sir John first of all gained government confirmation of Whitehaven's right to hold a market. Then he set about buying more land, made a successful claim to the foreshore, acquired the mansion called 'The Flatt', and laid down the basic street-plan upon which the town still stands today. By the time he died, in 1705, Whitehaven had a population of over 2,000*, a large coal trade with Ireland and the beginnings of an export and import trade with America.

All this continued to expand under Sir John's heir, his second son, James (later Sir James) Lowther, locally known as 'Farthing Jemmy'. By the mid-eighteenth century, the town had become one of the three or four most important ports in England and looked like developing into a great North-country centre for trade with the New World. Men like Walter Lutwidge† sent out ship-loads of English goods to Virginia and imported rum and tobacco in return. The importing of tobacco, in fact, became for a time one of Whitehaven's principal trades and was the special concern of Wordsworth's uncle, Richard Wordsworth, Controller of Customs‡ in the town.

The tobacco trade dwindled, and was finally killed by the American War of Independence, but the coal trade continued to grow, so that when 'Farthing Jemmy' died in 1755 he left his successor what amounted to a small but very powerful industrial monopoly. That successor was another James Lowther, later the first Lord Lonsdale, the 'Wicked Earl' whom we met in Chapter Six. (In fact, Sir James did not originally intend that this other James should be his heir, since in his will he bequeathed the Whitehaven estates and coal mines to Sir William Lowther of Holker Hall near Cartmel, who died before him, in 1753. If Sir

* See Daniel Hay, *Whitehaven: A Short History* (Whitehaven, 1966), to which I am indebted throughout this section

† See Edward Hughes, *North Country Life in the Eighteenth Century*, Vol II (Oxford, 1965)

‡ The same post was offered to the poet himself, in 1815, but he declined as it would have meant that he would have had to leave Rydal for Whitehaven. See Mary Moorman, *William Wordsworth: A Biography* (Oxford)

William had lived longer, or had left a son, the subsequent fortunes of Whitehaven might have been very different.) By the time that the future first earl succeeded to the property the town already claimed a pottery and a glass-works, a ship-yard and all the sail-making and rope-spinning and other trades that went with it. The population was flourishing, but the town was so jammed in between the sea and the three hills round the harbour that it could not easily spread. Instead, the squares and open spaces between the streets of the original seventeenth-century plan were filled up, and hundreds of families were packed into narrow, airless courts cupboarded behind the wide and imposing main streets. Today, when these courts are being pulled down, you can see the thick walls of rubble or cobble-stones, the dungeonlike basements, the twisting stone steps that led to the upper rooms. When you remember, also, the starvation wages, the recurrent epidemics and the appalling conditions in the mines, with their dangers from fire-damp, explosion, fall of roof or in-rush of water, you begin to fill in a picture that is distressingly familiar. One other thing should be remembered. Men and women did not flock into Whitehaven because they wanted to live in degradation, but because the wages, miserable as they were, were better than those they could get on the farms. The growth of Whitehaven in the seventeenth and eighteenth centuries is, in fact, a comment on the kind of poverty which then existed in the cottages and hovels of what the Romantics were beginning to call a pastoral paradise.

From all this it may seem that there was little to choose between Whitehaven and any other industrial town of the North of England. Yet this was not so. It retained a strong individuality, a sense of being not so much a region as a colony, separate from the rest of the country. This was partly due to the monopoly of the Lowther family in the town, but the feeling of separateness was just as strong in the outlying districts where the Lowther influence was challenged.

The leader of this challenge was a man very different from the first earl, both in politics (he was a Whig and the Lowthers were Tories) and temperament. John Christian belonged to a Manx family, former supporters of Cromwell, who came to Cumberland at the Restoration and settled at Ewanrigg near Maryport.

(Fletcher Christian, who led the mutiny on *The Bounty*, came from the same family.) As a young man John Christian seems to have been neither ambitious nor industrious, but in 1782 he married his cousin, Isabella Curwen, heiress to the Workington coal-fields, and at once began to wake up. He moved from the family house at Ewanrigg into Workington Hall, took the name of Curwen, and threw all his energies and enthusiasm into Whig politics and the development of the coal trade*. It is clear that Christian Curwen was a man with a quick grasp of the problems that were arising in this new industrial society. From the very first he showed what, for his time, was an unusual concern for the welfare of his employees. He began some imaginative workmen's insurance schemes, encouraged Friendly Societies, bought food wholesale and sold it cheaply to his own workpeople, and campaigned for the repeal of the Corn Laws. Yet, in spite of his paternalism, the Whitehaven-Workington area remained split into two violent, vituperative and thoroughly unscrupulous party factions.

Some people, nevertheless, managed to live fairly comfortably between the two. Wordsworth, who remained a loyal supporter of the Lowthers while marrying his son to Christian Curwen's daughter, was one example. The Senhouses of Netherhall were another. They could claim, moreover, to be more truly a west-coast family than either the Lowthers or the Christians, for their name, which means seven hills (from *haugh* or howes) is connected with Hall Senna, near Seascale, from which the family originally came. Humphrey Senhouse (1706-70), the middle one of three of that name, is best remembered as the founder of Maryport, which he named after his wife, Mary Fleming, daughter of the Dean, later the Bishop, of Carlisle. (Before this the village had been called 'Ellenfoot', being at the mouth of the River Ellen.) His uncle, Captain Richard Senhouse, was the man who built the splendid seventeenth-century town house (now The Waverley Hotel) at Whitehaven, calling it Tangier House after the port in which he had served as a quarantine officer during his days in the navy. His sister, Bridget, married her cousin, John Christian of Ewanrigg, and became the grandmother of John Christian Curwen.

* See Edward Hughes, *North Country Life in the Eighteenth Century* for much fascinating information about Curwen

The Senhouses, therefore, were in a strategic position to build up a powerful anti-Lowther alliance, had they so wished. They were closely intermarried with the Christians and the Curwens; they controlled Maryport harbour which looked like making up for the failure of the Parton harbour scheme; and, from the family mansion at Netherhall (now the site of a new comprehensive school), they could overlook the whole of the northern part of the Cumberland coal-field. But the Senhouses refused to fit into the pattern: they were Tories instead of Whigs, and every man of them was loyal to the Lowthers.

The latter, for their part, knew how to reward loyalty, and the story* of how they did so in one case is typical of their political string-pulling. The Humphrey Senhouse who founded Maryport was a somewhat indecisive, unimaginative man, with little of the Lowther stamp. His eldest son, the third Humphrey, had even less, and it seems to have been partly through his lack of enterprise that Maryport failed to develop as it might have done. Nor were his three sons more successful to begin with. The second son wanted to be an artist, and there was talk at one time of apprenticing him to William Hogarth, whose father came from Kendal. The two younger sons languished unprofitably at sea until their father, like a prince in a fairy tale, remembered the magic ring in his pocket and applied to Sir James Lowther.

Now it happened that, in 1763, the Lowther nominee for the parliamentary seat of Westmorland (Sir James's own brother, Robert) had voted against Sir James's wishes in a division, and was promptly told to apply for the Chiltern Hundreds. In January 1764 the new Lowther nominee, John Robinson, was returned, in spite of the opposition of the Curwens, and by 1770 had risen to the position of Secretary of the Treasury. He now received his orders from Sir James, and the wheels began to move. Almost immediately the elder of the two Senhouse brothers was appointed Surveyor-General of the Customs in Barbados and the Leeward Islands, and he, in his turn, was able to appoint the younger to a similar post in the Windward Islands. The younger man accepted his good fortune with amused cynicism, saying that he had once been little more than 'an arrant Smugler', so that, if you set a thief to catch a thief, he ought to make a good Custom-house

* See Edward Hughes, *North Country Life in the Eighteenth Century*, Vol II

Officer. The elder son, on the other hand, cherished a reverential gratitude towards his patron for the rest of his life. He christened his son James Lowther Senhouse, named his home in Barbados Lowther Hall, and proceeded to fill the Customs service in the Caribbean with men from Cumberland.

This last act is not nearly so surprising as it may seem, for, though Whitehaven may have looked remote from the rest of England, the merchants kept very close trading connections with the New World, and especially with Virginia and Maryland.

Take the interesting case of George Gale, dealer in tobacco and, as might be expected, a cousin* of the Senhouses, who, on one of his business trips to Virginia, met and married a widow, Mildred Washington. Gale returned to Whitehaven, bringing his wife and her three children, two boys and a girl, by her first marriage, but Mrs Gale died the following year and was buried in St Nicholas's Churchyard. Her two boys, in the meantime, attended Appleby School, but, after her will had been contested by relatives of her first husband, they were sent back to America. Had it not been for this, the father of the first President of the United States would have been brought up as a Whitehaven boy, and the Stars and Stripes of the Washington coat-of-arms might not have become the American flag.

Whitehaven has yet another association with American history through the career of John Paul of Kirkbean in Kirkcudbrightshire, who was bound apprentice to a merchant of the town, and, later, took the name of Jones, accepted a commission in the American navy, and, in April 1778, raided Whitehaven Harbour and set fire to shipping anchored there. The story may be too well-known to need telling again, but it should not be dismissed merely as a romantic episode, quite irrelevant to the Whitehaven of today. Nor are the affairs of the Lowthers, Curwens, Christians, Senhouses and Gales irrelevant either. For the town they built holds on to much of its eighteenth-century mercantile and maritime appearance. In spite of the devastated colliery landscape round about, and in spite of the grime which has drizzled down for 200 years, the harbour still has an adventurous, Westward-Ho look about it. From the new loop road, just behind the plain-Jane

* Later on, the Gales became related by marriage to the Wordsworths, since Captain John Wordsworth, son of Richard, married Ann Gale

St James's Church*, the two outer piers can be seen, enclosing fifty acres of water in their huge crab-like claws. In a smoky winter sunset, the lights glimmer up from the quayside, giving it the blurred beauty of an eighteenth-century steel engraving. The lighthouses at the end of each pier were built, in fact, in the first half of the following century, and look like white chess-men, bishops or castles, controlling the diagonals and lines. But lighthouses, bollards, steps and parapets, all have the same unconcerned neatness, as if they belonged to too good-mannered a family to look awkward in any company—and some of the company is embarrassing enough! Then, on a brisk day in summer, with the wind on the tide, the scene takes on the bustle of a Rowlandson print brought up to date, with maybe one of the Marchon boats in the harbour, and lorries by the quayside, youths fishing, children running along the very edges of the piers, and everybody looking as if they are about to tumble headlong into the water.

The town itself is altogether more sedate, more mundane, less fanciful, less archaic. You must forget the usual association of the word 'Georgian'. Whitehaven has none of the fashionably old-fashioned stylishness of the county town or cathedral close. Instead, it is practical as an account book, and as orderly too, ruled in good straight lines, both sides added up and seen to balance.

I am talking now of the main streets—Lowther, Duke, King, Scotch and Irish. The first three of these have suffered much from rebuilding, the introduction of incongruous shop-fronts and the like. Above the Scotch Street intersection, however, both Duke Street and Lowther Street retain some good buildings. Duke Street has on one side the rather ornate house, now the council chambers, and, on the other, the very handsome Somerset House. Lowther Street has one admirable terrace, from the crocketed little non-conformist church almost to the castle, which, with the corresponding stretch of Scotch Street, make up two sides of what might have been a fine Georgian square. Alas, the other two sides are filled by the humdrum Public Hall and the untidy car park.

This kind of contrast is continually cropping up in Whitehaven.

* Inside, however, it is far from plain, with some delicate Italian plaster-work

A little further down Scotch Street, for instance, opposite the decorously-florid iron gates of Holy Trinity Churchyard*, is a place where the end house of a terrace has been pulled down. Weeds and soil and rubbish accumulate on the old foundations; old fireplaces and flues jut out of the gable-end of the next house. And, ironically, the offices of the Cumberland Development Council, with their imposing portico, look out on to this sorry specimen of dilapidation.

It is the same throughout the irregular quadrilateral of the old town. Queen Street and Church Street are long narrow streets looking, in one direction, right up the hill—Queen Street gazes, up a long canyon, to the dead-pan front of St James's Church. But in the other direction the streets both bend, and beyond the bend seem to be shut away in a forgotten, sealed-off quarter. This is cramped, dark, not immediately inviting, yet there are many good houses if you persist in looking for them, homes of the old merchants and traders—square, thick-set, unornamented, consequential yet unostentatious, with bold doorways, stone steps up to the doors and iron railings round the basements. Looking at them you become aware of the solid comfort enjoyed by the middle classes of their time, even in the dirt and huddle of a coal-mining town. Some houses are in surprisingly good condition, the stucco bright with new paint. Others have declined into twilight property, or are botched up into warehouses, or lie empty, with doors boarded up and dust fuming out of the gaping window-spaces.

There is nothing much that the council can do about most of these buildings except to pull them down. Forty years ago it might have been different. If an attempt had been made then to renovate the better houses, demolish the worst, and let the light in, it might have been possible to preserve a district that any town could have been proud of. But, forty years ago the people of Whitehaven were finding it a hard enough struggle merely to keep alive. Yet even today, though you can't close your eyes to the decay and disappointment, this older part of the town remains the most intensely interesting built-up area in all Cumberland—a whole folk-museum of urban industrial life which has escaped

* The church itself, a good, solid, galleried building, was pulled down soon after the war

the catalogue and the glass case. It has not escaped much else, however, and those who want to see it should not wait too long.

But if Whitehaven is inevitably losing many of its eighteenth-century buildings, not all the change is loss. The town is healthier than ever it was and cleaner, and the demolition of the old slums is letting the sun into the quayside streets and opening new vistas. Moreover, the town has two new buildings which are worth boasting about. The first is the Rosehill Theatre. Like most provincial towns of any importance, Whitehaven had its theatres in the eighteenth and nineteenth centuries, one of which survived, intact if inactive, right up to the 1950's. This was 'The Royal Standard', actually a music hall, in the West Strand, built about 1870 as an extension to a public house of the same name. 'The Royal Standard' has often been described as a 'Georgian theatre', and some people have even tried to trace it back to the Restoration, but Mr Daniel Hay, Whitehaven's librarian and historian, assures me that this is nonsense. 'It was,' he says, 'a Victorian music-hall, nothing more.' Nevertheless, it seems to have been a building of real charm, so that attempts were made to save it and turn it into a West Cumberland centre for music and drama. The attempts failed and 'The Royal Standard' was hauled down, but its demolition seems to have inspired Sir Nicholas Sekers with the brilliant idea of making a theatre out of an eighteenth-century barn in the grounds of his house, a mile or so to the north of the town*. Sir Nicholas's main interest was in music, and the concerts he has initiated have gained such a high reputation that before long I expect Glyndebourne to become known as the 'Rosehill of the South'. But the hall is small, the prices are high, and the concerts are held late at night, so that for most people—especially those of us who live thirty or forty miles away—visits, however delectable, are bound to be rare. The case of drama, however, is rather different. To begin with, there is usually not one performance but five or six, often with one or two matinées, so that the seats are cheaper and it is easier for non-members to get in. Moreover, by a sensible arrangement with the Cumberland Education authorities, senior school children can get tickets for sometimes as little as five shillings, with the result that the audiences at the plays, as compared with those at the concerts,

* The very pretty proscenium at Rosehill comes, in fact, from the 'Standard'

are younger, less middle-class, less formal and more ready to let themselves go. Of course, the standard of performance is not as high in drama—obviously it is much easier to accommodate the Amadeus Quartet than the Old Vic Shakespeare company. But there are plans to enlarge the stage and hopes of enlarging the membership, and if both these can be carried out then Sir Nicholas's lovely little theatre may benefit a much wider section of the Cumberland people than has so far been able or been ready to take advantage of it.

The other notable new Whitehaven building is the West Cumberland Hospital at Hensingham, which was the first entirely new hospital to be opened in England since the war. It is built like a Tibetan monastery, clasped close to the steep side of a hill, well above the smoke and the sea-mists. You drive in at the out-patients' department, take a lift down two or three flights and emerge at ground level many feet below. This building, with its Ideal-Home furnishings, its plants in tubs and luxury-cruise décor, its outdoor sculptures ('Togetherness', outside the maternity department, looking like a huge concrete safety-pin), its informal wards and picture windows framing half West Cumberland, is so colourful and pleasant that it makes other hospitals look like medieval lazar houses. Relatives, coming up from London to visit patients, are almost taken ill with envy. The hospital has a special importance for all Lakeland visitors, of course, because it is where they will be taken if they fall off Pillar Rock.

The mining towns* of West Cumberland fall into two groups. First of all there are the iron-ore towns and villages of lower Ennerdale: Beckermet, Egremont, Moor Row, Cleator, Cleator Moor, Frizington, Arlecdon, Rowrah. Many of these are familiar to visitors since they lie along the Egremont-Cockermouth road that carries the tourists from Keswick to the western dales. Not many of the tourists give the towns a second look, nor even, in some cases, a first. Yet to me this is the most romantic landscape in Cumberland. Not, of course, the prettiest, the grandest, the wildest nor the loneliest. But here you can see man, a defiant Byronic figure, struggling against the elements, each separate

* For a fuller account see N. Nicholson, *Portrait of the Lakes* and *Cumberland and Westmorland* (Robert Hale)

Maulds Meaburn

town being a small ship tossed against the stormy sea of the fells.

You can see, also, the history of that struggle. First the iron rush, before the middle of the nineteenth century, and the sinking of shaft after shaft along the line of the limestone. Then the springing up of towns around the shafts, some no more than a row or two of cottages close to the pit-heads, others, quite sizeable, like Cleator Moor, with its blast furnaces as well as mines. But before the end of the century the boom was over, and from then to nearly the end of the 1930s the towns slowly mouldered away. The blast furnaces were dismantled; the mines closed one by one, until today only those at Beckermet are still raising ore. For many years these towns stagnated and scarcely one new house was built during the first quarter of this century. Then came the first council estates, the shoring up of old cinemas and chapels to make small factories and workshops, and the opening of new, more ambitious factories and mills. They stood, as they still stand, in a landscape of broken-down pit gear, flooded quarries, crumbling slagbanks and sullen terraces that glower at one another across narrow streets.

Post-war prosperity has poured lashings of paint over the old houses; the concrete-grey, blockhouse-like estates are now prettified with forsythia and made private with privet; the new garages are more commodious than the old cottages. But the iron towns still stand on the edge of the elements. The quarried outcrops of limestone, the dusty screes of slag, the slithering barrows and tumuli of ore-heaps and rubble tips are a continual reminder of the rock beneath, and the swollen mole-hill of Dent is a reminder of the fells beyond.

Though several of the iron towns lie in the valley, one gets the impression, from almost any of the approach roads, that the whole area is thrust up on a plateau. Cleator Moor, in particular, looks high and unsheltered, with the roof and tower of the Co-operative factory seeming, from a distance, to be that of a great church. A friend, who did not know the district, once told me that Cleator Moor had the most attractive-sounding name in the Lakes. That remark is good for a laugh in West Cumberland. Yet Cleator Moor still has something of the air of Cleator's moor—the inhabitants speak of the main street as being 'on the moor'. And, if you walk past the little chapel at the head of Wath Brow you

Great Asby, Eden Valley

need go only a couple of hundred yards to reach the Ehen and a river scene as placid and Wordsworthian as any in the county.

Cleator itself, where the Keekle joins the Ehen is one cramped, intimidating street. To walk along it in the Slump, when every woman stood at the doorstep with her knitting or her gossip, was an experience fit to scare the life out of a stranger. Today the traffic shuffles through, from Cockermouth to the coast, and nobody bothers to stare. The traffic does not find Moor Row at all—a village reached by narrow, umbrageous lanes like those of Hampshire. Rowrah, on the other hand, is so bare that it makes you shiver to look at it; Frizington seems not yet to have rinsed the Slump out of its tattered shirt-tails; Bigrigg is balanced on the edge of empty craters and quarries among which the main road from Egremont twists like a causeway. I once saw a stoat, in the pure white of winter ermine, run across that road, from quarry to quarry.

Egremont, the only one of the towns with a history older than iron, is also the most obviously romantic. The backs of the decayed part of the town go down to the Ehen—what a lovely riverside it might have had! But the new town, and the oldest part of the old, climb up the little hill which is now a public park. Here is the Norman castle, with excellent herring-bone masonry in its walls. You can walk along tarmac paths between the dirtied red sandstone of the collapsed keep and look down on the dirtied red haematite of the abandoned mines. The ballad of the sword or the ballad of the pick—both tell tales of exploitation. You can take your choice, whichever you prefer.

I do not feel the same affection for the second group, the colliery towns. This, no doubt, is partly because I was brought up amongst iron, but it is also because coal makes a grubbier landscape.

Yet, if you take the train along the coast from Whitehaven to Workington, you pass through a most spectacular region of the industrial picturesque: hollow warehouses like sacked abbeys, roofless pit buildings, deserted coke ovens, old slag heaps as over-crowded with gulls as the stacks of the Farne Islands. It is a curiously unstable landscape, and after a week of heavy rain, the cliffs begin to slither down on to the railway line in a slow, treacly waterfall, delaying the trains and the mail. Here and there you will see slabs and buttresses of new brick let into the side of the cliff to stop the slide. Elsewhere, there are darnings of primroses in spring, with the metallic gilt of coltsfoot by the lineside, giving way to dusty, miniature rhubarb leaves in summer when the yellow of the bird's-foot trefoil dolls up the sandstone. And on the other side of the line, the tide siphons its cindery shingle over rocks gangrenous with black and green seaweed or warted with barnacles.

But the lifted hinterland that runs from Whitehaven almost to Maryport has nothing of this dramatic look. It is a land smirched by coal and then left to clean itself up as best it can. There are no collieries working today anywhere inland*, but old coal tips still stand beside the colliery towns like extinct volcanoes. And the old terraces, built of blocks of grimy sandstone, often plastered or roughcast, stubbornly continue to look like miners' cottages in spite of the fact that no one who lives in them may ever have been down a pit.

This northern part of the Cumberland coal-field is now largely a land of steel. Distington has the plant of the high-duty alloys; Workington has the large Moss Bay works of what, before nationalisation, was United Steel. Workington seems to me to be a place which has less individuality than most of the West Cumberland towns and villages, though maybe I would not think so if I lived there. Its streets have a might-be-anywhere drabness about them, with nothing of Whitehaven's maritime look and next to nothing of its eighteenth-century look. St John's Church, however, built in 1823, has a massive portico, modelled on that at Covent Garden where Eliza Doolittle sheltered from the rain, while Portland Square, with its trees and cobbles and prim, bare propriety, reminds one of Ibsen rather than Shaw, for it looks far more like Bergen or Trondheim than anywhere in England.

The coast from Workington to Maryport is the most dismal in Cumberland—so flat that after a very high tide there seems to be more water on the landward side of the road than the seaward side. In the raw, sooty, salty fog that so often clogs this part of the Solway, the pit-heaps near Flimby loom up like black parodies of the Scottish hills blotted out on the other side of the firth. Maryport is a paradoxical town. When you approach it, by road or rail, it looks too prosperous for West Cumberland, almost

* The pits still working are both on the coast, at Workington and Whitehaven

opulent—smart new factories to the south, and to the north the Netherhall estate and villas and terraces of the plum-red, bourgeois-looking sandstone of the Carlisle Plain. This part of the town is built on the inward slope of a small hill or ridge on which the Romans built one of the forts that guarded the English shore of the Solway. Go to the top of this hill, and you can look down into what was once one of the most distressing slums in Cumberland—a clutter of miserable houses shovelled on to the waste land between the harbour and the slope of the hill.

A few years ago I visited Maryport to see the fine collection of the works of L. S. Lowry owned by a Maryport banker with whom the artist had often stayed. My wife drove me up the hill and down the slope so that I could look at the new housing estate which has taken the place of the old slum. Then she found herself in a *cul-de-sac* and had to back the car to get out, and, while she was doing so, I caught sight of a flight of stone steps tacking its way up the slope. 'Look', I said. 'That's just what Lowry would have painted.' And when we went into the exhibition, there, on one of the first canvases we saw, were the same steps.

North of Maryport the scene is almost rural. But not quite. The railway runs chummily along the side of the little River Ellen, passing the ruins of old collieries in the woods—birches beginning to scramble up the pit-heaps, and anemones and marsh marigolds in the sumps below. At Bulgill the railway station, now closed, is built at a bend in the line, so that passengers on the down-platform could not see those on the up. The road runs along the ridge, through the optimistically-named Prospect (close to the village of Oughterside), where a small community is grouped round an iron water-tower, lifted high above the roofs, as if the village people were all water-worshippers.

Road and railway meet at Aspatria, which really is the end of West Cumberland. It is a kind of frontier town. The pits have been closed for a long time, and the country is creeping up again. Farms back on to the main street, and a stranger who dropped in from a balloon would find it hard to tell if he were in a mining village or a country market town. This is the extreme northern tip of the industrial west where the regional dissimilarities of the Lakes clash close one against the other. The town has its roots in the coal seams, and the coal has put its mark on streets, houses, farms and church. But the old forest of Inglewood seems not entirely uprooted in the country round about, and the fells are not far away to the east nor the Solway to the west.

And Aspatria has its own special distinction, for it is the birthplace of Sheila Fell, daughter of a retired coal-miner, and an artist whose work has been placed by critics in the great English landscape tradition. Her pictures are sombre, brooding, often dark, with the human figures hardly to be differentiated from the soil and rock on which they work. No other Cumbrian-born painter has been so successful in interpreting the basic character of our landscape.

Now I live in Millom, on the extreme southern tip of the industrial west, and though—Heaven knows!—I do not claim the gifts of Sheila Fell, yet I, too, as a poet, have tried to interpret that same landscape. And it seems to me no coincidence that it is two such places as Aspatria and Millom which have produced two such people as us.

Aspatria, moreover, provides a good example of the social and economic problems which are now facing West Cumberland. For with the closing-down of the pits Aspatria has really lost its purpose. It has even lost its postal address, and letters have to be sent 'via Carlisle', though in straight mileage Carlisle is no nearer than Kirkcudbright. The story has often been told of how West Cumberland was rescued from the sleeping sickness of the Slump by Jack Adams (later Lord Adams of Ennerdale) and the Cumberland Development Council. Their achievement was, indeed, immense. Many now famous firms came to the district (Sekers silks, Kangol berets and so on) and there was the spectacular success of the Marchon anhydrite (calcium sulphate) mine and chemical works at Whitehaven. As long as the post-war boom in coal and steel continued, the new factories were sufficient to provide work for women and girls and for any men not wanted by the heavy industries. For a while prosperity seemed to have come back to Cumberland. But the coal-field is fast declining, and steel is scarcely in a better way, and some economists regard Workington as too isolated to fit into the steel-production plans of the future. New industries, new developments, new opportunities and new communications are urgently needed if West Cumberland is not to slip back into a second Depression.

There is, of course, an alternative, which is to let the whole region slowly run down: to cut off the trains, to leave new roads unbuilt, to encourage the younger people to move from the district, and to allow the others to doze away the rest of their lives in underpaid jobs or on the old-age pension. In Cumberland we suspect that this is what many planners and economists would really like to do, though few have the guts to say so. But quite apart from the crime of killing a community that has been alive for nearly 300 years, and quite apart from the foolishness of driving more people into the already overcrowded Midlands and South, this is a policy which has tremendous dangers for a part of the country which the planners *are* concerned about: the Lakes National Park. For, as I keep saying, industrial Cumberland and rural Cumberland are part of one whole. You don't treat a patient for pneumonia by leaving his feet out of the bed.

I had better say it now and have done with it. From industrial Cumberland right up to the mouth of the Eden, the chief feature in all western views is Scotland. Only I shall not have done with it; I shall keep on repeating myself. And for this I need not apologise, since it is the continual repetition of the view that astonishes the visitor, which is what I am when I get north of Maryport. Perhaps if I lived there I should become inured to the view. When you pointed it out to me I should say: 'Good heavens, I haven't noticed that for years!' But as a visitor I find myself seeing it for the first time all over again every five minutes.

There is, of course, an undebunkably romantic look about hills seen across water. Dry up the Solway Firth, join Kirkcudbrightshire to Cumberland by twenty miles of good farming land, and I'd be quite ready to turn my back on Galloway and stare at Skiddaw. As it is, the hills unroll themselves along the whole horizon, remote from Maryport, close at hand from Burgh, but at both places looking as foreign as ever France does from Dover. Along the colliery coast, the centre of the view is Cairnsmore of Fleet and the moors above Gatehouse—a jagged marquee of mountains not unlike those of the Lakes. North of Maryport Criffel bullies itself into the front, looking, from this distance, as if Robert Bruce had stolen Black Combe on one of his raids. Then, when you get beyond Bowness-on-Solway, Criffel seems to have floated out to sea, and the opposite shore is made up entirely of the bread-and-butter hills above Annan.

Take away this view and the shore of Allonby Bay would become rather dull. I certainly thought so the first few times I saw it, which were all in summer, with a hot, dirty haze on the Firth, cars parked between the road and the shore, bathers plodding stickily among the sandwich papers, and young girls hacking jaded ponies through the skimpy grass. I came there again, however, in early November, when the sky was like washing-blue and the white-washed barns might have been starched. The golf-course, at the Maryport end of the bay, was a series of green discs of turf among the rough, brown marram. (How can any golfer keep his eye on the ball with that enormous view tempting him to lift his head?) The parking places were empty, and if a car stopped anywhere on the road the begging gulls gathered up from miles around.

Allonby is a village assembled round a green with a beck flowing through it—rather like one of the Pennine villages with the sea in the place of the fells. About the beginning of the nineteenth-century it became quite a popular little resort for sea-bathing—then, of course, a matter of medicine rather than pleasure—and it seems to have made just the faintest attempt at a seaside elegance. Today this has all given way to cafés and souvenir shops and the battering of the Solway weather.

Silloth*, on the other hand, has clung on to its elegance and is by far the best-looking seaside resort along the whole length of Greater Lakeland. The town was laid out in the mid-nineteenth century and stands well back from the shore, with the main promenade, as it were, opening on to a perpetual full tide of grass like the Stray at Harrogate. But the houses are prettier than those of Harrogate, as if the men who built them might once have spent a weekend at Brighton. The square terraces behind the promenade are spread wide and dour as the streets of Kirkcudbright, Silloth's sister town across the Firth, while the parish church seems to have been dumped down like one of those cardboard churches left on shop counters to collect money for missions.

When Silloth first began to be developed, following the opening in 1856 of the railway from Carlisle, it was planned as a port

* The sea-*hlatha* or sea-barn—i.e. of Holm Cultram Abbey

rather than a seaside resort. There were, at one time, regular passenger services to Liverpool, Dublin and the Isle of Man, and even today the harbour is used by cargo ships. Visitors see very little of the shipping, but the seafront still has a serious look about it, dominated, as it is, by the huge flour mills. It is not until you pass beyond the Green towards the road to Skinburness that frivolity breaks through in an anthology of about every kind of bungalow and villa that can decorate or disfigure a coastline.

We have arrived, now, at the second of the 'Moricambe' Bays of the north-west, the dual estuary of the Waver and the Wampool. This is the fen country of Cumberland: dead flat agricultural land, the silt of centuries; pasture and mangolds; long straight roads, with the villages slumped beside them, their brick foundations sunk deep in the mud. The whole landscape has the tatty look of the Fens, too: broken-down barns and corrugated iron sheds visible for miles above the flatness, while north of Silloth there are the old, blotched hangars of the wartime aerodrome, now serving as storage depots for commercial firms. This is a scene which needs the low winter sun to ginger up the willows in the hedges and add a glitter to the otherwise dreary emptiness.

The old capital of Moricambe Bay was the village now called Abbeytown, once the site of Holm Cultram* Abbey, the wealthiest of Cumberland's monastic houses. All that remains of it today is part of the nave of the abbey church, now used as the parish church of the village, and at first sight it looks rather disappointing. Indeed, the first time I saw it I did not bother to go inside. The north and south walls are of the eighteenth century, plain as a non-conformist chapel, with two rows of round-headed windows far too small for the size of the wall. The west doorway is enclosed by a sixteenth-century porch, which, with the odd-looking gable-end and bellcote above, makes the whole west end seem cluttered. It is not until you go into the porch that you see the point of it, for it shelters a magnificent Norman doorway, well worth travelling miles to see. The light from the several windows falls full on the columns of the door and on the tombstones set up against the

* The original place-name was probably a British word meaning 'isthmus', to which the Old English *ham* was added. The Old Norse *holmr*, 'an island', was prefixed in the twelfth century

walls, including one to the Earl of Carrick, father of Robert Bruce.

To go through that door is to have a strange experience. You feel that you are in a ruin, magnificently preserved and roofed over from the rain, but still a ruin. You are, in fact, in the centre of the abbey church, with the two wall arcades of red sandstone (not visible from the exterior) striding along on either side. In between the pillars, and in a kind of clerestory above the arcade, are the eighteenth-century walls, plastered and cream-washed, and pierced by the round-headed windows which now look not a bit too small. The line between medieval and comparatively modern is sharp; the effect incongruous but not unpleasing. Whereas the abbey churches at Carlisle, Lanercost and St Bees have been altered and adapted with the years, Abbeytown seems, like Calder, to have remained in the Middle Ages, though protected from the weather of time by an eighteenth-century shell.

Holm Cultram was a Scottish abbey to begin with, founded in 1150 at the time when Cumberland was ceded to Scotland by King Stephen. Chroniclers say that the founder was Prince Henry, son of David, King of Scotland, but the English Alan, son of Waldeve, Lord of Allerdale, probably had quite as much to do with it. It was, at first, a daughter-house of the Cistercian monastery of Melrose, and the great medieval wizard, Michael Scott, buried at Melrose, is rumoured to have been at one time a monk there.

The abbey had extensive possessions in Scotland, both in Annandale and in Galloway, with others scattered throughout Cumberland, but it was primarily an abbey of the marshes. Holm Cultram, as the name implies, was then practically an island, hemmed in by tidal waters and approached by a narrow isthmus on which the abbey stood. This island was regarded as a kind of detached outpost of Allerdale Forest, so that the deer repeatedly made their way across the abbey lands, causing so much damage that in the reign of Edward I the monks appealed, unsuccessfully, to have the island deforested. Nor was this their only reason to grumble at the forest regulations, for every Friday the foresters had the right to claim dinner in the servants' hall of the abbey, and to take away one flagon of wine, two tallow candles, a bushel of oats for each horse and a loaf of black bread for each dog. Yet, as Henry II had given the monks pasturage for swine in the forest and had allowed them to take wood for building, they were probably none the worse off in the end.

But they were certainly worse off from the nearness of Scotland. No religious house in Cumberland, with the possible exception of Lanercost, suffered so much from Border raids. In 1216 the Scots pillaged the abbey in revenge for King John's invasion, stealing vestments, chalices, horses and cattle, and even stripping a monk who lay dying in the infirmary—the chronicles say that retribution overtook them on their return journey and that 2,000 of them were drowned in the Eden. In 1327 Robert Bruce laid waste the abbey, in spite of the fact that his father was buried there; in 1385 the monks paid 200 pounds to the Earl of Douglas as protection money against raids; and as late as 1527 they petitioned the English parliament to be relieved of taxes on account of their repeated losses through the Scots. Edward I, 'The Hammer of the Scots', more than once made Holm Cultram his headquarters, and he was probably on his way from there to Carlisle in 1307 when he was taken ill and died near Burgh-by-Sands. (The traditional place of his death is marked by a pillar set up in the early nineteenth century by the Earl of Lonsdale.)

Danger from the Scots has helped to shape the landscape almost as much as the tides and the weather. For this is pre-eminently the country of the pele towers, though peles are, of course, frequently to be found further south in the county. They were oblong or square buildings, with walls of five to ten feet thick, and a basement entered by a low doorway, gated and barred, from which a narrow staircase gave access to the upper storeys. A pele was regarded not so much as a small fortress, able to withstand a siege, but more as a place of temporary refuge, giving protection from a hit-and-run raiding party, and, above all, giving protection from fire.

Most of the peles were attached to the homes of the landowners, but along the Solway there are two fine examples of church towers which have been strengthened for defence. The first of these is at Newton Arlosh, about three miles north of Abbey Town.

As you approach the church from the road you see the west

tower and the south wall, looking much as they must have done when they were built in the early fourteenth century. The tower is massive, with walls four feet thick in parts, pierced only by slits for windows, and with no door at all on the outside—entrance was by an inner door at first-floor level. But when you go in the church you will have a surprise. For what from the outside looks like the south wall of the nave turns out to be the rear wall of a nineteenth-century chapel facing south to north—a mission-type of church, neat, prim, and three centuries removed from all thought of danger.

From Newton Arlosh it is easy to move north to Bowness-on-Solway, either approaching it directly from Kirkbride, or by Anthorne (where you look back across salt water to the Cumberland fells) and around the edge of the Cardurnock Peninsula. The latter has been taken over as a NATO radio station, under the jurisdiction of the GPO, and, though you are allowed to drive through, among the pylons and aerials, you are not allowed to get out of your car.

Most people, however, will come to Bowness from Carlisle, and this is what I, too, propose to do. Anyone who has accompanied me from Abbey Town and wants to keep to the route followed in this chapter, should take the road that winds between sandy-willowy hedges from Kirkbride to Moorhouse and joins the Carlisle-Bowness road at Kirkandrews-upon-Eden. Or, if he has more time to spare, he can scoop further inland, ferretting his way among the rabbit-warren of roads that lie in the 'V' between the Kirkbride-Carlisle and Wigton-Carlisle roads. This is a little plateau, mostly between the 100 and 200-foot contours. It is richly farmed, full of hamlets and patches of woodland, so that you seem to have got miles away from the fenland by the shore. In fact the level of the land has only to rise ten or twenty feet for you to be aware, immediately, of the change. The chief village is Great Orton, perched on a little hump, with its squat, homely church looking across a dip of country so unemphatic that it might almost be in Suffolk. The East Anglian comparison seems all the stronger because Orton is one of the few places where you can see examples of 'cruck' barns and cottages—buildings with 'cruck' or timber supports, and walls, often two feet thick, made of the local clay and known as 'clay dobbins'.

So on he fares, and to the border comes
Of Eden . . . .

Paradise Lost, Book IV

It was Satan who made the journey to that other Eden, but we, coming to our Eden in the neighbourhood of Kirkandrews, are also coming to a paradisal land. In whatever direction you leave Carlisle, except by the squalid, lorry-ridden road to Gretna, you quickly come into pleasant countryside, and the route along Eden-side gives the quickest and most pleasant escape of all. Perhaps it is because I live in one of the starker parts of Cumberland that I find the change so unexpected. The estuarine silt is spread over the ground, thick as butter on hot toast. There are meadows swilling over with grass and buttercups, hedges erupting into trees, huge piled-up skies and, in winter, the wrought-iron patterns of the willows against a sunset that begins soon after midday.

The prosperity of Eden-side, however, is comparatively recent, for before the eighteenth century the Border was too turbulent for agricultural enterprise. But after the union of the crowns things settled down, and eventually the Enclosure Acts of the second half of the century led to much draining, clearing, improvement and development of the rural estates. It is to the Enclosures that we owe both the orderliness of this landscape and its many handsome farm-houses, which are a continual delight to one who comes, as I do, from a district where farms are piled roughly together out of slates from the fellside or cobbles from the shore.

The *Official Guide to Cumberland*, published by the county council, includes, in some of its editions, an article by Arthur Millard illustrated by photographs of several fine farm-houses at Dalston, Burgh, East Curthwaite and Street near Wigton. But there is no need to go in search of these particular farms, for others are to be found almost everywhere between the fells and the Eden shore. They are four-square buildings, built of local sandstone or handmade bricks. Sometimes there are extended wings, but more often the façade is just a plain two-storey of three windows up and two down, one on either side of the front door. Usually that door has a semicircular fan-light, often a stone pediment with columns, sometimes a portico. Sometimes, too, you will find either a Venetian or a tall round-headed window at the side, running through the two storeys, to give light to the stairs. And almost always you will see that each corner of the house, whether of brick or of stone, is bound-in, as it were, with a bold pattern of 'in-and-out bands', sandstone quoins of about a foot thick, placed one on the other like children's bricks. Barns, haylofts, byres, stables and other outhouses are grouped round a large stackyard entered through an eliptically-headed archway, and if the stone is red sandstone, as it generally is, everything will be mossed and moulded and lichened to the compost colours of straw and decaying leaves. There are some larger eighteenth-century mansions in the district, too—one at Moorhouse and one on the main road right in the middle of Burgh—but it is the farms that really own the landscape.

When you approach Burgh*-by-Sands from Kirkandrews you wonder where the sands are, for the village has a rich, red, snugly-inland look. It takes its name from the *burgh* or fort on Hadrian's Wall, on the site of which it stands. Indeed, stones from the Wall went to the building of the church, which, appropriately, possesses one of the finest of all the fortified towers of Cumberland. As with its neighbour at Newton Arlosh, there is no doorway on the outside, while the door on the inside still has its massive iron gate, with slits above it so that the defenders could shoot into the nave if the raiders broke into the church.

Yet to me the outside is even more interesting for the graveyard holds the most entertaining collection of tombstones I have seen anywhere in Cumberland. They belong largely to the nineteenth century—Regency and mid-Victorian. The earlier ones, of around 1810, are restrained and even elegant, in so far as carving in this crumbly sandstone ever can be elegant. The decoration is mostly of the kind you see engraved in the books of that time—excellent lettering, set in raised ovals, with trails of formal leaves. The Victorian stones are heavier, often sentimental, always didactic—the huge draped urn, books piled one on another, all labelled 'The Bible', heavy laurel wreaths and a formal tudor rose. The same ideas and motifs are repeated over and over again, combined in different ways, making me wonder if there can have been a family of local stone-masons who worked in the district, perhaps

* Pronounced 'Bruff'

through several generations, changing slowly with the times. But whether or not this is the case, Burgh churchyard remains a remarkable display of the pop art of the past.

A little way beyond Burgh the road dips between trees; you cross a cattle grid and immediately find yourself not so much beside the Solway as actually on it. High tides wash over the road and black-and-white posts are planted there to measure the depth of the water. Acres of saltings lie to the right, pink with thrift in summer, and a muddy, oily green all the rest of the year. And across the water on the Dumfriesshire shore one huge leek of steam unfolds from what seems to be a single concrete stalk. This is the atomic station at Chapelcross, and it is only when you move further west that you see the stalk widen and split into four cooling-towers set one behind the other.

At Drumburgh, where the fortified farm-house at the side of the road is said to be the 'White Ladies' of *Redgauntlet*, you move out of sight of the sands for a little while. (It is worth while, incidentally, crossing the railway just before you reach Drumburgh in order to see the very companionable group of farms and houses at Easton.) But soon you come back to the Solway and find that it has now grown narrower. You are approaching Port Carlisle, and, in spring and summer, you will see the haaf-nets propped up at the side of the road. These nets are constructed on rectangular wooden frames divided in the middle, so that when the fishermen stand in the channel, facing the current, each net billows out behind him in two large pockets. The haaf-fishers work in groups at low tide, and the basic principle seems to me to be very similar to that of salmon-drawing on the Duddon.

Port Carlisle, like Silloth, was an attempt to make the Solway into one of the shipping centres of the North. It came before the more westerly town, however, being linked to Carlisle by canal as early as 1823. Ambitions then ran to an extension of the canal to Newcastle, but the new steam-engine soon put water-transport out of date, and railway lines were laid on the old, dried-up bed. Finally, the harbour silted up, and all that can now be seen of this once-hopeful mercantile adventure is a row of stiff-collared, clerklike houses, continually adding up the figures of an empty ledger.

Bowness, where the Eden Estuary opens out into the sea, is,

in fact, the only one of the Edenside villages that really seems to belong to the coast. It is built mostly of big sandstone blocks that look as if they had been found lying about the shore among the shingle. We are now at the very end of the Roman Wall, and, as at Burgh, stones from it were used in the masonry of the church, which houses a fine Norman font. The building has been much restored, but still retains enough of its Norman character to take its place as the last of the chain of medieval churches of the Greater Lakeland coast which began, in Chapter Seven, with St Patrick's of Heysham.

Beyond Bowness, on the way to Cardurnock, is what I consider the loveliest stretch of the Solway. The coastline slants a little to the south, so that the inland hills recede and Criffel swings into view with the winds blowing across from Galloway. The Solway is at its narrowest at this point and is fordable at very low tides. My god-daughter, then about 9, and her sister, who were spending a holiday at Bowness, went out for a paddle one day and returned casually saying that they had walked to Scotland. In the days before the war tramps used to walk to Scotland in another way, leaping from sleeper to sleeper of the old Solway Viaduct from Bowness to Annan. The viaduct was opened in 1870 to serve West Cumberland, and at one time the company had hopes of making it part of a new west-coast route from London to Scotland. But it was closed to traffic in 1921 and dismantled in 1934. Once, when I had my lunch at a very attractive guest house on this shore, I was served by a woman who, as a schoolgirl, had travelled over the viaduct every day to attend the Annan Academy.

CHAPTER TEN

CARLISLE AND INGLEWOOD

GREATER Lakeland ends at Carlisle, and though the city is the historical county town, it still seems to me to be almost outside Cumberland, the capital of a debatable land that stretches along the Solway and the Roman Wall and the Bewcastle Fells. This northern fling is beyond the scope of my book, though it contains some of the most attractive and least publicised landscapes in the county. The valley of the Irthing holds Lanercost Priory, the most romantically beautiful of all Cumberland's ruins, together with a fine stretch of the Roman Wall at Birdoswald, and, at Brampton, a town of most un-Cumbrian refinement with a Pre-Raphaelite church, built by the artistically-minded George Howard, ninth Earl of Carlisle, who lived nearby in the family fortress-home of Naworth. Unlike the earl, his wife Rosalind had little leaning towards art, yet she, too, made her mark on the district, devoting herself to Votes for Women, Home Rule for Ireland and Liberal politics in general—during elections she went about dressed entirely in blue, the Liberal colour in Cumberland*. But what perhaps mattered even more was the fact that she was a fanatical teetotaller. All the licensed houses on Howard estates were shut down, and, in 1883, over 1,300 of the inhabitants of Brampton were persuaded to take the pledge, and the Countess prophesied that even the main public house of the town (called, amusingly, 'The Howard Arms') would one day have to be closed for lack of custom. Later on, Lady Carlisle became President of the National British Women's Temperance Association and a passionate opponent of Lloyd George's wartime proposal to nationalise the drink trade, so it is ironical to find that Carlisle became the only city in Great Britain where the beer, the public houses, and all but one of the hotels are under state management.

* See *The Radical Countess* by her son-in-law, Charles Roberts. Steele Bros, (Carlisle, 1962)

Carlisle is one of the few places of importance in Greater Lakeland that still holds on to a mainly British name. The Romans called it Lugovalium after the Celtic sun god Lugus, and by the tenth century this element had been prefixed by the Welsh *caer*, a fortified place. The Romans had reached it in the first century, and, after the building of Hadrian's Wall, they made the city into one of the greatest military centres in Britain—the camp at Stanwix being, in fact, the largest along the entire frontier of the Roman Empire.

The original British *caer* probably stood on the knoll beside the Eden where William Rufus began the building of the castle in 1092. During the early twelfth century, Carlisle, like the rest of Cumberland, was ceded to Scotland, but after it was reclaimed for England in 1157, Edward I made it into a most formidable fortress, the king-pin of the defence of the Border.

As the reader may have guessed, I have no great love for castles. I have walked beside the courtyard at Naworth and heard a granddaughter of the Radical Countess tell me how, as children, she and her cousins used to hop along the walls of the battlements, never worrying about the dizzy drop beneath—and, except for regrets in the case of my kind and informative guide, I would not have worried if they had all fallen off.

Had I lived on the Border in the later Middle Ages I should, no doubt, have been grateful to the castles for protection against Scottish raids. But my ancestors came from the south of Greater Lakeland, well out of reach of the Scots, and if any of them ever entered a castle it would be as a servant to be ordered about or as a tenant to pay rent. Most of the larger castles, in fact, were built by an alien aristocracy to help them dominate the people and hold on to the land they had grabbed. So far as I am concerned, they look better in ruins.

The main gateway of Carlisle Castle is, nevertheless, a grimly imposing block. I passed through it once, at the age of about 10, and saw the dungeons and one cell where the walls were decorated with the figures of naked women with hugely exaggerated sexual organs—perhaps the work, as I learned later, of Major Macdonald (the Fergus McIvor of *Waverley*) who was imprisoned there after the Jacobite defeat in the 'Forty Five. That is all I can remember. But when I look at the brick parody of the fortress, built by the

Salvation Army not far from the main gate, I cannot help feeling that this is the more endearing and more lastingly useful structure.

I have no such sense of alienation when I turn to the other great medieval building of the city. To say that for an Anglican the cathedral of his diocese is his spiritual home probably sounds a bit too pious. Better say that he goes there like a child visiting the house of a well-to-do grandmother, feeling that he has his own small claim to the pictures and the china and even to the old-fashioned stuffiness of the place. That is how I feel about Carlisle Cathedral. So I will leave to others the job of recording and assessing the architecture, and will merely try to sketch down impressions gathered from a good many poppings-in, kneelings-down and walkings-round.

To begin with, Carlisle is one of our smaller cathedrals as it now stands. Once it was much larger. The original Norman nave alone was 140 feet in length, in eight bays, six of which were pulled down during the Siege of Carlisle (1644-5), the stones going to repair the defences of the city. The arches of the two remaining bays are buckled and bent, since there seems to have been some subsidence soon after building began, but they still give an idea of the dark, heavy, repetitive strength of the old nave—short, elephant-legs of pillars carrying a horizontal band of plain wall, with triforium arches and clerestory above.

This part of the nave is almost completely blocked off from the choir by the rood screen, and stands, now, as a kind of entrance hall, housing the Chapel of the Border Regiment, which had its headquarters in the castle—after the well-known practice of honouring the men of war in the temples of the Prince of Peace. When you pass through the screen you pass into another age. The choir aisles still belong, in part, to the earlier time, and are dark, cloistral, and at a lower level than the main choir. And, on the back of the choir stalls in the north aisle you can see a series of monastic paintings which illustrate, with the aid of rough rhymes, incidents from the lives of St Anthony of the Desert, St Augustine of Hippo and Northumbria's own St Cuthbert—an extremely interesting example of a medieval strip-cartoon, though Professor Pevsner* casually dismisses them as 'all of *c.*1500 and all bad'.

* In *The Buildings of England: Cumberland and Westmorland* (Penguin Books, 1967)

All this belongs to the past. But when you walk up the steps into the choir you see at once that Carlisle Cathedral is a living church which many people in the city regard as their parish church.

First of all you notice the colour. If it is morning, the sun may be pouring through the east window, a magnificent Decorated work, inspired by the great west window of York. The glass—some medieval in the upper tracery but Victorian below—has much blue in it, and there is a sky-blue roof with gold stars. Gold appears, also, on the reredos and canopy of the altar, set against the white stone of the pulpit, the khaki stone of the floor, and the lovely pink sandstone of the arcades. It is a swirl of colours with cross-beams of sunlight touching up the blue and the gold.

The eye is dazzled, almost hurt. But if you turn your back on the east, you will face the soothing shadows of the choir stalls—a doll's-house Gothic cathedral of soaring turrets, pinnacles, gables, steeples and crockets, all carved in the fifteenth century seemingly out of solid black liquorice. And, underneath, if you go along turning up the seats of the misericords, you will find the usual medieval wood-carver's menagerie of angels, men and monstrosities, some devout, some comic, and all as lively as Charlie Brown.

Seen from the outside, however, the cathedral may look rather disappointing. This is partly because, without its nave, the building is too hunched and bunched together, merely the head and shoulders of a church; and partly because the fifteenth-century crossing tower looks more like a Border keep than a work made to the glory of God. The present deanery, once the prior's lodge, is, in fact, built round a pele tower: i.e. the refuge tower of the old priory. On this deanery side the precincts do have much of the expected peace and propriety of a cathedral close, for as well as the deanery there is the sixteenth-century gatehouse, some Georgian houses for the resident canons, and the fratry, once the monks' refectory, now the cathedral library, with its beautiful undercroft, sometimes used for exhibitions.

But from the opposite side, from Castle Street the cathedral looks bare and exposed to the traffic, especially if you approach it from the north from whence the fine east end is not in view. It is true that Castle Street contains some good eighteenth-century houses—and so, too, does the parallel and quieter Abbey Street, which may also claim the handsome Tullie House, now part of the city museum and library. But Castle Street has been allowed to become knocked about and stained far more than it should have been. Carlisle has too little left of the eighteenth century to be ready to lose what it has: apart from the two streets mentioned, there is really just St Cuthbert's and a town hall which looks as if it belonged to a south-country butter-market rather than a Border garrison. In fact, take the long rectangle that lies between Castle Street and West Walls, extend it as far as the Castle itself, and you have fenced in practically all pre-1800 Carlisle—including the medieval tithe barn in Heads Lane, the much altered guildhall near the market-place, and what very little remains of the city walls. For Carlisle, in spite of the 2,000-year ring of history behind its name, is largely a nineteenth-century town. Not that it has forgotten its history. Instead, it proclaims at every corner that it is a Border city, a medieval city, a martial city, but most of the proclamations are in nineteenth-century Gothic.

It is best to arrive in Carlisle by rail, for it was as a railway centre that the city became famous in Victoria's reign. (It was in a railway hotel in Carlisle that the Eustace Diamonds were lost or not lost in Trollope's novel of the name.) The station, designed by William Tite, is as Tudor as Windsor Castle, with mullioned windows and a clock-tower, though, from the outside the effect is rather spoiled by its being overtopped by the buildings round about. Tens of thousands of starlings roost every night on its glass roof. Inside, the Border-castle game is played out to the last stone, from the great drive-in porch to the baronial hall of a dining-hall, with its vast fire-place and coat-of-arms, where, alas, you can no longer dine.

When you emerge from the station you come at once on Carlisle's most spectacular prop of Gothic scenery, the assize courts, designed in 1810 by Sir Robert Smirke, the architect of Lowther Castle, and built on the site of, and to some extent on the plan of, Henry VIII's sixteenth-century citadel. It takes the form of two enormous round towers, like the castles in a chess-set, with battlements on top, and archways on the pavements for pedestrians to walk through. That citadel must be an odd place to work in—one fancies that the tables are all oval, the desks curved and that the clerks all develop round shoulders. But it leaves you in no doubt that Carlisle thinks of itself essentially as a Border stronghold.

Three hundred years after the merger of the two crowns, the city still seems to be in an uneasy state of Border truce. It is the great check-point between the kingdoms, both by rail and by road. In summer, especially at weekends, if you try to sleep in a room overlooking the Botchergate-Lowther Street route of the A6, you are kept awake by the continual gear-changing of all-night lorries and motor-caravans, though this should ease off when the new motorway is completed from Shap to Gretna.

Away from the main traffic it is an unexpectedly quiet town. If you step into almost any of the side streets branching off Warwick Road, or east from Botchergate, you will find nineteenth-century terraces, not particularly stylish perhaps, but sedate, sound-looking, with Greek porches, often too big for the rest of the façade, and basements that can be made into surprisingly comfortable rooms. And nowhere in these streets do you feel boxed in, for you need walk only a hundred yards or so to find some place where you can look out into the wildness that encircles the city—from the railway viaduct to Back o' Skiddaw, and, elsewhere, to the Caldbeck or Bewcastle or Dumfriesshire hills.

Industrially, Carlisle has little in common with West Cumberland and has perhaps stronger links with Tyneside. Its industries—textiles, furnishing fabrics, clothing, biscuits, chocolates, metal boxes, and engineering—are, on the whole, not those of the Cumbrian mining belt. Some people envisage the Carlisle of the future as the administrative centre of a new industrial region, based on a Solway barrage, full of atomic-power-driven factories, and smokeless towns and sky-scraper blocks of flats. This may or may not come to pass: but whether or not, Carlisle is likely to go on being a busy, bustling, self-important, thriving place in which the Scots and the English mingle as perhaps nowhere else in either kingdom.

Typical of this mingling is Border Television, one of the smallest of the independent television companies, which serves a very large but sparsely-populated area stretching from Stranraer to Kendal and from Whitehaven to Berwick-on-Tweed. For the people of Carlisle city, Border TV offers a lively evening newspaper, on which, any day, they are almost certain to see someone they know personally or at least by sight—to go into an hotel with one of their more popular interviewers is to find yourself treated like royalty. From the organisers it demands, of course, continual tact in the balancing of Scottish and English interests. I was once caught up in this balancing act. It was at the time of the quatercentenary of Shakespeare's birth when Border Television decided to stage a tribute to the Bard from two locally-born poets. The Scottish representative was Hugh MacDiarmid, born at Langholm, just a few miles over the Border, and one of the finest poets writing today in any form of the English language; the English representative was only me. So the viewers had the experience of hearing the Scotsman declare that the English had never appreciated Shakespeare and never would, while the Englishman, overawed by the company in which he found himself, hardly dared to contradict!

The older part of Carlisle lies almost entirely on an all-but-island moated round by three rivers, the Eden and its two tributaries, the Caldew and the Petteril. Remember also that the Eden is joined only a few miles back by the Irthing, and you will realise that the city stands on a great plain of alluvium washed down from the Pennines, the Lake District and the Caldbeck Fells. It is a spacious and fertile landscape. The rivers are certainly not sluggish, but they are no longer mountain streams. Look at the Irthing at Newby, just before its confluence with the Eden. The bridge, rather like Twizel Bridge near Flodden, has a fine, high-leaping arch, and the river runs well below field-level, deep down in a trough, with no rocks or shallows, nothing to break the steady flow. The steep banks are of red sandstone soil, almost sand, in fact. In places they are quite bare; in others, muffled up in a woolly scarf of bushes and butterbur. If you gaze downstream in the evening, you see willows and alders beside the water, and larger trees around the meadows, a recession of twigs and branches under a sky borrowed from Lincolnshire. The villages, though now mostly commuter-owned, are rooted in prosperous furrows, and the farm-houses look as if they are not bothered about the rent. At Rickerby, just outside the city boundary, the country children attend school in a converted Georgian mansion, surrounded by enough stables and barns in make-believe Tudor Gothic to give them pleasant daytime nightmares of thumbscrew and stake.

Yet, in spite of the richness of its riverside environs, Carlisle, until the Reformation, was a city between two wildernesses: the Border on the north and the forest of Inglewood on the south. Inglewood is, of course, 'English wood', but that does not mean English in contradistinction to Scottish, but the wood of the Angles as against that of the Britons of Strathclyde or Cumbria. In fact, the name probably derived, in the first place, from the invasion and settlement of the Northumbrian English in the early seventh century. Yet pre-Anglian associations are particularly strong in this part of Cumberland. I have already mentioned the British *caer* in Carlisle. The British *cumba*, or its Welsh equivalent *cwm*, a valley, can be heard in the village-names of Cumrenton, Cumwhinton, Cumwhitton, Cumdivock and Cumrew, which sound like a line of Edward Thomas's, while Cummersdale records the Cymry who gave their name to Cumberland itself.

Carlisle also has its place in the legends of the British hero, King Arthur. It is true that Geoffrey of Monmouth does not mention the city, nor does Wace nor Layamon, but Chrétien de Troyes, writing in the twelfth century, puts Arthur's court there, probably dimly remembering the time when Cumbria was still ruled by British kings. And later on a whole group of Middle-English romances, many of them about Sir Gawain, are set in 'Merry Carlisle' and the forest of Inglewood.

Why Carlisle should be called 'merry' is hard to say. The Border, to the north, was a no man's land of war and pillage, while the forest laws, to the south, made Inglewood a far from jolly place to live in. The city stood, in fact, right on the boundary of the forest, which may be said to have lain, roughly, between the Eden and the Caldew, though it stretched further west as far as the present Carlisle-Thursby road. The southern boundary ran just below the Sebergham-Penrith road, reaching the River Eamont south of Penrith. Penrith, therefore, was within the forest, as were Dalston and Great Salkeld, while the name still persists at Hutton-in-the-Forest and at Heskett-in-the-Forest, or did until Heskett* dropped the 'forest' in 1934.

This, however, was by no means the full extent of Cumberland's forest area. To begin with, there was the smaller forest of Allerdale, stretching to the west of Inglewood as far as Wigton and the River Waver. Then Henry II afforested or 'put in regard' (i.e. subjected partially to forest laws) a vast new area: on the west, the whole of the land between the Derwent and the Solway, and on the east, the land from the Eden to Geltsdale and the slopes of the Pennines, making this one of the largest hunting forests in all England. Not all of this was woodland or heath. There were manors, cultivated land and privately-owned woods within the forest boundaries. Indeed, Inglewood as a whole was a well-managed royal estate, and the Crown collected a good revenue from grazing rights for cattle and pannage for swine, from fishing rights (especially in the ballad-sung Tarn Wadling) and from the sale of dead wood and of bark for tanning, though, significantly, no tanner was allowed to set up business within the forest.

Owners and tenants were subject to rigid restrictions. They were not allowed to put up adequate fences in case these trapped the deer, which therefore continually strayed on to farmland and damaged the crops. It was an offence, also, to fell a tree or cut down a bush which might give shelter to the game. No undergrowth could be cleared ('ridded' was the word often used, hence the number of farms called 'Riddings') nor could land be brought into cultivation without a licence. No one was allowed to set up a mill within the forest or even put up a hut or shed—such rulings will sound not unfamiliar to anyone living today within the boundaries of the National Park.

It was strictly illegal, of course, to kill a deer or a wild boar, though certain officers of the forest, such as the Foresters in Fee (an hereditary office usually held by members of the Boyvill family and the Huttons) were allowed to hunt lesser game, such as hare, fox, wild cat, pine marten, badger, otter, squirrel and wolf. Of the deer, all three, red, fallow and roe, were found in Inglewood, the red being the commonest and the roe, as in most

* Heskett is derived from Old Norse *hestr*, a stallion and *skeith*, a way or course, meaning racecourse

St James's, Great Ormside

(overleaf) *Temple Sowerby Manor, the gates and* (facing) *the nine-bay front*

northern forests, the scarcest. From accounts of kills, it would seem that the fallow kept to the north and the east of the area, preferring woods and undergrowth. Certainly, game was plentiful enough at the time of Inglewood's greatest fame, and there are accounts of some tremendous hunts. It is said that when Edward I visited the forest in the eighth year of his reign, he hunted for four days, and on the first day alone killed 400 harts and hinds. Even as late as the reign of Henry III, the Pipe Rolls show that 200 harts and 200 hinds were taken in two successive seasons.

Penalties for breaking the forest law were extremely severe, but F. H. M. Parker, the author of the comprehensive study* of Inglewood to which I owe much of this information, insists that they were not carried out nearly as vindictively as tradition and the ballads would make us believe. The deer-stealer, by the time of Edward I, was fined heavily, imprisoned for a year and a day if he failed to find surety for the money, and was liable to be banished at the end of that period. But, of course, the nobles and rich tenants readily paid up. Moreover, there was no social discredit attached to poaching. Charges of breaking forest law were made, not only against the nobility, but against the bishop, the prior of Wetheral, and several clergy, though the bishop and the prior may not have been personally responsible for the acts of their servants. In fact, poaching was so much taken for granted, that Adam Turp, lord of Edenhall, near Penrith, and a repeated offender, was later made into an official verdurer with the task of administering the law he used to break.

The laws pressed more heavily, however, on the common people. Henry II made it an offence even to be found carrying a bow and arrow within the forest, which meant that the poor man lost most of his chance of picking up a rabbit or a wild duck which was often the only fresh meat he enjoyed from one year's end to the other. The lawing of dogs—a cruel practice by which three toes were struck off the forefoot with an axe—was another particularly unpopular measure. Though the ballads may have exaggerated, there is no doubt that the forest laws gave rise to centuries of resentment and to a hatred of officialdom and outside interference which has not yet quite died out among the people

* Printed in Volumes 5, 6, 7, 9 and 10 of *The Transactions of the Cumberland and Westmorland Archological Society*, New Series

Millom Ironworks 1968

of rural Cumberland. I think I have inherited some of this myself, so that to me it seems quite understandable that the Cumbrian ballad-makers chose to celebrate, not the men who fought against the Scots, but the men who defied the laws of the forest:

Mery it was in the grene foreste
  Amonge the leves green,
Wheras men hunt east and west
  Wyth bowes and arrowes kene;

To raise the dere out of theyr denne;
  Suche sightes hath ofte bene sene;
As by thre yemen of the north countrey,
  By them it is I meane.

The one of them hight Adam Bell,
  The other Clym of the Clough,
The thyrd was Wyllyam of Cloudesley,
  An archer good ynough.

They were outlaw'd for venyson,
  These yemen everych-one;
They swore them brethren upon a day,
  To Englysshe-wood for to gone*.

The ballad goes on to tell how Wyllyam went to Carlisle to see his wife and was there captured and condemned to be hanged; and how Adam Bell and Clym of the Clough (or cliff) entered the city by a trick, rescued Wyllyam, and killed the Justice, the sheriff, and 300 men; and how they went to London to ask pardon of the king, before whom Wyllyam performed Robin Hood's feat of splitting a hazel rod with an arrow and William Tell's feat of shooting an apple off his son's head. And the ballad closes with sentiments not perhaps quite typical but well-suited to a forest where even a bishop might be a poacher:

Thus endeth the lyves of these good yemen;
  God send them eternall blysse:
And all, that with a hand-bowe shoteth:
  That of heven they may never mysse!

* *The Oxford Book of Ballads*, edited by Arthur Quiller-Couch (Oxford)

Of the three rivers which flow north to Carlisle, the Petteril is my favourite. This is partly because Wreay, on the Petteril, is one of those spots—like Cartmel, Little Langdale and St Bees—which the friendships of many years have made into a second home. But it is also because the Petteril is so comfortable and cosy, so pleasingly hedged-in like a Victorian rectory garden. The A6 and the Carlisle-to-London main line both run almost the whole length of the valley, but the road keeps to the ridge, and the railway, though one of the busiest in England, is surprisingly unobtrusive. The projected motorway will certainly be more obtrusive, but that, too, seems to be going to leave the valley-bottom little changed.

Road (not A6 but a minor one), railway and river, the railway always in the middle, keep fairly close company from Wreay, through Southwaite and Calthwaite, until the river turns west, by Newton Reigny, towards the limestone hills around Greystoke where it has its source. At Wreay*, the three through-routes of road, rail and river almost coincide, so that this seems a convenient point from which to view the valley, as well as being, for me, the most familiar. And when you start to take that view you find it hard to believe that the oak at Wragmire near Wetheral, reputed to be the last survivor of Inglewood, fell as long ago as 1823. For here you still seem to be in the forest. There are woods along the river-banks, pouring down the river-carved slopes in brown or green cataracts. The hedges are like Wordsworth's 'little lines of sportive wood run wild', and if you go up to the flat ridge that divides the valley from that of the Caldew, you will find large new enclosures and plantations of young trees. Even the long, straight parallel roads running along the ridge-land are, indirectly, a sign of the forest, for they mark the large-scale enclosure that took place, in this almost village-less countryside, in the centuries after it was deforested.

From Wreay Vicarage, the home of the friends to whom this book is dedicated, you look south into what must be about the snuggest valley in Cumberland. The village is built on a hill above a bend of the river (the *vra* of its name) so that, though you

* Pronounced in two syllables to rhyme with 'Leah', and derived from Old Norse *vra*, a nook or corner. There are a number of villages or farms in Cumberland called Wreay, together with one Wray (pronounced 'ray') at Drigg, several more in Westmorland, and Wray Castle on the Lancashire shore of Windermere

are looking up-dale, you still look downhill. The fields on the slope are of parkland, landscaped with trees, some of them fenced round with iron railings, and all of them, many a winter morning, fenced in with mist. When the old steam-trains ran past, out of sight in the cutting, the mist was thickened with smoke.

The hills on either side are not very high and barely earn a change of colour on a contour map, yet the valley is as private as an armpit, half hidden under the hairy tufts of woodland. The trains, which come into sight on a curve of the track some distance above the old station, skitter in and out like a mouse darting from its hole and back again. Above the eastern slopes of the valley Barrock Fell balances its sharp triangle, as individual as Great Gable, though it is less than 800 feet in height. Further away, at night, you can see the Aurora Borealis of headlights on A6, and, in daytime, the line of the Pennines as far as Cross Fell.

Except in its upper reaches, the Petteril flows, like the lower Eden, through sandstone and, again like the Eden, cuts its course several times through what I can best describe as a one-sided gorge. Take the gate by the bridge below the railway station, walk beside the river through one or two fields and past a farm, and you come to a sweep and tumble of riverside, a chasm every bit as romantic as the more celebrated National Trust woods near Wetheral Abbey, on the Eden. There is not a great deal of rock—at least, by Lake District standards—but the hillside rears up, steep as a haystack, with trees clinging to the soil for dear life. The river itself is half-choked with smooth sandstone boulders, of a rusty grey more often than red, and the banks are paved and kerbed with water-worn slabs, pock-marked with dubs and hollows, often holding a basin-full of water for the wagtails to drink from. Yellow hawkweeds, pink mountain willow herb, and Scotland's bluebells grow all around in little plantpots of soil, and, where the floods have washed away the clay, tree roots writhe out into the air and back to the bank again. If you continue along this way for about two miles, you can walk or scramble beneath hanging woods, until you come into more parklike country at the narrow bridge only a few hundred yards from the noise and rush of the A6 at 'The Golden Fleece'. And yet, on the whole journey, you may have heard nothing but birdsong and the sound of water.

Wreay itself is a village of a red-green sandstone, the colour of mouldy gooseberry jam. It is a place that puts on no airs and looks as indigenous as a sour-docken. It is also one of the few spots in Great Britain to retain its old village parliament, 'The Twelve Men of Wreay', who still meet every Candlemas to discuss village affairs. During these discussions each member was expected to smoke a churchwarden pipe, but, as these were broken and could not be replaced, the tradition was dropped for a few years until, in the spring of 1968, the vicar, who is chairman of the Twelve Men, was at last able to find a new stock.

Up to now, speculative builders and housing planners have let Wreay alone, so that you scarcely realise that it is only five miles from the centre of Carlisle. Recently, however, it has gained a new local fame from the publication of Professor Pevsner's book on the *Buildings of Cumberland and Westmorland*, in which the author devotes three pages to the village church as against, for instance, one and a half to St Bees Priory, one to Greystoke and Kirkby Stephen, and only half a page to the lovely Holy Trinity, Millom. For me, St Mary's, Wreay, has strong personal associations. The vicar is an old friend of mine, and the last service I attended there was the funeral of a dear god-daughter. Yet I cannot close my eyes to the fact that the church is a freak. Indeed, it is probably this very freakishness which intrigued Professor Pevsner, challenging him to turn architectural detective and try track down the many styles—Lombardic, Rhenish, Romanesque, Byzantine and Lord knows what else—that contributed to the design of this fascinating ecclesiastical 'folly'.

To begin with, it is the fancy of one woman, Sarah Losh of Woodside, daughter of the James Losh who was a lifelong friend and correspondent of Wordsworth. Miss Losh built the church between 1840 and 1842, using local craftsmen (including her own gardener, a remarkable wood-carver) who worked directly to her instructions. When you first see the church, half-hidden by trees, it looks dumpy and unexceptional. It is only when you come close that you notice the extraordinary character of its decoration. The west windows, for instance, have surrounds crawling with huge butterflies and beetles, separated from one another by flowers, leaves and ears of corn, while the gargoyles that bend down from the roof are in the form of snakes, crocodiles, tortoises and the like. Inside, the effect is even odder. The nave—I am tempted to call it the auditorium!—is plain, but the raised sanctuary looks for all the world like the setting of an Italian opera, with an apse, backstage, surrounded by an arcade of fourteen pillars, and tiny windows, filled with coloured glass, that heighten the theatrical effect. The altar, which looks more suited to a pagan temple than a Christian church, consists of a marble slab held up by two enormous brass eagles, which, together with another eagle and a pelican doing service as lecterns, and an owl and a cockerel on a bracket (birds of night and day), led the late Canon Aiden Hervey to call Wreay 'the ornithological church'.

Professor Pevsner sees in Sarah Losh an amateur architect of real originality who anticipated fashions which were not to appear in England until much later in the century. He also tells us that the church was built as a memorial to her younger sister, who died in 1835. But this is not the whole story. For Sarah Losh had been in love with a young man of the district, Major William Thain, who went with his regiment to India and was killed by a poisoned arrow on the Kyber Pass, and the church is really as much of a memorial to him as to Katherine Losh. The arrow became for Sarah a symbol of death, and iron arrows are built into the church door, and form the railings to the old St Ninian's Well, while one, which formerly held a lamp, is shot into the interior of the north wall as if the choirboys had been playing Robin Hood. Moreover, before he died Major Thain had sent his fiancée the cone of a pine tree, and the pine-cone was then for her the symbol of life after death, so there are stone pine-cones inside and outside the church, and in the mausoleum built for Katherine Losh in the churchyard there is a white marble statue of the girl, seated, holding a pine-cone in her hand—it is just possible to see this by peeping through the tiny window at the east end.

So the two memories are brought together again. But it is the memory of Major Thain, not that of Katherine, which explains why, among all the butterflies and roses*, Sarah Losh was haunted by strange tropical images—the crocodiles and snakes on the roof, and, above all, the otherwise preposterous palm tree that

* And also the alabaster candle-sticks in the shape of lotus-flowers. Professor Pevsner complains that these have been removed but they are, in fact, fully on view at the back of the sanctuary. They were quite out of place on the altar, of course

holds a light to the gnarled tree-trunk of the pulpit. Professor Pevsner does not mention the palm-tree nor the arrows nor Major Thain, feeling, perhaps, that a romantic story like this has no place in the criticism of architecture. But, without the romantic story, it is quite impossible to understand how Miss Losh's imagination was sparked off in such an odd way; without the story, the church just does not make sense.

When I think of the Cumberland Eden I feel not like Adam, looking back to his lost home, but like Satan, who was only an occasional visitor. I am, in fact, a stranger to Eden, and by strangers the lower river is most often seen from one of three bridges.

The first of these is in Carlisle itself, the fine early nineteenth-century bridge designed by the architect of the Citadel. Although this has become one of the focal points of the city, the buildings round about hold themselves respectfully back, leaving the river room to sweep in leisurely loops round peninsulas of parkland, an ordered, orderly *rus in urbe*—though perhaps not so orderly as all that, since the riverside cricket ground is one of the most frequently flooded of any in the North Lancashire and District League.

The second bridge is that which carries the main road at Warwick. The Eden, here, is a wide river, very much contained within itself and giving the impression of *passing through* the landscape like a water motorway, rather than of belonging to it. You get a better view if you walk along the footpath to St Leonard's, which has been described as 'the most memorable Norman village church in Cumberland'. On the day when I called, very early in the morning, it was not open, yet the description seemed justified by the apse at the east end, with its lovely pattern of pillars or pilasters and tiny round arches no wider than the pillars. (Incidentally, on your way to the church you pass the old Methodist chapel—a classical front that would have been a credit to any town. Today, the building is a joiner's and undertaker's workshop, with offices upstairs in the old gallery, and woodshavings piled on the floor where the pews used to be.) Go along the path beside the church-yard, and you reach a wood, hanging by its toe-nails to the over-river escarpment. Here the

Eden makes a large, right-angled bend, and you look first across it and then along it, as if you were looking from below the bottom stroke of a capital 'L'. And, right at the point of the angle is Warwick Hall, a handsome, Georgian-looking mansion of red andstone, sharing the same view from lower down.

And the third bridge is that of the Carlisle-Newcastle railway at Wetheral. Wetheral is a village, if you can call it a village, quite different from any other in Cumberland. It stands round an ample green, with scarcely a sign of anything so lower middle-class as a shop, but only the kind of houses you expect in the more opulent suburbs of an industrial town—large, yellow-brick, nineteenth-century villas, turretted, gabled and sometimes even towered. The church, built on the site of part of the old Benedictine priory, is noted for a memorial to Lady Maria Howard by the eighteenth-century sculptor, Joseph Nollekins, whose name makes it hard for one to take him very seriously*, or this memorial either, to judge from photographs. (There are, by the way, still quite a number of notable churches in Cumberland that I have not yet entered, for I do not believe in going on a systematic church-crawl, preferring to slip in when opportunity arises and the spirit impels. And, so far it has not impelled me into Holy Trinity, Wetheral, though I expect that one day it will.) As for the once extensive priory, all that now remains is the gatehouse, beyond which are the famous woods.

But to return to the bridge. The view, seen as you cross in the train, is so splendid that it would be well worth the five pounds to pull the communication cord for a longer look. However, this can be enjoyed more cheaply by taking the little footway, riveted like a balcony to the side of the railway bridge, and reached from the railway station, now closed down. This view is the most remarkable thing in Wetheral. You are perched, like a crane-driver, high above the water, looking straight upstream. The river curves gently to the right, its banks bolstered with trees. Closer, you see the red of water-carved sandstone, and, almost at your feet, old quarries, scooped back from the banks, with cottages fitted tightly into them like boxes pushed into a drawer. On the Great Corby

* Wordsworth, however, did, and wrote two sonnets about the memorial, the first of which begins:

> Stretched on the dying Mother's lap, lies dead
> Her new-born babe; dire ending of bright hope

side of the river, there are, in fact, a series of man-made caves which, according to tradition, were once the hermitage and refuge of St Constantine, an early Christian king of Scotland. There is evidence that they were in use at least as early as the fourteenth century.

And that is the last most people see of the Eden, at least until the Penrith-Alston road crosses it at Langwathby. For there is no main road down this Cumberland stretch of the valley and no town of any size. Compared to the lower Lune, the Eden is an unfrequented river. It differs also from the Lune in that, while Lonsdale is always and obviously a valley, at times a narrow one, Edendale spreads out so widely below Appleby that it hardly looks like a valley at all. On the east the Pennines stand rather aloof; on the west there is only the lowish swelling between Eden and Petteril, which, nevertheless, does open out quite often into grouse moors and upland plantations. What lies in between is not so much a valley as a wide, shallow indentation, along which the river casually pushes its way, without the trouble of cutting a course for itself.

That, at any rate, is what the valley looks like when seen from Hartside or Lazonby Fell. But the truth is that, for much of its course, the Eden is a surprisingly secluded river that buries itself out of sight, like a mole in an open field. Between Armathwaite and Kirkoswald, it is so muffled up in thick woods that it is completely hidden from the roads on either side of it, so that to follow it you have to leave the road and take to the track along the celebrated Nunnery Walks.

Now the whole two miles or so of this walk is too rough and too long for me, but luckily, it is quite possible for those who are short in wind or limb to get a most satisfying glimpse of the Eden woods—though without actually seeing the Eden—by stopping at Nunnery, two miles south of Armathwaite. The nunnery of today is an eighteenth-century mansion built on the site of the old Benedictine convent. You pay a toll at the gate, circumnavigate the gardens, and walk about a quarter of a mile across fields into a wood. Choose, if you can, dry weather in spring, for the path is slobbery after rain and in a ferment of flies in the heat of summer. The woods are less dark in spring, too, and the path is marked out and enlivened by many tufts and bunches of little white flowers, the common and the lesser stitchwort, and also the meadow saxifrage, which I have not, in fact, found very common in our parts.

You come now to Croglin Beck, a tributary of the Eden, flowing down from the Pennines. Here the beck, which has dropped 1,500 feet in five miles, has drilled into the rock like a brace and bit. There is a gorge quite unlike the splintery, boulder-cluttered gills of the Lake District—e.g. Aira Force, which is not very far away. Instead, the water has bored deeply and smoothly into the rock, making a chasm narrower at the top than the stream which has cut it. Further down, at water level, the rock is scooped back into caves and hollow basements, out of sight from above. The waterfalls—there are more than one—drop sheer, like water poured from a bucket, in the manner of the falls of the millstone grit. And the whole scene is scaffolded and girdered with trees—beech, oak and rowan. In spring, before the leaves are too thick, the varying greens glint and click together, and the light infiltrates right down to the lower dungeons of the chasm, flashing on water that continually turns over on itself.

We have penetrated, now, to the secret heart of the sandstone country, or, if that sounds too romantic, to its bowels, which, after all were once regarded as the seat of compassion. Let us be still less romantic and say that here we see the internal plumbing of the sandstone country—the water flushing and circulating; the rock scoured and swilled. Everything seems to be of the same element. The mud is sandstone watered down; the dead ferns are mud drawn out into a pattern. Much, too, is of the sandstone colour—not red, for there is not enough light to bring out the red, but rather a rich mouldy-brown, mossed over with green or lichened with grey. We have dug down to the growing root of the landscape.

Out in the sunlight again we can see what that root has produced. The Eden Valley lies like a long pavement of sandstone between two limestone escarpments, compared to which it seems rich, lush and ripely-coloured. The villages are all of a stone as warm as a tawny port: Armathwaite, homely and closely gathered about itself; Lazonby, with its upward-twisting main street and an unexpected blue-tiled swimming pool where the children swarm like tiddlers in the hot weather; and Kirkoswald, on

Croglin Beck, which Collingwood describes as 'a decayed market town'. What one feels about it, however, is not a sense of decay, but of a past dignified out of proportion to its present size. The church has a Norman nave, with the very short round pillars and low arches typical of the Eden Valley churches, and there is a bell-tower set up separately on a hill. St Peter's was a collegiate church, and the residence of the clergy, beautifully rebuilt in the seventeenth century, became the home first of the Dacres and then of the Festonaughs, who, from the monuments in the church, would seem to be the only people who ever lived in the village, or, at least, the only ones who ever died there.

But, perhaps what I remember best about Kirkoswald is the way the meadows wash right up to the walls which are built, most precisely, like the best drystone walls of the fells, with through-stones running the whole length of the wall like a shelf. Above Kirkoswald—or, rather, above Lazonby—the river is more open and, so far as I am concerned, more familiar. For Great Salkeld, the next village to the south, was the home of a greatly-valued friend, Canon Aiden Hervey, one of that line of parson-naturalists that springs from Gilbert White of Selbourne. Canon Hervey could direct you to within a yard or two of almost every rare flower in Cumberland and Westmorland. He took great amusement in the thought that his huge, rambling rectory was built round the remnants of a pele, and was proud of the fact that his parish church included one of the finest examples of a fortified tower in the Border counties. Moreover, only about a mile away from the rectory is Long Meg and her Daughters, another of the more remarkable 'places-of-worship' in the county, if, indeed, it *was* a place-of-worship. Long Meg is the largest of the three major stone circles of Cumberland, though its setting is one of less grandeur than either Castlerigg, near Keswick, or Swinside, near Broughton-in-Furness, while the trees planted inside it and the cart track lying across it seem to reduce it in size and mystery. To me, the most mysterious thing about it is the fact that—apart from Long Meg herself, an external, sandstone menhir—the stones are all of the volcanic rock of the fells, though they stand on sandstone ground with large outcrops of limestone on either side. Probably the explanation is merely that it was easier for the Neolithic people to collect and transport the glacial erratic boulders of the volcanics than to hew or dig out rocks of sandstone or limestone, even though these were nearer at hand. But may it not perhaps have been that the volcanic rocks seemed a more appropriate building material for the circle simply because they were part of the stuff of the hills?

(Long Meg, Castlerigg and Swinside—which Wordsworth, somewhat fancifully, called

. . . some famed temple where of yore
The Druids worshipped—

are all that now remains of what was once a large number of stone circles set up by the megalithic building people who came to Britain between 1800 and 1500 BC. There are records of five vanished circles in South Cumberland, of two more near Keswick, and of four or five in the north, including one called the Grey Yards, near Carlisle, which must have been the second largest in England. Presumably most of them were pulled down either to make way for the plough or to give building material for walls and barns. But for this Cumberland would now be one of the country's greatest centres of pre-historic interest.)

Long Meg is in Little Salkeld, next door, as it were, to Great Salkeld, but on the opposite side of the river. So that when Canon Hervey wanted to visit it, he had to go round by the bridge either at Lazonby or at Langwathby, 'the village by the long ford', travelling six to eight miles, to end up only a mile from home. Had he chosen to swim, he could have walked from the rectory gates and down a rough track until it peters out in meadows edging the river. This is the view of Eden that I most like to recall. There are flat fields, willow hedges along the lane, and yellow crosswort in the dyke bottoms—like the cowslip, this flower seems to thrive on sandstone almost as well as on limestone, but is rarely found on slate. On this side, the meadows ease off gradually, giving place to the water, but on the far side mud cliffs rise quite sharply, with the railway slicing in and out of them. When the engines shunt up and down they look like genial burrowing animals as much at home as a badger.

* *Prelude* (1850), Book II, lines 101–2. Ernest de Selincourt, in his notes on the *Prelude*, even more fancifully applied these lines to Conishead Priory near Ulverston

I cannot say much about the eastern strip of Inglewood. For one thing, it is scarcely in Greater Lakeland at all. For another, books must have their boundaries as well as regions, and for every further page that I now write, a page must be deleted from what I have already written.

I have spoken before of the many different routes that may be taken by a motorist driving south from Carlisle. And now I must find space to mention at least one other route, which, though it belongs to the Pennines rather than Lakeland, gives a most comprehensive and breathtaking view of Eden. From Carlisle you reach it through Wetheral, Cumwhitton and Cumrew—though this means that you will miss Geltsdale, Cumberland's one limestone dale, which looks as if it were a tributary of the upper Wharfe rather than of the Irthing. At Cumrew you strike the road which joins together the small fellside villages that lie along the 500-foot contour. They mostly stand beside becks, where the water has scooped out a small valley to give shelter—and shelter is much needed for we are approaching the district of the Helm Wind. The road is easy-going, unhurried, narrow, enclosed mostly by hedges that give way, higher up, to walls. You are, in fact, following the line that divides the sheep country from the semi-arable land below. On your right, as you go south, there is the wide, spreading trough of the Eden. On you left, are bumps and knotts and 'dodds' like Dufton Pike—steep-sloped, broken-off out-thrusts which catch the eye far more than the flat range of the Pennines proper.

You are in limestone country now, but the villages themselves are built entirely of standstone, and this contrast between the red of the buildings and the white of the rock becomes more and more noticeable as you move towards Westmorland, where the escarpments are sharper and the rock much readier to show its teeth. From Cumrew you pass through Croglin and Renwick, both typical fellside villages, the former mostly on a side road that worms its way up the gill made by Croglin Beck. Gamblesby has less of the remote fell look about it; Melmerby, once famous for its midsummer wrestling, lies a quarter of the way up the climb to Hartside. Skirwith and Milburn are villages more aware of the nearness of towns, though Milburn, in particular, is a good-looking, planned village, standing off-road, with eighteenth- and nineteenth-century houses placed deliberately round an angular village green. We have crossed into Westmorland by now, and those who have had enough of these fellside roads can go through Long Marton to Appleby. The rest should continue through Dufton—another village round a green, though this time the road bisects the green—to Murton, joining the A66 near Temple Sowerby.

All these are fell-flank villages, not dale villages. You have no sense at all of being in the Eden Valley, but only of hanging on at the highest practicable level of cultivable land. Hartside, however, is a different matter. Here you pass high above all cultivation. In fact, Hartside is higher than any pass in the Lake District. It is the highest classified road in England, and the one most frequently blocked by snow, yet crossing it can be a disappointing experience. Though you reach nearly 2,000 feet, the land around you never looks much more than undistinguished moorland such as might be found almost at sea-level. Of course, if the pass is clear of cloud, there are the distant views: on the west, the whole landscape dropping away from you, as if you were looking down from the moon, Eden rolled out underneath and Skiddaw erupting on the horizon; and on the east, a landscape of the moon itself, the strange, unearthly, dead, lead hills of Alston. Alston is the highest market town in England—the 1,000 foot contour runs right through it. It is still in Cumberland, but its river flows down to Newcastle, and from the speech of its people you can tell that they, too, belong to the Tyne. I have made Greater Lakeland stretch to include a very large area but I cannot stretch it to include Alston. I wish I could, for it is certainly one of the strangest towns, most unexpected, most disturbing to the imagination of any I have ever seen. Even Hammerfest, the most northerly town in the world, looks suburban beside Alston.

CHAPTER ELEVEN

EAST WESTMORLAND

WE have come at last to the outermost boundary of Greater Lakeland: or, rather, to no boundary at all. I have written in previous chapters of places that lie as far or even farther from the central dales—the Solway, for instance, or Furness, or the southern shores of Morecambe Bay. But if these do not belong to the Lakes they belong to nowhere else for beyond them there is only the sea. The Eden Valley, on the other hand, and the upper Lune, are as close, or closer, to the Pennines as to the Lakes. I enter them as a robin enters the neutral strip between its own territory and that of its neighbour: it may not be driven out, but neither will it be allowed to settle down and claim the site for its own.

So I will no longer go on showing the reader round as if I owned the place, but will be contented merely to recall some spots, some associations, some memories that make the Eden valley, if not home, yet at least a cousinly country.

I will begin with the greatest view East Westmorland has to offer—that of the escarpment of the Pennines, above the Eden, from Brough to Temple Sowerby. But I should not call it a view. The term is too static, too detached, too photographic. It puts one outside the picture from the start. And I cannot look at the Westmorland Pennines in this detached way, for I have stayed many times in the home of a friend, just west of Brough, and have felt those same Pennines move up close until they become part of the hour-to-hour environment of the changing day. The cottage stands in an old garden, overloaded with gooseberry bushes, that juts out into a field only one hundred yards from A66, the main road from Yorkshire to Carlisle. Cows come up and scratch themselves on the barbed-wire of the fence, and the roofs of delivery vans seem to slide along the top of the high field hedge. But for the latter, you would not know a road was there. Beyond it the fells rise up quite steeply—not the highest fells of the

Westmorland-North Riding border, for you are too close to see them from here, but the outriders, running parallel with the main range: Middle Fell, Long Fell and Roman Fell. They are all high hog-backs, flattish and long-drawn-out, standing separate one from another as if they were not on speaking terms. Further down the valley, not quite visible from here, the more conical Murton Pike blocks off all sight of the gill that leads to the, to me, inaccessible corrie of High Cup Nick.

On the lower slopes, especially of Middle Fell, there is a good deal of scrubby wood, but the hogbacks are bare, and, when the full light falls on them, may seem bald and featureless. It is different at sunrise. Then, when the light begins to squirm over the tops and through gaps and gullies, it catches, not the main outline of the fell, but the protruding limestone ridges that lie along the curve of the contour. One moment, the fellside is in complete shadow; the next, the sun has run a yellow pencil along the full length of it, perhaps a third of the way down from the top. Then the tips of the trees in the woods, lower down, catch the light, till the whole slope is striped with horizontal lines before the full sun pours down like a waterfall. In autumn, the woods are fuzzy and ginger, whiskering up the jowls of the grey rock; in spring, woods and rock are equally grey, except where the larches spurt into green. This is the landscape that for years compelled the imagination of W. H. Auden:

> The limestone moors that stretch from Brough
> To Hexham and the Roman Wall,
> There is my symbol of us all.*

And he goes on in a long geological metaphor, to equate the Pennine escarpment with original sin, which is not so surprising since Eden, after all, was the place of the Fall.

When I remember the Lake District, I think, first of all, of the dales; of the Lake coast, I think of the headlands; of Morecambe Bay, of the estuaries. But in the case of the Eden valley, I think first of the towns and villages. For this is a landscape which does not easily subdivide, as that of the Lakes does, into smaller memorable features that can be recorded each in a separate snap-

* W. H. Auden: New Year Letter. Faber & Faber, 1941

shot—a lake, a tarn, a crag. If you think of it at all you've got to think of the lot.

Appleby is both the capital of Eden and the capital of Westmorland, though Penrith is the largest town of the one while Kendal is the administrative centre of the other. Yet Penrith* is not in the Eden valley at all. Neither is it in the valley of the Petteril, though it lies on the line of road and railway that leads from that river. In fact, it is very hard to know where to put it. It stands within the boundary of the old Inglewood, yet it has little of the character of the forest. It is now a popular tourist centre for the Lakes, yet with its solid sandstone streets it is totally different from any of the towns of the central fells. It lies, moreover, in Cumberland, and here am I dealing with it in the chapter on Westmorland!

It is this very ambiguity which is, for me, the main characteristic of Penrith. After visiting it many times, I still can't make up my mind about it; I don't quite know where it belongs. My strongest impression comes, not from my own but from another man's experience: it was the town where Wordsworth was unhappy. And it was on Penrith Beacon that he found what he thought were the initials of a murderer carved on the turf close to the spot where the body had hung in chains. Wordsworth was mistaken: the initials, 'T.P.M.', were those of the victim: 'Thomas Parker murdered'. The name of the murderer was, in fact, Thomas Nicholson (he had been hanged at Carlisle before the corpse was suspended on the Beacon), and I am proud to think that a Nicholson, and quite possibly a distant relative of mine, may have helped to inspire one of the finest passages of *The Prelude*†. The town itself is as well-made as a piece of eighteenth-century farm-house furniture. It has some fine Georgian houses and probably the best Georgian church in the county. For years it has been raked from end to end by the conveyor-belt of A6, but this should lessen now that the new by-pass has come into use. The price of this diversion, however, was such shovelling and bull-dozing that the land near Eamont Bridge came to resemble the site of the Battle of the Somme, while the once-pleasant road through the limestone country

* Accent on the first syllable
† Book XII, lines 225-47

round Penruddock looks as if it, too, is going to be 'improved' into a mass-produced, grass-verged, concrete-kerbed, semi-suburban carriage-way.

Yet I have one memory of Penrith which even Wordsworth might have envied. On Palm Sunday, April 1966, I was engaged to read my poetry at the Newton Rigg Farm College beside the Penrith-Wigton road. The day before there had been, unseasonably, a snowstorm. Sunday, however, was a day of cloudless skies—the air still freezing but the sun as warm as in June. I was driven over Kirkstone Pass, between high barricades of snow, down the length of Ullswater to Penrith. Everywhere the snow was unscratched, unblotted, like a clean sheet of paper. Once or twice in every winter you can expect to see the fells snow-covered from base to cairn under a bright winter sky, but not more than twice in a lifetime under such a flood-light of April sun. The dazzling contradiction of two seasons made the whole landscape look artificial. Around Penrith the red sandstone barns and farms were plopped out on the fields like red glacé cherries decorating a white-iced cake. My face grew damp with sweat from the heat of the sun on the windscreen, yet outside not a drop of thaw could be seen on wall or twig or grass-blade.

And now, having done my dubious duty to Penrith, let me return to Appleby.

The first thing to be said is that there is nothing at all ambiguous about it. It so obviously belongs just where it is: a sandstone town in sandstone country, built round a castle set on a hill in a crook of the river. There was a keep at Appleby as early as 1174, when it is said to have been besieged by William the Lion of Scotland. King John, in 1203, granted the estate to the family of Veteripont or Vipont, and by the late thirteenth century it had passed into the hands of the Cliffords, one of whom was 'The Shepherd Lord' whose adventures were turned by Wordsworth into 'The Song at the Feast of Brougham Castle'. Then, in the seventeenth century, it came to the last of the Cliffords, the Lady Anne, who, in both stone and story, left more to be remembered by than any other woman of Westmorland.

Yet it was only after years of waiting and legal wrangling that Anne Clifford came to her own. Her father, the third Earl of Cumberland, who died when she was 16, had quarrelled with her mother, and, as an act of spite, disinherited his daughter. King James upheld the will, and it was not until the last of the male line of the Cliffords died, in 1643, that Lady Anne came into the Clifford estates. By this time she was 53 and was the Countess of Pembroke by her second marriage, having already been the Countess of Dorset by her first. She quarrelled with both husbands, and, having left the second one, travelled north in 1649 to her great inheritance. In Yorkshire she had two castles: Skipton, where she was born, and Bardon Tower in Wharfedale. In Westmorland, she owned castles at Appleby, which she chose for her main home, at Brougham near Penrith, at Brough-under-Stainmore, and at the remote Pendragon, in the valley of the upper Eden, which looks as if it cannot have been inhabited since the time of King Arthur let alone that of Lady Anne. All these she repaired or rebuilt and made each her place of residence from time to time, though Appleby and Skipton remained her favourites. She was almost equally conscientious about the rebuilding of churches. As well as restoring the parish church at Skipton, she largely rebuilt the older of the two churches at Appleby, St Michael's, Bongate, and repaired the parish church, St Lawrence's, where she erected an alabaster memorial for her mother and prepared a sombre, much-escutcheoned tomb for herself. She repaired the church at Mallerstang, and completely rebuilt both the chapel at Brougham (it was altered and refurnished in the mid-nineteenth century by Lord Brougham) and the isolated church of St Ninian, known as Ninekirks, on the banks of the Eamont, which, I am told, remains almost exactly as the countess left it—perhaps the most interesting seventeenth-century church interior to be found in the two north-western counties.

Lady Anne's biographers* tell how she regularly received the sacrament in all her churches, how she set up a pillar on the Brougham road at the point where she last saw her mother, and how she built and endowed St Anne's Hospital for the old women of Appleby. Piety, daughterly affection, charitableness—these are the virtues we are asked to admire. And, no doubt, they were

* George Watson, *Anne Clifford* (Penrith, 1901)
George C. Williamson, *Lady Anne Clifford* (Kendal, 1922)
C. M. L. Bouch, *The Lady Anne* (Penrith, 1954)

admirable. Yet George Watson, one of the earlier, though not the earliest, of her biographers, adds ominously: 'It is somewhat singular that a woman so high-minded, religious, and discerning should have made two such unhappy marriages.' It does not seem so singular to me. For, even allowing for the fact that her two choices were pretty bad ones, she can never have been a comfortable woman to live with. She was 13 when she watched the funeral of Queen Elizabeth, and she lived right through the reigns of James I and Charles I, and the Commonwealth, until well after the Restoration. By her second marriage she was related both to Sir Philip Sidney and to George Herbert, but poetry does not seem to have been one of her interests. In spite of her loyalty to the Church of England, there seems to have been something of the puritan about her, in temperament if not in politics. There is a seventeenth-century cross at the head of Boroughgate, just outside the walls of the castle, with the inscription: 'Retain your loyalty Preserve your rights.' Lady Anne would have approved, but the rights would most certainly been *her* rights.

When she looked down Boroughgate from the top of the castle hill, she could have seen a good deal of what we see today—the low, almost apologetic, alms-houses with their equally demure courtyard, the sixteenth-century Moot Hall, parked, thoughtfully, at the side of the street, the early seventeenth-century house which is now a chemist's shop, and the rather sprawling church of St Lawrence. She would not, however, have seen the fine Georgian houses which have been built since her time, or the Gothic-revival, cloister-like screen which divides the churchyard from the street, or the little market-hall, or the agreeably-Victorian 'Tufton Arms', named after one of the families connected with the Cliffords, where not even the garaged cars of the hotel residents can dispel the Dickensian charm of the old stable-yard. Boroughgate was originally laid out around the beginning of the twelfth century to be the New Town of Appleby, the Old Town having been centred on Bongate, behind the castle and on the other side of the river. From then to now the street has kept on growing and renewing itself, and signs of most of the intervening centuries can be seen somewhere along it. From the top, by the 'Preserve-your-Rights' column, where the street is at its widest, bordered by grass and trees, it drops like a water-chute right into the narrower canal of the lower street, with the cloisters to stop it from sweeping into the church. Look up, from the eighteenth-century cross at the bottom of the hill, and you will see a totally different view—a steep-sided funnel lifted upwards to trees and the sky, and the castle seeming almost to be above that. Seen from either end, it is surely the most beautiful street in Greater Lakeland.

When I think of the Westmorland Eden, three villages come immediately into my mind, each distinguished by its church, and each standing on one of the two main arteries of the Eden Valley, the river or the Carlisle-Settle railway. Great Ormside stands on both. It is only a few miles from Appleby and not hard to get to, yet it seems more remote than many of the fellside farms. You approach it by a road that burrows under the railway and seems about to give up the ghost at every turn. You can't quite call it a road to nowhere for you doubt if it will get you even there. Finally it peters out at the gates of the fourteenth-, fifteenth-, seventeenth-, eighteenth-century Ormside* Hall, now a farmhouse.

In Westmorland they are fond of calling pairs of villages by the same name—Great Asby and Little Asby; Kings Meaburn and Maulds Meaburn, Crosby Ravensworth and Crosby Garrett. But of all the 'greats', Great Ormside is surely the littlest! The church gates are opposite the farm gates, but the church itself stands high above on Orm's hill. The tower, of the thirteenth century, massive as a quarry-wall, doorless and almost windowless, was surely intended for defence against the Scots, like that at St Cuthbert's, Great Salkeld, lower down the valley. It looks even more like a fortress when you catch sight of the Eden flowing as if in a moat at the foot of the hill. Inside, the nave has an arcade carried on characteristic, short, bulky, Norman pillars. The chancel, partly rebuilt in the seventeenth century, has a fine example of a leper's squint and is, on the whole, not unpleasing, though, when I saw it, the walls were coloured in a rather repellent shade of yellow.

Crosby Garratt is another out-of-the-way village almost in-

* Orm's Hill or headland, from a Scandinavian personal name and Old English *heafod*, a headland

visible from any direction, hidden in deep folds of the hills like a flea in a pleat. As with Great Ormside, the church is built on a hill—so steep a hill, in fact, that you wonder how they manage to carry a coffin up the path. Unlike Ormside, however, Crosby Garrett has no river, though for consolation you can look across to the soaring arches of the railway viaduct, and survey the whole village as from a watch-tower.

Inside, the nave has a Norman arcade of three bays on the now-familiar, very short, round pillars, this time with finely-carved capitals. The arches are so low, the pillars so thick, that you feel as if you were in a crypt, as if this arcade held up the weight of tons and tons of masonry. The chancel arch is pointed, but again so low, so wide-straddled, that it almost cuts off the chancel altogether. Go through it, however, and you will soon realise that this lovely church is all of a piece. The mere difference of a couple of centuries has brought no incompatibility between chancel and nave. Indeed, the former round arch, signs of which can be seen quite clearly in the east side of the wall above the chancel arch, is older, even, than the nave and is thought to be Anglo-Saxon. There are few churches in the Carlisle diocese where the past presses more heavily on you than in this rough-walled, almost intimidatingly silent chancel—especially if you stand with your back to the more recent east window.

My third church is credited with little more than a mention by either Pevsner or the Royal Commission's *Inventory of the Historical Monuments in Westmorland*. Yet St Theobald's, Great Musgrave, has quite a bit in common with the churches of Great Ormside and Crosby Garrett. To begin with, it is near the Eden. You leave the road and walk down an unmetalled track and through an avenue of trees to the churchyard, right on the banks of the river. It is near the railway, too. Road and railway each cross the river on bridges near the gate to the avenue, though the railway is the old, disused track from Penrith, over Stainmore, to Barnard Castle. Again, Musgrave has its hill, but St Theobald's, for some odd reason, is not at the top but at the bottom. The graves on the higher side of the churchyard are on a level with the church roof, and an old farm, now used as a barn, overlooks the church bells. Two churches have already slid into the river, and there doesn't seem much to keep the present St Theobald's out—though the Eden looks as placid as a Midland stream, with lumpy mud banks, valanced over with trees.

The church itself is of the mid-nineteenth century but, in spite of the pointed windows, it manages to look almost Georgian. The most remarkable thing about it, however, is its thinness, as if it had been slimming. Its west tower is so emaciated that there is barely room at the bottom to let a door in to give access to the church. The interior is plain, neat, non-conformist-looking, except for the odd pointed arches. Not a church to which many will come either as visitors or worshippers, yet one which fits unobtrusively and even attractively into a setting as primly paradisal as any on Eden.

I have time now only for a glance at some of the other villages of this part of Westmorland—at those of the valley of the Lyvennet* for instance, perhaps the least hurried stream in the fell-country, which rises about two miles north of Orton and flows past Crosby Ravensworth, Maulds Meaburn and Kings Meaburn, to join the Eden near Temple Sowerby station. Crosby Ravensworth is like a village out of Trollope, with a hall and a large, spiky, much-gabled church, approached by a little bridge, possibly dating back to monastic days, over the shallow, yet quietly-lively beck. Maulds Meaburn is really Maud's Meaburn, both in local pronunciation and in historical fact, since, round about 1174, William de Veteripont gave the estate to his wife, Maud. 'Meaburn' is, of course, 'meadow stream', which still accurately describes the site of the village, round a green or common, on either side of the Lyvennet, which is crossed here by road-bridges and foot-bridges and one set of stepping-stones. Maulds Meaburn is so handsome in the picture-calendar style, so much a townsman's dream of a village, that it scarcely looks real to one used to the cheerful higgledy-piggledy of the fell communities. And just outside it is the skilfully-renovated Tudor mansion of Meaburn Hall, the ancestral home of the Lowther family.

On Temple Sowerby, however, I must throw more than a glance. Not on the village, though this is pretty enough in spite of being so close to A66 that it looks like an elaborate service

* Pronounced with the first syllable long as in 'life'. The name is probably of British origin, and may mean 'slippery root or elm'

station, but on Temple Sowerby Manor, also called Acorn Bank, which stands about three-quarters of a mile from the village.

The last private owner of this house was Mrs McGriggor Phillips, better known as Dorothy Una Ratcliffe, the Yorkshire dialect poet and travel writer, who, in the early 'fifties, handed it over to the National Trust with an endowment for its upkeep. Just before she left Temple Sowerby—she was living, at the time, in a caravan in the grounds!—she invited me over to see the house, but I was ill and had to cancel my visit. I did not greatly worry, however, as I knew that it was going into the hands of the National Trust and presumed that it would be accessible to the public. I was most surprised, therefore, when at last I was able to go there (not until 1967) to find that only the gardens were open to the public, and those merely on one afternoon a week. I make no complaint whatever about the present tenant, who, though I had not arrived on the permitted afternoon, courteously invited me to look round the garden and showed me part of the house. But this seems an odd way for the National Trust to arrange for the care of property which, after all, has been given to the nation.

And it is certainly something for the nation to be proud of. Indeed, in its setting, Temple Sowerby Manor is, for me, the loveliest house in Westmorland. Part of it is Elizabethan, and a good deal belongs to the seventeenth century. There are two wings, each with a staircase, one of the seventeenth and one of the eighteenth century, both leading up to a Venetian window. But this is all mere archaeological detail. What matters far more is the assured elegance of the south front, of three storeys and nine bays, all built of a sandstone so carefully and precisely laid that, at a distance, it looks like mellow Georgian brick. Perhaps the National Trust have been more cunning than I thought; perhaps they wanted to make us look at the house at a distance. Certainly, with its wide meadows that sweep right up to the forecourt, with its backing and side-screen of trees, and with the half-withdrawn authority of Cross Fell behind it, Temple Sowerby makes the Pennines look as suave and idealised as a Gainsborough landscape.

The one town of the upper Eden is Kirkby Stephen. When I arrive there I know that I have left Lakeland behind. It is Wild Boar Fell that dominates the skyline now. The Eden Valley still continues above Kirkby, under Mallerstang Edge, but it is now essentially a Pennine dale, even, in appearance, a Yorkshire dale, with the road on its way to Wensleydale or, forking left at Nateby, to Swaledale.

Yet I feel very much at home in Kirkby Stephen. Eric Nixon, a good and underrated poet who was born in the town, told me that it bears the same relationship to the Lakes on the east as Millom does on the west, and when, eventually, I came to the town, I saw what he meant. At a first glance Kirkby is a typical market-town of the northern hill-lands. It has a fine sandstone church with an early sixteenth-century tower, and the churchyard, like that at Appleby, has a screen of imitation cloisters, this time in a classical style. But Kirkby Stephen, as we see it, is really a product of the Industrial Revolution, for it grew rapidly in the last century when the limestone of the district was in demand for building material. The stone is everywhere to be seen—not only in the houses, but in the beautifully-made field walls, often with two lines of through-stones, as along the road over Ash Fell to Newbiggin and Tebay. Today many of the quarries are closed down, and Kirkby looks, at times, rather like a town which has lost its purpose in life. It still has its market, of course, and serves the farmers of Upper Eden. And it has some trade as a tourist town—in fact, being almost exactly at the half-way point on the route from Durham and the North East to Blackpool, the main street has become a popular stopping spot for cars and coaches. But this is not enough to support the population that once thrived on the quarries, and Kirkby, for all the breath-taking beauty of its setting, has something of the look of an industrial has-been, losing its young people, and finding it hard to attract new employment to a town where the railway station is a mile and a half away, and on a line which seems likely to be closed down.

Of Brough* there is much that could be said. It is one of the great entrance gates into Greater Lakeland, and has been used from at least the time of the Romans. Stainmore, to which it leads, is without doubt the dullest of all crossings of the Pennines, but is also one of those most frequently snowed up. Over and over again the houses and even the schools are packed with lorry-

* Pronounced 'Bruff' like Burgh-by-Sands

drivers and motorists who have had to abandon their vehicles. A friend of mine, who came to the area as Medical Officer of Health, found that her first job was to organise relief to the travellers in a train snowed-up in Mallerstang. And, in the winter of 1964, the main road at Brough was so completely blocked, from bedroom window to bedroom window, that a tunnel was driven through the snow and the traffic moved under it.

Brough has its Roman fort, its castle, its church, but I want to take leave of it with an anecdote which shows that, though it is probably the most distant from my home of any place dealt with in this book, it still belongs to the unity of Greater Lakeland. In the autumn of 1965, on our way back from Durham, my wife and I visited the church. It was round about the time of harvest festival and there was a huge bowl of michaelmas daisies near the altar, and, flitting among the flowers, obviously frightened and distressed, was a blue-tit. We opened the church door to let the bird escape, but, though it flew towards the opening, it swooped upwards each time it came near us and was lost again among the rafters. We soon realised that the only way to persuade the bird to escape was to go away, leaving the door open, so that it could fly out in its own time. We decided, however, that we ought to tell the vicar about the open door, so we went down to the vicarage, which lies in a kind of moat, well below the level of the church. We rang the bell. The vicar answered the door and my wife began to explain our visit. But soon I realised that the vicar was not listening to her but pointing with his finger at me. 'Norman Nicholson!', he said. I looked up. He was, in fact, a Millom man, who, thirty years earlier, as a journalist on the local paper, had poked quiet fun at my first appearance in print.

When I enter the country of the Westmorland Lune, I feel that I am trespassing. The Lune may form one of the outer boundaries of Greater Lakeland, but Lonsdale does not really belong to the Lakes, and I shall not allow myself to go much beyond the line of the Kendal-Kirkby Stephen main road.

To the west of that line, especially in the Orton area, the landscape is typical of the outer edges of the Lakes. If you come by road from Appleby, you leap quite suddenly out of the sandstone of Eden-side, into limestone moors that would not seem out of place beside Morecambe Bay. Orton Fell, for instance, though in places a good deal of stone has been removed to make rock-gardens, has the kind of limestone pavement that can be seen on Farleton Fell in lower Kent-dale, or on Birkrigg near Ulverston. And Orton village could be set down beside Beetham without seeming obtrusive.

To me, however, the greatest delight of coming to the Orton area is finding myself once again among the flowers of the limestone. I speak not of rare species, interesting primarily to the botanist, but of the obvious, showy, abundant flowers which dress up this landscape for anyone who has eyes at all. First, there are those which one has already seen in the limestone of southern Westmorland—huge masses of meadow cranesbill and the large scabious. Then, in the hedges around Brough, you can see marjoram and the giant bell-flower; and in those west of Appleby, the white flowers or the red berries of the wayfaring tree; while the purple chimneysweep's brushes of the greater knapweed grow actually on the grass verges of A66.

But for me one flower above all typifies the Orton limestone: the bird's-eye or mealy primrose (*Primula farinosa*), a flower not so rare that I dare not mention where it grows, yet one that few people will see in the whole course of their lives. It is a flower specially associated with Teesdale, but it also grows in places to the west of the Pennines, and, in particular, around Sunbiggin Tarn which can be reached by car from Orton, or from Newbiggin-on-Lune. The tarn itself is quite unlike the tarns of the Lakes. It is a shallow pool, sunken into peat, half filled-up with reeds, and surrounded by an enormous waste of dreary, anonymous moorland. But close to the tarn, and all along the sides of the road from Raisbeck, there is, in June or July, a faint fume of colour, like a pink-mauve ground-mist among the sundew, the tormentil, the stone bedstraw and the heathers. The flowering time is short and varies from year to year, and you are lucky if you have, as I have, a friend who will drop a postcard telling you when the flower is out. Gardeners may perhaps not be over-excited about it, finding it only a smaller version of the primula they grow in pots or in the herbaceous border. But to me, the small but very lovely blooms evoke curlew-cry and plover-creak and the loneliness of those in-between lands that are neither mountain nor valley. And, even if the flower is not in bloom, there is still the pleasure of discovering Sunbiggin itself.

When you reach Tebay you are back on Lake District slate again, after having travelled almost the whole length of the Eden, from Carlisle to Appleby or even Kirkby Stephen, on sandstone or limestone. Tebay is on the Lune, and the river here cuts deeply into the Silurian slate which lunges east from Windermere as far as the Howgills in Yorkshire. At this point, it is a very dark rock, almost black, and sometimes dusted with bronze metallic grains. Tebay was once an important railway junction and depot—travelling home to Millom, from my uncle's in County Durham, I changed trains at Durham City, Barnard Castle, Tebay, Oxenholme, Carnforth and Barrow. Until recently most of the inhabitants of the village depended on the railway for their work and lived in railway houses. But the line to Barnard Castle was closed long ago, and Tebay, like Shap, is soon to cease to be a passenger stop, so that today the chief occupation seems to be that of watching the fishermen trying to hoist salmon out of a river that is itself as slippery as a fish.

For Tebay is at the head of the Lune Gorge—not a gorge, really, but a glaciated trough through which the Lune flows from the spreading country north of Tebay to the widening valley south of Sedbergh. The river leaves the road at Low Borrow Bridge and continues in comparative solitude, towards Lowgill and Firbank. The road, for its part, climbs up the fellside, towards Greyrigg and Kendal, slowly angling away from and above the river, till the vast bulk of Langdale Fell* looms up, its almost completely bare sides scooped and hollowed with gills, corries and empty valleys looking less like a landscape than a blown-up papier-maché model of a landscape! Down in the rut is the river with sometimes a goods train (we would call it a *luggage* train!) chugging aimiably along. This is one of the great views of the Lune, or was until about a year ago. Now the bull-dozers are slicing it up to make the motorway as an alternative route to Shap. Thank God I knew it before that happened.

The Lune now flows due south, past Sedbergh to Kirkby Lonsdale. To the west of it is the lumpy, knobbly country of the Silurian slate—Docker, Lambrigg, Killington and Old Hutton—

* Not, of course, to be confused with Great Langdale near Ambleside

which is bare, stubborn-looking and open to the snow. Killington has a reservoir, built to feed the old Kendal-Lancaster Canal. The new motorway will go through this country, too, but there is more room than at the Lune Gorge, and these uplands will not take so much notice of it. In fact, the land between Kendal and Sedbergh, if not very spectacular, is 100 per cent Westmorland and not inclined to apologise for it.

But at Kirkby Lonsdale the Lune strikes limestone once again—the eastern arm of that major deposit that stretches from Kendal as far south as Carnforth. Kirkby Lonsdale does not look like a town of the Lakes. The beautiful, yellowish limestone of which it is built reminds one of the Cotswold villages, though it is less rurally 'quaint' and more urbanly elegant. In fact, there is scarcely a house in the main street or around the old Swine Market which is not a pleasure to look at—the stone crusted and dusted with orange or olive-green. Alley-ways lead to courts and wynds, and gaps between the buildings give views of Barbon Fell across the Lune. And the whole town, in contrast to much of Kendal, is clean, uncluttered and well cared-for. In some ways Kirkby Lonsdale has almost been annexed by Yorkshire, being the first Westmorland town on the main route from the West Riding to the Lakes, and the shops show the kind of prosperity which comes from catering for the well-to-do suburbs of an industrial population.

Yet it still has close connections with the Lakes. It is built of Kent-dale limestone, and it owed its early growth to the wool trade centred on Kendal. I will say little here about the other attractions of the town—its church with the superb Norman nave (almost a little Durham) and good wood-carving; the far-stretched grave-yard and vicarage green; the famous 'Ruskin' view, and the Devil's Bridge over the Lune, which, rather sadly, has been turned into a car park and stand for pebble-throwers now that the very necessary new road bridge has been built nearby. For what more concerns me is that we have now encircled Greater Lakeland; we have come back where we started. Go just a short way along the road to Crooklands, and Morecambe Bay comes in sight again and all the fells around Kirkby Kendal. In fact, except when we have dipped into a valley or gone into a church, the central fells have never really been out of the view: one or two have always been there, at least on the horizon—Coniston Old Man, Scafell, Pillar, Skiddaw, the Mardale Harter Fell, or Helvellyn. Perhaps Greater Lakeland could be defined as the country where the Lake fells are in sight. But the unity is greater than that. It comes from the rock, from the shape of the land, from its history, and from the stock and breeding of its people. It embraces places which the visitor to the Lakes may not want to see and aspects of life and society which he comes here to forget. But it is no good trying to forget them. Greater Lakeland does not just mean Derwentwater, Blea Tarn and the Wasdale Screes: it also means Windscale Atomic Station, the Marchon chemical factory at Whitehaven, Workington Steelworks, Barrow Docks and Carlisle Railway Depot; wharves, warehouses, bus-stops and parking-places; schools, adult-education centres, the county libraries; churches, chapels, Sunday schools, cinemas and dance-halls; sports fields, allotments and cemeteries; the new housing estates and the old, shabby Victorian terraces; hardware stores, chemists', fish-and-chip shops, pubs and coffee-bars; the dairy herds, turnip fields and pig-sties of a thousand lowland farms; one cathedral, one teachers' training college, one Polaris-submarine ship-building yard—in fact, all that goes to the life and death of the people of the old kingdom and the new county of Cumbria. Forget all this, and what all the rest of the country calls 'Lakeland' will turn moribund, dying slowly from the edges inwards, to become in the end little more than a beautiful, embalmed corpse in a rotting coffin.

INDEX